Understanding and Developing Student Engagement

Enhancing the student experience, and in particular student engagement, has become a primary focus of Higher Education. It is in particularly sharp focus as Higher Education moves forward into the uncertain world of high student fees and a developed Higher Education market. Student engagement is a hot topic, in considering how to offer 'value' and a better student experience. Moreover, it is receiving much attention all over the world and underpins so many other priorities such as retention, widening participation and improving student learning generally.

Understanding and Developing Student Engagement draws from a range of contributors in a wide variety of roles in Higher Education and all contributors are actively involved in the Researching, Advancing and Inspiring Student Engagement (RAISE) Network.

While utilizing detailed case examples from UK universities, the authors also provide a critical review and distillation of the differing paradigms of student engagement in America, Australasia, South Africa and Europe, drawing upon key research studies and concepts from a variety of contexts.

This book uncovers the multi-dimensional nature of student engagement, utilizing case examples from both student and staff perspectives, and provides conceptual clarity and strong evidence about this rather elusive notion. It provides a firm foundation from which to discuss practices and policies that might best serve to foster engagement.

Colin Bryson is Director of the Combined Honours Centre at Newcastle University, UK.

D1344320

The Staff and Educational Development Series
Edited by James Wisdom
Academic and Educational Development

**Research, Evaluation and
Changing Practice in Higher Education**
Edited by Ranald Macdonald and James Wisdom, 2002

Assessment for Learning in Higher Education
Edited by Peter Knight, 1995

Benchmarking and Threshold Standards in Higher Education
Edited by Helen Smith, Michael Armstrong and Sally Brown, 1999

Changing Higher Education
The Development of Learning and Teaching
Edited by Paul Ashwin, 2006

Computer-Assisted Assessment in Higher Education
Edited by Sally Brown, Phil Race and Joanna Bull, 1999

Developing Effective Part-time Teachers in Higher Education
Edited by Fran Beaton and Amanda Gilbert, 2013

Education Development and Leadership in Higher Education
Implementing an Institutional Strategy
Edited by Kym Fraser, 2004

Educational Development through Information and Communications Technology
Edited by Stephen Fallows and Rakesh Bhanot, 2007

Enabling Student Learning
Systems and Strategies
Edited by Gina Wisker and Sally Brown, 1996

Enhancing Staff and Educational Development
Edited by David Baume and Peter Kahn, 2004

Facing Up to Radical Change in Universities and Colleges
Steve Armstrong and Gail Thompson, 1997

Flexible Learning in Action
Case Studies in Higher Education
*Edited by Rachel Hudson, Sian Maslin-Prothero and
Lyn Gates, 1997*

A Guide to Staff and Educational Development
Edited by Peter Kahn and David Baume, 2003

Inspiring Students
Case studies in Motivating the Learner
Edited by Stephen Fallows and Kemal Ahmet, 1999

The Management of Independent Learning
Edited by Jo Tait and Peter Knight, 1996

Managing Educational Development Projects
Effective Management for Maximum Impact
Edited by Carole Baume, Paul Martin and Mantz Yorke, 2002

Quality Issues in ICT-based Higher Education
Edited by Stephen Fallows and Rakesh Bhanot, 2005

Researching Learning in Higher Education
An Introduction to Contemporary Methods and Approaches
Glynis Cousin, 2009

Reshaping Teaching in Higher Education
Linking Teaching with Research
Edited by Alan Jenkins, Rosanna Breen and Roger Lindsay, 2003

Resource-Based Learning
Edited by Sally Brown and Brenda Smith, 1996

Teaching International Students
Improving Learning for All
Edited by Jude Carroll and Janette Ryan, 2006

The Realities of Change in Higher Education
Interventions to Promote Learning and Teaching
Edited by Lynne Hunt, Adrian Bromage and Bland Tomkinson, 2006

SEDA is the professional association for staff and educational developers in the UK, promoting innovation and good practice in higher education. SEDA offers services to its institutional and individual members through its Fellowship scheme, its Professional Development Framework and its conferences, events, publications and projects. SEDA is a member of the International Consortium for Educational Development.

SEDA
Woburn House
20–24 Tavistock Square
London
WC1H 9HF
Tel: 020 7380 6767
www.seda.ac.uk

Understanding and Developing Student Engagement

Edited by Colin Bryson

Routledge
Taylor & Francis Group

LONDON AND NEW YORK

First published 2014
by Routledge
2 Park Square, Milton Park, Abingdon, Oxon OX14 4RN

and by Routledge
711 Third Avenue, New York, NY 10017

Routledge is an imprint of the Taylor & Francis Group, an informa business

British Library Cataloguing in Publication Data
A catalogue record for this book is available from the British Library

Library of Congress Cataloging in Publication Data
Understanding and developing student engagement / [edited by] Colin
Bryson.
— (Seda series)
1. College student development programs—United States. 2. College
students—United States—Psychology. 3. Student affairs services—
United States. 4. Academic achievement—Social aspects—United States.
5. Education, Higher—Aims and objectives—United States.
I. Bryson, Colin.
LB2343.4.U64 2014
378.1'97—dc23
2013035128

ISBN: 978-0-415-84338-6 (hbk)
ISBN: 978-0-415-84339-3 (pbk)
ISBN: 978-1-315-81369-1 (ebk)

Typeset in Galliard
by Swales & Willis Ltd, Exeter, Devon, UK

MIX
Paper from
responsible sources
FSC® C013056
www.fsc.org

Printed and bound in Great Britain by
TJ International Ltd, Padstow, Cornwall

Contents

Illustrations

Figures

Tables

Contributors

Zoë Sarah Baker is currently a PhD student at the University of Sheffield with her research being funded by the Economic Social Research Council. Prior to this, she graduated from Sheffield Hallam University with a degree in Education Studies and Sociology, and subsequently completed her MA in Educational Research at the University of Sheffield.

Dr Michaela Borg works in the Centre for Academic Development and Quality at Nottingham Trent University. She leads a team working on aspects of academic development. Michaela's research interests include assessment and feedback and the experiences of international students and staff. She has published and presented on these topics.

Viola Borsos, after travelling and working in education internationally, became a mature student in 2011 when she began to study BA (Hons) Fashion Design at Nottingham Trent University. She is Hungarian, speaks seven languages and is particularly interested in different cultures, languages and learning styles.

Colin Bryson is Director of the Combined Honours Centre at Newcastle University. This role allows him to practice student engagement, after researching that for 10 years or more. He is Chair and co-founder of RAISE. He was awarded a National Teaching Fellowship for this work, but the real reward comes from working in partnership with great students.

Emma Chadwick, who had previously worked within the National Health Service, is currently working within a small physiotherapy practice within the Manchester area which specialises in musculoskeletal physiotherapy. Being a recent graduate her previous study at Manchester Metropolitan University provided her with the skills to treat patients holistically and successfully.

Christopher Demirjian is studying BA (Hons) Fashion Design at Nottingham Trent University, which he commenced in 2011. Prior to this he completed a Foundation course in Art and Design at Nottingham Trent International College. He is from Cyprus and likes to use his Cypriot traditions and cultural values in his work.

Dr Sam Elkington is a senior lecturer in Sport Management and Teaching Fellow at the University of Bedfordshire. Sam's practice and research interests centre on creative pedagogy and innovation in curriculum design as they play out in academic engagement and student–tutor partnerships.

Ed Foster works at Nottingham Trent University. Ed is a generally useful person in a tight spot; particularly if that tight spot requires a knowledge of student transition, engagement, learning and teaching or retention and success. He also owns his own screwdriver (not sonic unfortunately).

Ruth Furlonger recently graduated from Combined Honours at Newcastle University. Throughout her degree she took on leading roles in the department's schemes of engagement, including mentor leader, Combined Honours Society president and Peer Assisted Study Support leader. This work helped her secure a full-time post as the Student Engagement Coordinator for the Combined Honours Department.

Linda Graham lectures in the Department of Social Work and Communities at Northumbria University. Formerly the Student Development Officer in the university's Centre for Excellence in Assessment for Learning, she has extensive experience of developing and supporting student engagement in a range of disciplinary contexts.

Claire Hamshire is a Senior Learning and Teaching Fellow at Manchester Metropolitan University (MMU). This role combines faculty teaching with a cross institutional contribution to technology innovation. Her research interests include student engagement and learning transitions; she was awarded a Higher Education Academy National Teaching Fellowship in 2012.

Dr Christine Hardy is a Principal Lecturer in the School of Art and Design, Nottingham Trent University. Her teaching focuses on research methods and supervising postgraduate and research students. Her current research interests are academic writing and student engagement, taking a student perspective. She is co-founder of the international network RAISE.

Dr Andrea Jackson is the Pro Dean for Student Education for the Faculty of Environment at the University of Leeds and holder of a Higher Education Academy National Teaching Fellowship. Andrea has experience of designing and delivering practical-based teaching provision and is an advocate of evidence-informed approaches to enhance learning and teaching practice.

Ji Kim commenced studying BA (Hons) Fashion Design at Nottingham Trent University in 2011. After graduating high school in Korea she chose to study in the UK to learn English and discuss ideas in an open forum. She found it difficult to settle in and got involved in research to help other international students.

Daniel Johnson recently graduated from Combined Honours (CH) at Newcastle University. During his studies Daniel took a lead in managing a university listening service and the student representative system within CH, providing him with valuable volunteer management experiences as he looks to pursue a career in the third sector.

Sarah Johnson is a Learning and Teaching Officer at Nottingham Trent University, with responsibility for a team of Student Mentors who work in schools supporting students to develop their academic writing and study skills.

Dr Ellie Kennedy works in Academic Development at Nottingham Trent University. She has a PhD in German literature and has published articles in the fields of Gender Studies, English for Academic Purposes, and Learning and Teaching in Higher Education. She is also an editor of the International Student Experience Journal.

Sarah Lawther has extensively researched student transition, retention and engagement and is currently working to use these findings to improve the learning and teaching experience for students at Nottingham Trent University. Sarah is particularly interested in the use of mixed methods in research.

Katie Livesey is the Student Experience Officer for the School of Earth and Environment, University of Leeds. Her work involves working with students to understand how they engage and developing initiatives to encourage student involvement in co-curricular activities to enhance their educational experience.

Susan Lund completed her BA (Hons) Education Studies degree at Sheffield Hallam University in 2011. She now works as a Disabled Student Support Assistant, and is proud to note that a student had nominated her in the National Student Survey 2013 as someone who made a positive impact on her life.

Jane McNeil is Director of Academic Developments at Nottingham Trent University. She leads a team of specialists who support the university's academic and quality structures. She is an experienced academic with research interests in assessment, feedback, academic writing and the use of technology to enjoy learning and teaching.

Rebecca Murphy is studying at Nottingham Trent University for a BSc (Hons) in Computer Science, with a year in industry. As a Student Academic Writing Mentor, she worked with other students providing one-to-one support for writing and study skills.

Nga Wun Mok is studying BA (Hons) Fashion Design at Nottingham Trent University, which she commenced in 2011. She comes from Macau, China, and, as an international student, has experienced difficulties studying in a foreign country, so is keen to improve the experience for all international students through involvement in research.

Beth Parker graduated from Combined Honours in 2013. She began her engagement journey as a peer mentor, later becoming a mentor leader and attending many conferences and university events. These experiences not only enriched her student experience but equipped her with numerous skills for the future.

Sarah Parnham is studying for the BA (Hons) in Psychology and Educational Development at Nottingham Trent University. She is also a Student Academic Writing Mentor supporting students with their academic writing and study skills in order to help them to reach their full potential.

Sean Prince is a Senior Lecturer on the undergraduate and postgraduate Fashion Design courses in the School of Art and Design, Nottingham Trent University and at the Hong Kong Design Institute. He has an MA in Fashion and Textiles from Nottingham Trent University, is a fellow of the HEA and a member of RAISE.

Carol Robinson is a Principal Research Fellow in Education at the University of Brighton. Her research interests combine theoretical and empirical work and focus on student engagement, voice, ethics and rights. Carol is also programme leader for the Professional Doctorate in Education.

Professor Kay Sambell is widely published in the field of teaching, learning and assessment in higher education. She has directed a number of large-scale research and development projects investigating and enhancing students' experiences of learning, and was a co-director of Northumbria University's Centre for Excellence (CETL) in Assessment for Learning.

Shanna Saubert is currently pursuing her PhD at the University of Leeds. Her research focuses on international experiences and student engagement. Coming from the USA originally, she recognises the importance of positive international exchanges on both personal and collective levels.

Jo Southwell-Sander is President of the Nottingham Trent Students' Union. She graduated with a degree in International Business at Nottingham Trent University and has served one term as the Vice President of Education and Representation.

Carol Taylor is a Reader in Education. She has researched and published on student engagement policy, practice, voice and ethics. Her other research interests include Higher Education, gender, philosophy of education, and collaborative research methodologies. Carol teaches on the BA (Hons) Education Studies degree, and supervises MA and doctoral students.

Dr Christopher Wibberley is a Principal Lecturer at Manchester Metropolitan University. He has worked in Higher Education for over 20 years in a variety of roles. His current research interests include narrative explorations of: health conditions/disorders; transitions into healthcare education and employment; health and social care service use.

Julie Wintrup is a Principal Teaching Fellow in the Faculty of Health Sciences at the University of Southampton. Her teaching interests include workforce development, leadership, ethics and decision making in health services. Julie has reported and published regularly, and presented to health, ethics and education conferences nationally and internationally

Oliver Worsley is from the UK and commenced studying BA (Hons) Fashion Design at Nottingham Trent University in 2011. He was a teaching assistant in Germany and has studied in Hong Kong. Internationalisation has always been an interest and a strong focus in his design practice. He is a member of RAISE.

Foreword

Mantz Yorke

'Student engagement' has always been an issue in higher education, but only latterly has it gained prominence in the discourse on teaching and learning. The National Survey of Student Engagement (now well into its second decade in the US) has arguably been the most potent influence in this respect, and has spawned derivative versions elsewhere. The key to its success has been the focus on what students actually do in their studies rather than on what has been done to them by the institution in which they are enrolled (roughly the standpoint of surveys of student opinion that are embedded in some higher education systems).

Surveys have their uses, but more is often made of their output than is warranted: one has only to look at the naive use made of the findings from the National Student Survey in the UK to appreciate the point. To search for a 'measure' of *the* student experience or *the* level of student engagement on a programme is to chase a chimera, for there are as many student experiences and levels of engagement as there are students (and, as Bryson reminds us in the opening chapter, engagement itself is a complex construct bearing a number of interpretations). Using a 'measure' of student engagement would be like focusing on the statistical mean whilst ignoring the 'messages' suggested by the standard deviation. If we are to understand student engagement, we have to engage more closely with students' lived experiences in higher education than any survey will permit. The qualitative data presented in *Understanding and Developing Student Engagement* enables us to do this.

This book juxtaposes the experiences of staff and student voices in an interesting way, and shines different and intriguing light on a familiar academic scene. The students' voices confirm, at first hand, some aspects of experience in higher education with which many academics are familiar, such as potential students' limited knowledge of what higher education will really be like; the importance of friendship groups; difficulties with group work (such as free-riding); anxiety about assessment; and unhappiness with being awarded lower grades in higher education than those they had gained at school or in further education.

Diversity is a thread running through the varied chapters of this book, and the evidence presented here implicitly invites readers to reflect on how well they might do on a tough test of pedagogic imagination – how to cater for a cohort that is heterogeneous in characteristics such as age, gender, ethnicity and nationality, and whose domestic arrangements may not always facilitate academic and social integration. Indeed, the book is full of material that provokes thought about how educational programmes should be conducted in a massified higher education system in which, because of the recent rise in tuition fees, the perspective of the 'student as consumer' has come to the fore: those involved in postgraduate certificates in learning and teaching in higher education are likely to be engaging in the issues explicitly and implicitly addressed in this book.

From the students' comments the importance is clear of the personal characteristics that they bring to their studies, such as how determined they are to succeed. But even committed students are vulnerable to negativity in their experience: those with relatively slender reserves of academic and social capital are particularly at risk. The issue for teachers is whether they can pick up, early enough to make a difference, those students whose experience is militating against their success. The co-curricular use of mentors can make a valuable contribution here – and contribute to the mentors' curricula vitae.

Work placement is a 'step-change' for some students, when they suddenly find a level of engagement far higher than they had previously managed to achieve. For some, this is likely to mark a shift from performance goals (where the focus is, instrumentally and crudely, on 'getting the grade') towards learning goals of various kinds – or, relatedly, a shift away from dependence towards autonomy. Perhaps this is why, on returning to university for the final year's academic study, some students find themselves almost in stasis as they anticipate work after graduation. Herein, maybe, is another challenge for those responsible for designing and implementing curricula.

This brings us back to the crucial role of the teacher and to teacher engagement. In the UK the former Teacher Training Agency used as an advertising slogan '*No one forgets a good teacher*', forgetting that the same applies to a bad teacher (I remember both, in roughly equal measure). It is a truism that good teachers commit themselves to ensuring that students succeed to the best of their ability. It is equally a truism that students' success depends on their willingness to engage with the demands of their programmes of study. Whereas teachers cannot guarantee the success of their students, they can – indeed, should – bend the odds in favour of success through their moral commitment to student learning, the attitudes they convey and the methods that they use. Our students deserve (and expect to pay for) no less.

Acknowledgements

This book would not have been possible without the many students who consented to share their experiences with us through all the studies undertaken by the contributors to this book, to whom the authors are deeply grateful. As editor I am also deeply grateful to the students who gave time and commitment to writing their own personal stories and reflections as chapters, and also to Eugenie Johnson, who did such fine work as my editorial assistant in the preparation of this book.

Introduction

Colin Bryson

In 2009, I was attending yet another conference, which had student engagement as a major theme, yet did not contain many presentations that were rooted in a conceptual basis on the topic or had much evidence or evaluation applied specifically to engagement. Therefore, it seemed a very good idea to try to build a network with a specific focus on engagement, and thus Researching, Advancing and Inspiring Student Engagement (RAISE) was born (with thanks to my daughter for the name). A very early collective project was to pull together a book and here it is.

Enhancing the student experience, and in particular student engagement, has become a primary focus of Higher Education. It is particularly in sharp focus in the UK as we move forward into the uncertain world of high student fees and a Higher Education market. Student engagement is a hot topic, in considering how to offer 'value' and a better student experience. Moreover, it is receiving much attention all over the world and underpins so many other priorities such as retention, widening participation and improving student learning generally.

Staff views on student engagement are often based on anecdote or belief rather than good evidence.

Therefore this book is for both staff and students. We offer a critical evaluation of the nature of student engagement, and range of practices that provide opportunities to foster student engagement. RAISE espouses the doctrine of partnership and we have to put that into practice by involving students in the creation of this book.

The book begins with a critical exploration of the most illuminating theories and research drawn from the international literature with a view to mapping the concept. This is followed by three sections:

1   Outcomes of recent studies about 'students engaging' – interpretations by researchers based on rich evidence from students.
2   Students writing directly about their engagement – and what engages them.
3   Policies and practices across a range of levels, which are effective in 'engaging students'.

Part I comprises three chapters from researchers who undertook separate longitudinal studies following students across the full period of their undergraduate or foundation degrees in three different universities from across England. The students were in a range of contrasting environments and the qualitative studies have uncovered rich and detailed accounts of their experiences; all are unique but some similar themes emerge.

Part II is an unusual and rather special contribution because the eight chapters were very much written by 15 students; five chapters entirely by students. These are powerful narratives of the students reflecting on their experiences, in particular the impact that undertaking roles and projects have had on their engagement and development. There are several themes around student engagement; the value of peer mentoring, student representation and other peer roles; students as researcher inside and outside the curriculum; what students value on learning and teaching; and the perspective of international students.

Part III has five chapters written by staff practitioners who have sought to enhance student engagement. In every case they have gathered and reflected on direct experience of applying these innovative practices and thinking, and this evidence very much reflects the voice of the students involved.

Finally I present some reflections about common and powerful themes emerging from this book and conclude by discussing the concept of student and staff partnership, which I suggest is the likely future of student engagement, as partnership embodies all the principles of student engagement and genuinely places it where it should be: at the centre of Higher Education.

Chapter 1

Clarifying the concept of student engagement

Colin Bryson

Introduction

This opening chapter seeks to explore the nature of student engagement (SE) in Higher Education (HE), to map SE conceptually and to articulate the key principles that underpin it. I shall draw on both research evidence and literature and on discussions over the last eight years with colleagues from across the world. My starting position for uncovering the nature of student engagement is premised on the goal of HE being about enabling the individual to learn and develop in powerful and transformative ways. I am positioning the student as active learner, not as consumer of a product such as acquiring a qualification. We may note that even within that definition there are many contestable issues and that students are diverse in every way imaginable. Equally disparate are the lenses commentators have applied to student engagement, as these perspectives reflect diverse traditions of research methodology, philosophy, discipline, and not least location within different educational settings, national and local.

Deciding how to structure all these conceptions and themes around diverse interpretations of the nature of student engagement is challenging. There is no obvious coherent path through this complexity. My criteria for including ideas in this chapter are that they offer an interesting and insightful perspective on SE, not simply because they fit neatly into a coherent framework. There are a few overarching models to present, but also a plethora of research on a single aspect or on issues which relate to SE.

I shall begin with the body of work which is most dominant, at least in volume. There has been over 50 years of research in the United States (US) on this topic, producing a mountain of evidence and publications. This conception of, and approach to, SE has influenced strongly the development of the concept in Australia. Research in other countries on SE tends to be much more recent but emerges from rather different origins and character. Note that some US and Australian research does not follow the dominant paradigm.

A likely explanation for the longstanding interest in the US in SE is that mass participation in HE has had a much longer tradition there and created issues of persistence and attainment among a diverse body of students which drew the attention of staff, policy makers and researchers. The focus in the United Kingdom (UK) and Europe has followed a different path, with much more emphasis on seeking to understand how students learn rather than on transitions and student success (Solomonides, Reid and Petocz, 2012). Therefore, research specifically on SE in the UK has been much more recent. SE has been construed in quite different ways in the UK from the US paradigm, as has other valuable research within national settings, for example, New Zealand, South Africa, France, Holland and Finland. Another issue which creates confusion within the UK stems from the point that engagement is used to refer to another area which seems quite distinctively different. Specifically, this is SE defined as collective student representation in university governance and decision making.

Seeking to review the relevant research evidence and analysis about SE requires another key consideration. Much excellent and insightful work does not emerge from a trawl of the search term 'student engagement', as issues and themes which are highly pertinent are not always described as SE or linked to SE. Thus, so called 'comprehensive reviews' of SE, such as Trowler (2010) undertook, can (and did) neglect this wider research base.

Another problem with seeking to be comprehensive is that so many studies on learning and teaching and on the student experience use the term 'engagement' very broadly and loosely. Such studies are really about practices or curricular approaches which the authors claim 'engages students' but without any conceptualization or evaluation of SE to substantiate such a claim. This 'background noise' can influence a reviewer of SE to adopt too narrow a research base in another way too. Thus, Trowler's rejection of virtually all the UK research studies (and many from elsewhere) on SE on the basis they were based on qualitative evidence, or case studies based on single institutions, or had not been disseminated through particular journals, was deeply flawed. This approach ignored the very useful conceptions of SE that emerged from such studies. My aim here is to take a rather broader critical review to consider all relevant material that may inform the scholarship of SE.

The dominant paradigm – North America and the National Survey of Student Engagement

The roots of SE research in North America lie in the many studies on the 'whole college experience' of students. Becker et al. (1961) pioneered this work, and Feldman and Newcomb (1969) produced the first studies on 'college impact' on students. This was followed by Pace (1982), who argued that it was the quality and quantity of effort expended by an individual student that led to good academic outcomes. This included investment by the students in both curricular and co-curricular activity. Astin (1984) refined this through a theory of student involvement where he proposed that more involvement resulted in better learning and development; thus institutions and staff should focus on the inducing of motivation and 'virtuous' behaviours in the student. The metastudies of Pascarella and Terenzini (1991, 2005) supported this notion of the extent to which students engage being the determinant of their success at college and emphasize that this is *holistic*. Therefore, it is engagement across the piece by the individual that matters because it is mutually reinforcing. This is a powerful message to staff and management about ensuring that what they do to shape the whole experience of students in classroom and beyond is aligned to this objective. The breadth of this was distilled by Chickering and Gamson (1987) into seven principles to be adopted by staff to:

- ensure student-staff contact;
- promote active learning;
- develop cooperation and mutuality between students;
- emphasize time on task;
- give prompt feedback;
- communicate high expectations;
- respect diversity in talent and ways of learning.

Indeed, it was Astin (1991) who went on to develop the first holistic model of SE: Input-Environment-Outcomes (I-E-O). The input part is what the students brings: how they have been shaped by their pre-college experience. He identified 146 possible variables that might influence this. He then noted another 192 environmental variables (social, cultural, practical, educational, behavioural inter alia) that might influence how the college experience would impact on students. The outcomes component related to the changes on the student from these impacts: development, success, satisfaction and persistence. This final component had slightly less variables, with a mere 82!

Based on some of these ideas and principles, in 1998 Kuh developed a survey instrument to measure engagement which has had the most profound impact: the National Survey of Student Engagement (NSSE). This has been adopted in over 1500 colleges in the USA and Canada, with several million students now having completed it. It is intended to offer something rather useful to institutional management – a proxy for quality (Kuh et al., 2008b).

Well over 200 papers have now been published on analysis of sets and sub-sets of results from the annual iterations of the application of the survey in all these settings. Therefore, Kuh's definition of engagement has gained a dominant position not just in North America but also in Australia and New Zealand (with the AUSSE) and more recently South Africa (the SASSE), as well as to China (NSSE-China). Kuh (2001: 12) emphasized it is what the students *do* that matters:

> Student engagement is defined as students' involvement in activities and conditions that are linked with high-quality learning. A key assumption is that learning outcomes are influenced by how an individual participates in educationally purposeful activities. While students are seen to be responsible for constructing their own knowledge, learning is also seen to depend on institutions and staff generating conditions that stimulate student involvement.

Therefore, the survey was designed to seek manifestations (and to some extent, outcomes) of students doing 'educationally purposeful activities' (these are widely defined to capture the 'whole college experience'). The survey sought to address five benchmarks, all considered to be key components which encourage student engagement. These were:

- Level of academic challenge: extent to which expectations and assessments challenged students to learn.
- Enriching educational experiences: participating in broadening educational activities.
- Active and collaborative learning: students' efforts to actively construct their knowledge.
- Supportive campus environment: feeling of being legitimatized within the community.
- Student–faculty interaction: level and nature of students' contact with teaching staff.

This is operationalized through a set of questions of items under each benchmark asking students to self-report against of scale of participation in 'appropriate' activities, or to identify if opportunities are present to do so. There are some 'rating' questions about the quality of environment and services.

After 10 years of application, the survey underwent a major review and update. NSSE 2.0 was introduced in 2013 and changes made reflected the growing use of information technology, clarifying and simplifying questions and refining the benchmarks (McCormick et al., 2013). The revision emphasized factors which had emerged as important for good educational outcomes from earlier results, e.g. reflective and integrative learning, collaborative learning and such activities as study abroad and internships.

The application and analysis of the NSSE has been very powerful in demonstrating that higher levels of student engagement are associated with all sorts of virtuous educational, and other, outcomes. In addition, it has provided strong evidence to address organizational defects and to develop better educational strategies and policies. Kuh (2008) was able to identify 10 types of activity such as engaging in collaborative projects, undergraduate-led research or peer-assisted learning, which he argued were strongly associated with high engagement, i.e. students who achieved high 'scores' in the other sections of the survey tended also to have access and participate in such activities. Though this apparent correlation does pose a conundrum, the 'chicken and egg' question of: was participation in such activities a catalyst or consequence of manifesting 'higher' engagement?

SE in Australia: convergence with the US

The origins of the focus on SE in Australia lie in large-scale surveys carried out on the First Year Experience (FYE) undertaken every five years across the national

HE sector since 1994. Williams (1982) had preceded this with an index of 'Institutional Belongingness, Social Involvement and Alienation', which are three themes or concepts which have subsequently emerged as strongly linked to SE, but this did not gain much currency. From the FYE data gathered by the 1994 survey, McInnis and James (1995) developed the concept of 'connectedness' as being important for retention and persistence. McInnis (2001) subsequently refined this into 'negotiated' student engagement, giving salience to the interactive and dynamic nature of SE. McInnis (2005) argued that strong SE manifests itself when students:

- share the values and approaches to learning of their lecturers (academic orientation);
- spend sufficient time and energy on educationally meaningful tasks;
- learn with others inside and outside the classroom;
- actively explore ideas confidently with other people;
- learn to value perspectives other than their own.

McInnis (2001) has particularly emphasized the salience of the transition into HE in establishing good levels of engagement. He noted that there are more challenges to engagement emerging from a widening heterogeneity of HE experience, from student diversity and mobility, the changing nature of student courses, more and wider student choice, such as e-learning and distance learning options, as well the decreased centrality of campus life to students who work or have families, which makes integration more difficult. Horstmanshof and Zimitat (2003) discussed how such major changes have affected the construction of student identities, where the 'student self' has to compete with other selves, but note that does not necessitate lower engagement.

Kerri-Lee Krause took over responsibility for the FYE in 2004 when the survey was redesigned to include more items to assess specific 'dimensions' of SE. She defined SE as 'The time, energy and resources students devote to the activities designed to enhance learning at university' (Krause et al., 2005: 31). Nearly contemporaneously, Coates provided this definition of SE (2006: 26):

> The concept of student engagement is based on the constructivist assumption that learning is influenced by how an individual participates in educationally purposeful activities. Learning is seen as a 'joint proposition,' however, which also depends on institutions and staff providing students with the conditions, opportunities and expectations to become involved. However, individual learners are ultimately the agents in discussions of engagement.

Coates became the leading Australian proponent of the NSSE-inspired approach to SE and developed the AUSSE. The AUSSE questionnaire was almost identical to the NSSE and was used for the first time in 2007, with first year and later year students in 25 Higher Education Institutions (HEIs) in Australia and New

Zealand. However, in addition to the NSSE scales, a sixth dimension, work-integrated learning, was developed specifically for the AUSSE. This measured the opportunity for students to integrate employment-focused work experiences into study.

Krause and Coates (2008) brought the FYE data and NSSE conceptions together in a joint paper. Perhaps unsurprisingly, the focus they adopted was to present 'a complementary tool [with the NSSE] in the on-going quest to understand, monitor and promote student engagement' (ibid.: 503). Thus they produced seven scales of SE. Given the focus on the first year, they added 'transition engagement' to academic engagement (developing the capacity to manage one's time, study habits and strategies); peer (developing knowledge in collaboration with peers); student–staff engagement; intellectual (being challenged by the academy and challenging themselves); online (the use of web and computer software; to support learning and access resources; to promote independent and self-initiated learning; and to assist communicating and building community); and beyond-class engagement scale (students connecting with each other and the university community in activities beyond the classroom, both social and academic). However, they did recognize that qualitative and on-going measures were required in addition to surveys in order to understand engagement.

Although in 2012 30 Australian and New Zealand universities were still administering the AUSSE, another development has diminished its importance and threatened its future. The Australian government have backed the introduction of a mandatory instrument to measure and compare the 'quality' of HE provision. This is the University Experience Survey (UES) which was administered to all 450,000 students (gaining a 25 per cent response rate) in all 40 Australian universities. Although 'learner engagement' (with only a handful of questions about that) is one of five dimensions, the other four are much more focused on 'rating' the experience, staff and services, akin to the UK National Student Survey (NSS) about 'student satisfaction', albeit with the UES having far more items in comparison.

Critiquing this paradigm

This quantitative approach to measure SE may be based on 50 years of research and on well-founded principles. The designers of such survey instruments might not have intended to have the results aggregated or simplified into a single measure or continuum, which infers that judgements can be made about to what extent a student is engaged in their study or student experience, and only offers one snapshot moment to express that. But this simplistic outcome of the application of such instruments raises some methodological and methods considerations, as well as being rather problematic in conceptualising the nature of SE.

The NSSE and its imitators have gained a central position and focus in SE in HE. Such surveys may offer rather more insight than crude instruments, such as the UK NSS, into what universities and colleges are offering students in terms of achieving 'good' HE outcomes. The surveys offer benchmarking and cross-institutional comparison. That has its own dangers, as such measures become appropriated to become a management tool and performance indicator with all its consequent misapplications. But distilling the complex concepts of SE into a survey has some profound problems:

- such surveys can only offer a proxy about levels of SE and the promise of measurement is illusory;
- standardization of questions in pursuit of generalizability loses sensitivity to local contexts and undermines the validity of the responses;
- the closed questions of such surveys give no voice to the student at all. Their perspective is shoehorned to fit, with no opportunity to present an alternative view to any issue.

There is emerging critique about the NSSE within its own methodological paradigm. The construct validity of the five benchmarks has been challenged by LaNasa et al. (2009) who suggests an alternative eight dimensions, undermining the claim to robust psychometric properties. Other researchers who sought to associate the NSSE results with actual outcomes have found little correlation (Carini et al., 2006; Gordon et al., 2008). There are also issues about the variation in interpretation and self-reporting of the items by students, particularly between those in different contexts (Bowman, 2010; Porter, 2009). The AUSSE too has been subject to similar criticism about both its validity and reliability (Hagel et al., 2012).

Moreover, much care has to be exercised in developing dimensions and scales about SE. This is redolent of reductionism on the construct of which earlier researchers, such Pace and Astin, argued was holistic. These surveys do not uncover the richness and diversity of the student experience, or very much about the perspective of students. Trowler (2010) recently looked at over 1000 items on SE (nearly all based on this paradigm) and found very few where the voice of the student was permitted to emerge.

Alternative perspectives and paradigms

My own research over a 10 year period has involved three phases of work, and the evidence gained has shown SE to be both rather more complex and impossible to 'measure'. The first phase involved gathering qualitative evidence from students and staff in a single subject school (Bryson and Hand, 2007, 2008) and brought out the extent to which students were disengaged, rather than engaged, and the influences on that. The second phase, a longitudinal study across several subjects and schools, followed students' entire experiences over three or four years of their degrees, over the period 2007–2011. This evidence is extensively explored and analyzed in a later chapter of this book. The third phase draws on a different student cohort in another university and has been much more an action research approach over five years of iterations and cycles (Bryson, 2010, 2012, 2013). What these studies have shown, even though the number of students participating is tiny in comparison to the huge data sets of the NSSE, is that each student is individual and unique, and that their individual context is paramount. It has brought out how dynamic and fluid the sense of engagement can be within an individual and also, in some ways, so fragile, but also resilient in other ways. The initial focus of these studies was on academic engagement, on and around the classroom, but the second phase really brought out the salience of the social (Bryson and Hardy, 2012) and the whole lives of students. I have been able to identify a set of key influences on SE from the empirical evidence based on student accounts from these studies. This list has evolved and grown over the phases of research.

Influences on SE as identified by students

1   Their aspirations: why they choose to come to university and their goals.
2   Student expectations and perceptions about university, being a student and about their subject and degree: as they arrived and as these change during their degree.
3   Balances between challenge and appropriate workload.
4   Degrees of choice, autonomy, risk, and opportunities for growth and enjoyment.
5   Trust relationships between the student and staff, and student and peers.
6   Communication and discourse between student and others.
7   A sense of belonging and community.
8   The existence of supportive social networks.
9   Opportunities for, and participation in, activities and roles which empowered the student and gave them a sense of ownership, self-assurance and self-efficacy.

One other key point that emerged from these studies was the different perspectives on SE between students and staff. Generally, staff associated SE with virtuous behaviours (e.g. diligence on academic tasks) but ignored the emotional component of SE. Conversely, students highlighted 'feeling engaged' as most important. This mismatch has been explored further (Solomonides and Martin, 2008) and demonstrates the need for staff and students to have a stronger discourse between them and thus shared understanding.

My subsequent investigation of SE literature in the secondary education sector, in which there is much longer tradition of research, emphasized the breadth and depth of SE and emphasized the salience of emotion. Fredricks et al. (2004) noted that:

- SE is multi-dimensional, it is a 'metaconstruct', with at least several complex dimensions;
- SE needs to be considered as 'pattern centred' not variable centred (ibid.: 87).

Around the same time, Leach and Zepke (2012) developed a conceptual 'organizer' with six domains for SE, through reviewing the literature, and then analyzing their own empirical studies:

1   Motivation and agency: engaged students are intrinsically motivated and want to exercise their agency.
2   Transactional engagement: students and teachers engage with each other.
3   Transactional engagement: students engaging with peers.
4   Institutional support: institutions provide an environment conducive to learning.
5   Active citizenship: students and institutions work together to enable challenges to social beliefs and practices.
6   Non-institutional support: students are supported by family and friends to engage in learning.

This model is a genuine attempt to be comprehensive and holistic. Nick Zepke has described it as porous, in the sense that perspectives may overlap and should not be seen as fully distinct domains. Although the model may identify sources or locations where SE might be generated or enhanced, it does not uncover what is going on with these or why they might be important. There are other models which set to do that more explicitly. These shall now be explored.

Ways of being a student

Dubet (1994) derived three dimensions from many empirical studies in France, which he ascribed to 'ways of being a student'. He contended that the student experience and student identity is constructed, from the combination of:

•   The nature of the personal project; what is the purpose or outcome of their degree for them, i.e. why are they at university?
•   The degree of integration into university life.
•   The level of intellectual engagement with the subject.

Dubet emphasized that the positive or negative emphasis a student gives to these is fluid. The application of Dubet's model generates eight archetypes from the different combinations of positive or negative attributes. Jary and Lebeau (2009) applied this model to sociology students in UK HE. They found examples of all archetypes in all types of institution (demonstrating more similarities than differences in environment and experience), with the exception of an absence of students who were negative about all three: 'a case of anomy'. Jary and Lebeau (ibid.) emerged with a rather controversial finding; that all forms of archetype, bar the entirely negative 'anomy', are viable. For example, they suggest that students with very low integration or intellectual engagement are nonetheless engaged enough (presumably via the personal project) to be successful.

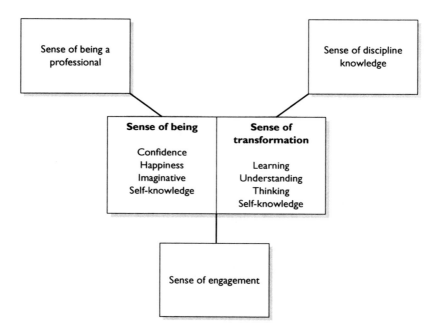

Figure 1.1 Relational student engagement
Source: adapted from Solomonides et al., 2012a.

Dubet's model offers much needed simplicity but obscures important complexity. He ignores context and diversity of students. The application of Dubet's typology seems a little problematic because each dimension (particularly the second) covers a wide area in which there is likely to be a complex mix of positive and negative factors, and ignores the dynamic nature of such domains in relation to the individual.

Relational engagement

Solomonides et al. (2012a) present a different model based on their qualitative research with students. They have particularly emphasized the ontological component of SE; how students develop a sense of self about aspects that are meaningful to them. They have identified that senses of professional formation and of discipline knowledge are likely to be salient (Figure 1.1).

The model is predicated on compelling notions about SE. The notion that SE is located within a sense of being was first devised in collaborative work between Ian Solomonides, Len Hand and me. These thoughts were strongly influenced by Fromm (1978) and the attractive idea that HE is about 'becoming', not 'having'. Thus the notion of 'becoming' permeates this model and all its components. The work of Barnett (2007) links the ontological with the epistemological through the concept of the 'will to learn' (ibid.: 70):

> The student's being, her will to learn, her strong self, her willingness to be authentic: all these are a set of foundations for her knowing and her practical engagements. Without a self, without a will to learn, without a being that has come into itself, her efforts to know and to act within her programme of study cannot even begin to form with any assuredness.

Exploring concepts in detail

There are a host of concepts that link to and underpin the dimensions and notions proposed in these models. These merit further discussion.

Belonging, integration and community

A student's sense of engagement with their experience is enhanced by feeling part of something: belonging, affiliating and feeling integrated. Tinto (1987) developed a model of student retention in which integration plays a key role in whether the student stays or withdraws. The model theorized that the student arrives in HE with a set of intentions, goals and commitments. These are influenced and reconstructed by the 'academic' experience the students perceive themselves to have (progress, performance and the impression gained of the commitment from teaching staff to that student) and by the 'social' experience (self-esteem and quality of relationships with peers and staff). Tinto suggested that sufficient integration results in student persistence.

Kember et al. (2001) drew on empirical work from interviews with part-time students to examine the concept of 'belonging'. The researchers noted that having a stronger affiliation to college and study appeared to enhance both retention and learning outcomes and that the teachers had an important role in enhancing a sense of belonging through establishing a good rapport and strong relationships. This sense of belonging links with earlier themes about involvement, connectedness and the salience of relationships as well as sense of being.

In my own studies, we found that students expressed that there were differing levels or spheres of SE as well as changing degrees of engagement within those spheres (Bryson and Hand, 2007: 359):

- within a classroom or in undertaking a particular task or assignment;
- within/to a particular module;
- within/to and across the course/programme of study;
- within/to the university or HE.

The construction of engagement at each of the levels will affect the other levels in a dynamic manner. We note that for the more 'local' levels such as a task, that engagement with that task might be quite transient given the timescale and nature of the task and that the notion of engagement with education is a much more diffuse concept.

Several of the key players in SE research (Kuh, Tinto and McInnis inter alia) have argued that the establishment of learning communities are crucial and that engagement is enriched to a significant degree by establishing a sense of community in the educational setting. Perry (1999) has concluded that although some students could achieve levels of development and independence of thought with very little support, 'for the majority [. . .] the most important support seemed to derive from a special sense of community [. . .] from reciprocal acts of recognition and confirmation' (ibid.: 238). Wenger (1999) has written extensively on the notion of community, particularly communities of practice, and espoused the importance of situated learning. Therefore, there would appear to be strong potential for SE if students perceive they are part of one or more communities of practice in which they feel competent and which accord with, in Wenger's terms, their 'learning trajectory'. McCune (2009) found some support for the existence of this in her study, but other research (Bryson and Hardy, 2010) has found that few students perceive they are part of, or have the opportunity to be part of, a community of practice in their university studies.

Thomas (2012a), based on the findings of a programme of work aimed at enhancing transition, retention and student success, argued that a sense of belonging is created through a responsive interaction between the student and other members of the university community. Thus, trust relationships between all parties are important. She identified a wide range of practices that foster belonging and, therefore, SE. Lefever (2012), in a contributory study to that programme, noted how the way students relate to the campus and 'spaces' within that (outside the classroom) influences sense of belonging.

Continuing the theme of the importance of the social dimension, Case (2007), in a South African study, raised the importance of relationships. She found that in addition to salience of students' relationships with studies, classmates and lecturers that those with broader university life, career and home were as important. She found a range of both engaging and alienating experiences, as a consequence of the degree of support, gained from such relationships.

The importance of integration in the student experience raises sharp questions about the transition process into and through HE, but that will returned to in the discussion of barriers later on.

Transformation

In making the case for students becoming as a goal of HE, we need to consider the question of 'becoming what?' Becoming also requires transformation, and this infers transformative and powerful learning, the sort of learning that engages, successfully, with threshold concepts and dealing with 'troublesome knowledge' (Meyer and Land, 2003). Therefore, the notion of intellectual and ethical development is useful, not least because it is one of the key goals of education and enables transformative learning. Two useful models are interlinked and have built on each other (Baxter Magolda, 1992; Perry, 1999). For example, Baxter Magolda's 'ways of knowing' requires students to transform their thinking about others, themselves and how they see the world.

Transforming is difficult because it requires movement out of comfort zones, taking risks and embracing uncertainly. Strong engagement is a prerequisite to that. The more advanced or sophisticated ways of knowing imply an open-mindedness, academic self-confidence, reflexivity and an ability to relate to others which infer that the individual both wishes to engage and is already engaged.

This raises the complex issue of student identities, which is a very major research area in its own right. Indeed, the student's journey to being a graduate can be seen as an 'identity project' (Holmes, 1995). There is insufficient space here to open up this topic properly but the identities that students bring with them to HE, and the malleability of these and the extent to which these are reconstructed while being a student, must impact profoundly on SE. This raises another important sociological concept of social and cultural capital, which also impacts considerably on student's transition and success (Reay et al., 2005).

The relational model of SE also includes professional formation and developing disciplinary knowledge. The latter links to the third dimension of ways of being a student: engagement with the subject of study. Although there has been some research of connections between SE and the development of generic graduate attributes (Reid and Solomonides, 2012) and with professional formation (Reid et al., 2011), this whole area is rather under-researched. For example, does strong SE lead to graduate 'success', however one might wish to define the latter? Clearly these dimensions do link with Dubet's notion of the personal project. Presumably, transformation may reinforce personal project development, or create new personal projects.

So what about the subject and discipline aspect of studying at university? To most academic staff the subject really does matter; arguably it might matter too much, in the view of many students, as they are unlikely to share quite the same degree of enthusiasm and aspiration to become a subject expert in the same way as their lecturers (Brennan et al., 2010). Nonetheless, there are studies which demonstrate the salience of the subject in students' perceptions. McCune (2009) demonstrated that to enhance students' 'willingness to engage', they needed to perceive they were undertaking 'authentic learning experiences'. The example of this she drew on was doing projects and roles in Biology that enabled students to feel they were genuinely undertaking the practices of a professional biologist. Thus, authenticity is engaging through the sense the student has of relevance and alignment to their own aspirations, in her example, 'becoming a scientist'.

McCune developed a model of influences which has much relevance for SE in that that it brings out the complex interactions between larger and local environments, communities of practice, 'what the student brings' and how these are mediated by social practices to create more or less opportunity for a sense of authenticity to be perceived.

Barriers and critiques

Mann (2001) focused on barriers to engagement and the polar opposite of engagement: alienation. Mann (ibid.) provided an insightful and persuasive analysis of powerful forces present in HE which can potentially lead to alienation of the student. She explored the ideas of classical and postmodern theorists to identify several factors present in contemporary universities, such as:

- Too much focus on performativity and functional serving of capitalist society; overemphasis on 'getting a useful degree' and employability. Academic discourses which constrain student identities.
- Students are estranged and disoriented by being 'outsiders in a foreign land'; they are entering an unfamiliar culture with different values and beliefs, which they are forced to adopt to be successful.
- Teachers exert disciplinary power over the student (e.g. through assessment). This combines with the student's inability to express their own creativity and the point that students have little control or choice over the learning process to create a Marxian 'exile from the self'.

Such pervasive forces not only create student disengagement, they may also disengage the staff. Even attempts to create a more welcoming community can have adverse effects. Mann (2005) focused on the pressure on the individual student to conform to codes of 'good student' behaviour by looking at examples of the communications and norms that occur in online learning communities. She warned of the danger of creating cultural practices that bind teachers and learners to an alienating social order. Zyngier (2008) adopted a rather more critical stance on SE. He challenges the deficit model of the student, where lack of engagement is seen as a problem *with the students*, i.e. that *they* need to change. He noted the contribution of gender, socio-economic, ethnic and class factors. He strongly opposed any interpretation of engagement as compliance, where students who do not conform are seen as disengaged. He was even sceptical of participation and involvement, and contends that may be compliance too.

Thus, as noted before, transition into HE becomes a vital stage. A student entering and experiencing HE encounters a culture where the beliefs and values of the members are likely to be very different from their previous experience and therefore present challenges and tensions (Ylijoki, 2000). Not only is the student under pressure to adopt the moral order of the academic discipline, in order to be accepted by the academics, but they have joined a new and unknown social group of fellow students that become significant others in the construction of their social identity, offering more scope for alienation.

Krause (2005) found related issues. She described 'inertia' among students which she prefers to disengagement because it is not active, 'which aptly depicts the state of being for the group of students who do not actively pursue opportunities to engage in their learning community' (ibid.: 7). She considered these students at risk of withdrawal, suggesting that even if they remain they will not benefit from HE. But she also noted another group (ibid.: 9): 'for some students engagement with the university experience is like engaging in a battle, a conflict [. . .] the culture of the institution is foreign [. . .] alienating and uninviting'. Such students are likely to be from disadvantaged backgrounds or be international. Her point is that such students are not unwilling to engage; indeed they may be trying hard to do so but find that the staff and institution are not prepared to accommodate their perspectives.

Other researchers have also raised concerns about taking too positive a tone with SE. Honkimaki et al. (2004: 447) noted 'that not even pedagogical innovations can make all students do their best' because some students were not responsive to interventions. Hockings (2010) found that a student-centred approach failed to engage some 30 per cent of students in her study. On further investigation, she found that this supposedly good approach had: 'challenged their approaches to and conceptions of learning, their conceptions of knowledge and ways of knowing and we challenged their sense of self. By challenging them we created an environment which engaged some students' identities and distanced others" (ibid.: 96). Similarly, Zepke and Leach (2005) argued that academics should not seek to force integration on students but meet them part way by acknowledging their pre-existing cultural values and beliefs, a view echoed by Bryson and Hand (2008).

Hockings (ibid.) did not suggest we give up, but that we need to adopt wider considerations of SE, sociological and epistemological aspects, in addition to approaches to learning, in order to open a dialogue with students on how to engage *all* of them. Hockings, in a subsequent study, identified 'artisan teachers' as those who deploy teaching approaches which enabled students to 'bring their own lives to bear on the subject of their learning making it personally meaningful, relevant and engaging to them' (2011: 4).The crucial point here is about creating the opportunity for students to bring and share their own experiences and perceptions into the classroom.

This exemplifies the need to recognize heterogeneity among students as the application of universal remedies to address SE will not succeed (Haggis, 2004).

Collective engagement

There is a whole focus of SE which is rather different from any of the discussion so far. This focus has a prominent position in the UK for a number of reasons. The English HE funding council have privileged 'student representation as SE' through commissioned work by Little et al. (2009) and subsequent imperatives. The Quality Assurance Agency (2012), in its Quality Code which all universities are expected to adhere to, acknowledges that SE may be defined as: 'Improving the motivation of students to engage in learning and to learn independently', but emphasizes a second definition to be applied to quality practices: 'The participation of students in quality enhancement and quality assurance processes, resulting in the improvement of their educational experience.'

Thus this approach to SE is about the collective role of students and their opportunities to influence the broader student experience through representation and involvement in governance and decision making (an 'industrial relations model') gaining student feedback, via questionnaires or student representation on committees, as part of the individual university's quality assurance framework. The Higher Education Academy (HEA) also privileged this definition in its initial policy on SE.

However, the HEA (2010), in collaboration with the National Union of Students (NUS), has transformed this focus on the collective to an emphasis on the partnership approach, which has enabled more inclusive and wider work on students involved at every level, e.g. in co-designing modules (NUS, 2010).

Healey et al. (2010: 22) proposed a framework for this form of SE:

- Micro: engagement with their own learning and that of other students.
- Meso: engagement in quality assurance and enhancement processes.
- Macro: engagement in strategy development.

This chapter is focused on the nature of individual engagement. We can note that student involvement and empowerment can create opportunities to foster student engagement both in those who take such opportunities up, and in the impact that these students and their work has on other students. Indeed, there are good examples later on in this volume of students acting to enhance SE within themselves, and in other students. In the final chapter, I will review that and look in detail at the emerging and growing phenomenon of 'students as partners' and its potential to integrate individual and collective student engagement.

Making sense of all this

I have sought to present a selection of the literature on SE and related topics based on useful conceptions that commentators have proposed, and/or compelling evidence. There are many, many ideas there and they demonstrate the variety of lenses that researchers have taken to this complex topic. However, some common themes emerge and these are offered below:

- Engagement is about both processes and outcomes.
- Engagement is socially constructed and reconstructed by the student and through the interactions they have with others and the environment.
- SE is broader than just about the academic and university environment – students need to make sense of their whole lives not just part of their identities.

- SE is much more than just about *doing*. *Being* and *becoming* are critical. At the heart of SE lie ontological considerations, although there are epistemological considerations too.
- SE is desirable for many reasons, but in HE what it offers is transformative learning. Through transformative learning SE is enhanced, leading to a virtuous circle of formation and development.
- SE is located in the individual and requires research approaches which bring out rich pictures.
- It is multi-dimensional and there are a host of issues and factors that influence SE. These are not amenable to reductionism (because it is their interaction and synergy that is important), thus a holistic perspective is needed and focus on patterns (idiographic rather than nomothetic).
- SE is dynamic and fluid. Although some aspects are resilient, others are fragile and this varies between individuals.
- Great caution must be exercised in seeking to judge whether an individual *is engaged* (and even harder to judge *how much*) because it is quality rather than quantity that is important.

A revised definition of student engagement might look something like this:

> Student engagement is about what a student brings to Higher Education in terms of goals, aspirations, values and beliefs and how these are shaped and mediated by their experience whilst a student. SE is constructed and reconstructed through the lenses of the perceptions and identities held by students and the meaning and sense a student makes of their experiences and interactions.

As players in and shapers of the educational context, educators need to foster educationally purposeful SE to support and enable students to learn in constructive and powerful ways in order to realize their potential in education and society.

Whatever method we use to study SE, we need to problematize the issues. There has been rather a lot of research which, though it may appear 'robust' in a narrow definition of the term, has not done this. Krause (2005: 4) critiques the student involvement paradigm as 'a positive and largely unproblematic theorizing of student engagement. In fact, student engagement is much more problematic than such a paradigm would suggest.' For example, it is clear that attempts at offering and 'doing' engagement are not enough to engage all students and requires much more considered approaches – approaches that consider what the individual brings, perceives and feels, desires and aspires to.

I suggest that part of the problem may arise, at least in part, because of the paradigmatic definition of SE that is dualistic, i.e. what both students *and* institutions do. Although I understand that it is the interactions of these aspects that are important, I propose that in seeking conceptual clarity, they should be separated into two distinct spheres: 'Engaging Students' and 'Students Engaging'.

Engaging students

This is about what the staff and other parties offer in creating opportunities for students to engage in educationally purposeful ways – to 'become' and develop transformatively. In order to achieve that, we need to consider wider issues so that we ensure we accommodate these in our offerings. We need to be mindful of all the alienating forces on individuals, and the context, and then mitigate these. The need to be inclusive to accommodate diversity argues for a set of principles, rather than any form of prescription. So offering a repertoire of approaches is as important as all these pet innovative ideas! I propose an agenda that puts engaging students at the centre of what we do and aligning all that we do with that.

These principles are not new ones. I have drawn on the excellent ideas from the literature covered earlier, as these are informed by what many students have responded to in such positive ways already (e.g. Bryson and Hand, 2008; Chickering and Gamson, 1987; Krause, 2005; Mann, 2001; Zepke and Leach, 2010). We should:

1   Foster students' willingness and readiness to engage by enhancing their self-belief.
2   Embrace the point that students have diverse backgrounds, expectations, values, orientations and aspirations, thus different 'ways of being a student', and to welcome, respect and accommodate all of these in an inclusive way.
3   Enable and facilitate trust relationships (between staff and students, and students and students) in order to develop a discourse with each and all students and to show solidarity with them.
4   Create opportunities for learning (in its broadest sense) communities, so that students can develop a sense of competence and belonging within these communities.
5   Teach in ways to make learning participatory, dialogic, collaborative, authentic, active and critical.
6   Foster autonomy and creativity, and offer choice and opportunities for growth and enriching experiences in a low risk and safe setting.
7   Recognize the impact on learning of non-institutional influences and value positive influences and accommodate or mitigate negative influences.
8   Design and implement assessment for learning with the aim to enable students to develop their ability to evaluate critically the quality and impact of their own work.
9   Work in partnership with students at every opportunity by seeking to negotiate and reach a mutual consensus with students on managing workload, challenge, curriculum and assessment for their educational enrichment,

without diluting high expectations and educational attainment, by developing mechanisms for all students to democratically participate in all aspects of the university that impacts directly or indirectly on them.

10 Enable students to become active citizens and develop their social and cultural capital.

Note that the principles are not just antecedents or influences on engagement; they are about creating a virtuous circle in which opportunities are offered (by the conscious effort of the staff) and enabled (by the appropriate wider environment being aligned with this and working with the grain rather than against it). This doesn't just foster student engagement but creates deeper interactions and new relationships that then change the community in fruitful ways. Therefore, it behoves us as educators to put student engagement at the very centre of what we think and do.

Students engaging

This has elements of process, agency and outcome, as it is dynamic and volatile. It is located within the being of the individual. The multi-dimensional nature of the concept and the diversity and variety of relevant concepts makes constructing a conceptual map rather challenging. SE is invisible and elusive to grasp. We can never see more than part of the picture and that picture is likely to change. It is a real hurdle to validity and reliability and a caution to placing too much faith in its manifestations.

Previous attempts to capture and map all the elusive complexities of the 'meta-construct' that is student engagement have not succeeded and tend to be coloured by the philosophical stance of the cartographer. Therefore, the I-E-O model from Astin (1991) is redolent with a reductionist approach (with 200 plus variables) and underplays the *pattern* nature of SE. It may attempt to be holistic, but it is not enough to be comprehensive as there is insufficient synthesis and interaction. The same can be said of the NSSE and the AUSSE.

The loose framework of Leach and Zepke (2012) has merit but does not seem to cover all the required ground, such as broader but important environmental and contextual influences, and some categories are rather vague. The more ontological 'sense of being' offers a different perspective (Solomonides et al., 2012a). The focus on being, becoming and transformation is a great contribution to conceptualising SE but, again, the model does not seem to cover the full scope of SE with full clarity. It fails to unpack the engagement 'component' and neglects components identified as important in other research. The sociological approach of Dubet (1994) and 'ways of being a student' may appear simple and straightforward but seems very difficult to apply with validity and reliability to evidence. It lacks sufficient nuance and, once again important dimensions are missing: there is nothing on the socio-cultural issues or on context (which Dubet deliberately omitted as he did not consider that they had any impact, in contrast to the view of so many other commentators).

Kahu (2013) has proposed an overarching conceptual framework. The introduction of this has been reserved to this point because her review of the literature and the structuring of the argument is of such excellent quality. This stems from the breadth of coverage of concepts and its relatively recent nature; it can draw on such a wide body of work from different traditions and paradigms. Kahu (ibid.: 758) set out her position thus:

> [. . .] a key problem is a lack of distinction between the state of engagement, its antecedents, and its consequences. While there is some overlap, four relatively distinct approaches to understanding engagement can be identified in the literature: the behavioural perspective, which focuses on teaching practice and student behaviour; the psychological perspective, which views engagement as an internal individual process; the sociocultural perspective, which considers the critical role of sociocultural context; and finally a holistic perspective, which strives to draw the strands together.

She contended that each of the first three perspectives is too narrow and that 'holistic' perspectives have confused antecedents (the influences on SE) and the 'state of engagement'. She then constructed a complex framework which locates all the issues into one, with macro socio-cultural surrounding the whole model which is 'embedded within' them:

1   Structural influences (more external to the student).
2   Psychosocial influences (including university, relationships and student variable) at its core.
3   The state of engagement (based on the 'psychological perspective': affect, cognition and behaviour).
4   Proximal consequences (academic and social).
5   Distal consequences (more indirect academic and social).

The model is more inclusive of all the issues and concepts that permeate the complex multi-construct of SE than any of the others that exist. However, it underplays the important and central concept of becoming and transforming. The model is also undermined by two other considerations. There is a strong element of linearity and discreteness, not enabling the framework to adequately describe the holistic reality of the individual, their experiences and how they make sense of that within an educational setting. Secondly, and even more importantly, Kahu critiques the notion that SE is both a process and an outcome, but then in the model states of engagement is an outcome, whilst contradicting herself in the conclusion by describing it as process.

I have contended here that student engagement is both a process and an outcome: it has features of both. My metaphor here is quantum mechanics, where one cannot measure all the properties of a particle, or even determine if it is particle or a wave. Zepke (2011: 9) has suggested the application of complexity

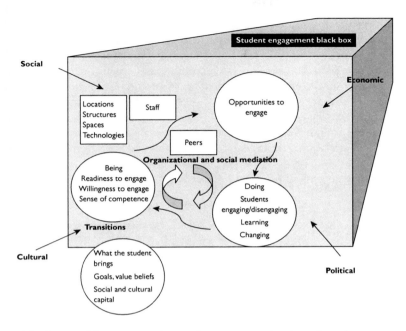

Social

Economic

Cultural

Political

Student engagement black box

Locations
Structures
Spaces
Technologies

Staff

Peers

Opportunities to
engage

Being
Readiness to engage
Willingness to engage
Sense of competence

Organizational and social mediation

Doing

Students
engaging/disengaging

Learning

Changing

Transitions

What the student
brings

Goals, value beliefs

Social and cultural
capital

Figure 1.2   A part of the conceptual map of engagement: the dynamic cycle

theory to SE. This notion of a dynamic, interconnected, non-hierarchal network in which all the issues and factors are both distinct but also connected is useful, but makes it even more problematic to clarify and map the conceptual nature of engagement.

It is the complex interactions and the constructivist nature of SE that prevents a conceptual map being drawn which shows all its properties. In addition, the dynamism and volatility at the level of the individual, allied to the rather tricky issue that as soon as the researcher interacts with the individual student in a meaningful discourse that the evidence about SE amenable to being gathered is likely to change, challenges clarity.

I offer the heuristic device of the black box. This is not a three dimensional box but contains rather more dimensions. We can slice this in a number of ways to produce a two or three dimensional cross section that shows some of the conceptions and how they might be 'associated'. However, we cannot illustrate all of them at once and it would serve no real purpose in doing so. The different models and linked concepts identified in previous research are likely to appear in this (but not in the same slice). One slice might look like Figure 1.2. Other slices might indicate: spheres/levels of SE; key influences in detail; some insight into patterns of SE within an individual at a given moment in time; et cetera.

We should be relaxed about the outcome that this complex idea is not reducible, or even possible to depict as a universal synthesis. Such is its very nature. But that does not lessen its critical importance in education and the fact that it sheds light on productive and positive ways of engaging students – such a worthwhile enterprise for all in HE. Therefore, any researcher or evaluator of student engagement can choose concepts and aspects of SE to explore. They should be mindful of the issues and arguments made in this chapter, but that should not inhibit their enquiry. So many of these studies have the beneficial effect of enhancing engagement through focusing on it and creating a potential discourse between students and staff, students and students and staff and staff. Some care needs to be exercised with surveys in this regard! However, we should never claim that we can measure engagement or create policies based on such a false premise.

Part 1

Students engaging

Perspectives from researchers

Chapter 2

Nottingham tales

Diverse student journeys through their undergraduate degrees

Colin Bryson and Christine Hardy

This chapter is based on a four-year study at a large UK university which followed students across a range of subjects through their whole degrees. Exploring their stories and perspectives at particular points in that journey offers insights into the complex pattern of issues across their complete university experience which mediated their engagement. The journeys that these individuals undertook were unique and diverse: some were a roller coaster ride, others had a smoother path, while for others still, the journey was not completed. We deliberately adopt an empirical approach to presenting the evidence, allowing the reader to interpret the students' own words. We have structured their stories in a chronological order through the path of their degrees but will seek to bring out the major themes identified in the preceding chapter of this volume. Although we would prefer to tell each individual story to maintain coherence, uniqueness and uncover a richer picture, space constraints require succinctness. Therefore, in the main, cross-sectional data is presented, focusing on commonalities and differences between individuals (Hockings et al., 2007).

We shall explore what expectations and aspirations the students brought with them, their personal projects (Dubet, 1994). There were powerful mediating factors which ebbed and flowed over the course of their journey, affecting some students to greater or lesser degrees depending on their context, perspective and agency. Primary among these were social and emotional issues and the salience of their social networks in supporting them through critical points when their engagement was in doubt. So the next focus is on early transitions, social and academic integration in the first year (Tinto, 1987). We shall examine the territory of settling in, building relationships and a sense of belonging. The alienating forces they identified will be compared with mitigating factors, which should illuminate if such barriers could be overcome. The second and third years were rather problematic for some students, and we shall note why this was so. The final section will overview the sense of becoming (Fromm, 1978), and their developing sense of being: becoming a professional, learning the discipline (Solomonides et al., 2012a) and becoming a graduate. We shall conclude by looking for evidence of transformation and identifying specific catalysts in that process.

The study

Investigations of student engagement often use questionnaires to identify relationships between student behaviour and outcomes, which assume that all students and institutions are homogenous, that student engagement is a fixed paradigm that can be quantified, and that all respondents have the same understanding of the questions asked. But based on our own research, and other studies, it would appear that student engagement is complex and holistic, requiring a different approach.

A qualitative approach addresses this by securing rich descriptions of student engagement, provided in naturalistic settings. We stress the socially constructed nature of reality, the intimate relationship between us and the students and situational constraints that shape the enquiry by seeking 'to make sense of, or interpret, phenomena in terms of the meanings people bring to them' (Denzin and Lincoln, 2005: 3). We 'mine the terrain' (McCracken, 1988: 17), recognizing that 'there are no universal truths to be discovered, and that all knowledge is grounded in human society, situated, partial, local, temporal and historically specific' (Coffey, 1999: 11). Therefore, the paradigm for this study is one of constructivism, with relativist ontology, subjectivist epistemology and a naturalistic set of methodological procedures (Denzin and Lincoln, 1994: 12). Our goal was to understand the complex world of lived experience from the point of view of the students who live it, 'that is, particular actors, in particular places, at particular times, [who] fashion meaning out of events and phenomena through prolonged complex processes of social interaction involving history, language and action' (Schwandt, 1994: 125).

We used in-depth interviews taking a phenomenological approach for collecting data. This method encouraged 'the respondent to tell his or her own story in his or her own terms' (McCracken, 1988: 22) over three/four years and several discussions. All the research was conducted in Nottingham Trent University, a large post-1992 institution in England, and ethical approval was gained from the ethics committee; all interviewees were given oral and written information about the project and signed a consent form. The interview guides were built around themes (Table 2.1 indicates these), 'allowing what was relevant to emerge' (Strauss and Corbin, 1990: 23). This inductive approach meant theories about student engagement could evolve during the research through the continuous interplay between data analysis/interpretation and data collection.

All interviews were carried out on university premises, lasting between one and two hours and were taped and transcribed. For this chapter narrative and paradigmatic analyses have been used. The paradigmatic analysis to 'locate common themes or conceptual manifestations among the stories collected as data [. . .] to generate general knowledge from a set of particular instances' (Polkinghorne, 1995: 13) was done by drawing together the findings of previous work, determining if they were applicable to this sample and also to postulate new categories. The narrative analysis is specifically directed to understanding human behaviour and is focused on 'the particular and special circumstances of each action' (Polkinghorne, 1995: 11) and has been written as mini case studies.

Table 2.1 Timetable and subject matter of interviews taken with students

Date	Areas for focus	Notes
Sept 2007 (pre-teaching week)	Their background, why they entered higher education and choose this university and course, their aspirations, their expectations about all aspects of university life. Also had a focus on intellectual development to establish a 'starting position' on ways of knowing (Baxter Magolda, 1992)	24 students were interviewed
Jan 2008 (first week after Christmas)	Their experience thus far and on transition	Coincided with a time that previous research has identified as important in student withdrawal decisions (Ozga and Suhanandan, 1997)
One student declined to take further part in the study
May 2009	Developed our previous themes further and sought to review the first year both in terms of how they were doing and how they had changed	Four students chose not to participate
March/April 2010	Focused on social and academic transition, for both the first and second year, including how they had changed and ways of knowing	14 students were interviewed (two dropped out of the study and three withdrew from university after the first year)
March/April 2011/2012	The themes remained the same as in the second year, with the addition of an oral self-characterisation, '. . . to see how the [student] structures a world in relation to which he must maintain himself in some kind of role' (Kelly, 1991: 243)
In 2012 with those students who did a placement, there was also a discusssion about their placement experiences.	Seven students were interviewed in 2011 and four (placement students) in 2012 (one had withdrawn in 2010)
June 2011	A focus group to review the whole degree including achievement of goals and professional and the future	Only three students from Fine Art attended, their work was also reviewed and discussed

Although there are many advantages to these types of interviews, we recognized and sought to minimise the limitations. It took an investment of both time and 'self' to be a respondent in our study and we lost some individuals along the way. We do not claim the 'sample' is representative, or generalizable. The relationships we developed with the students influenced the research process as 'we bring to a setting disciplinary knowledge and theoretical frameworks. We also bring a self which is, among other things, gendered, sexual, occupational, generational – located in time and space' (Coffey, 1999: 158). This gave us a 'privileged' position so we were careful to build relationships, based on 'trust, truth telling, fairness, respect, commitment and justice" (Hatch and Wisniewski, 1995: 119). Of course, this did run the risk of over-identification (Coffey, 1999) and we found some students 'over disclosed' leading to ethical problems regarding how much we should put into the public arena. We were also particularly cognizant of the need to be sensitive and non-judgemental when students were remembering events that were uncomfortable for them and were aware of individual variation regarding why certain things are remembered and how the memories are presented (Davies, 1999: 169). Due to these limitations, there can never be any absolute certainty about any event or fact, and no single source or combination of them can give a picture of the total complexity of the reality as the evidence is always fragmentary (Yow, 1994: 22), but this did not present an insurmountable hurdle as the data was triangulated by seeking out similarities and differences within all the data collected.

Two ethical issues were of particular concern to us in this study: privacy and representation. All respondents were assured of anonymity with pseudonyms, every care being taken to ensure that they could not be individually identified. Participant representation in writing, for an academic audience, was of concern to us as we wanted to have their 'voice' heard, the 'essential phenomenological essence of what is being said' (Goodall, 2000: 139), therefore we made some editorial decisions based on a desire to protect their dignity and a sense that if they do read their own words they will read a representation that is true to their original meaning.

Findings

We lost some of the students along the way. Several opted out and declined to do another interview and three withdrew from their courses before completion. Table 2.2 shows the students for whom we were able to follow their complete journey through their degree, and three who did not complete their studies.

It should be noted that entry into the Applied Business degree was very competitive. The degree involves the first year being taken on campus with the second and third years being an industrial placement interspersed with study blocks. The students were sponsored by companies, with fees paid, and salaried while on placement. The General Business degree and Fashion Textiles Management involve undertaking a one-year work placement in the third year for most students.

Beginnings and initial personal projects

Most of the students entered Higher Education because they believed a degree is required to offer them the sort of job and career opportunities they sought.

Table 2.2 The students, their subjects and university status

Student	Start Age	Course	Status
John	18	English	Graduated
Keith	18	History	Graduated
Ella	18	Applied Business	Graduated
Frances	19	General Business	Graduated
Kevin	18	General Business	Graduated
Martin	18	General Business	Withdrew after second year
Jack	18	General Business	Graduated
Terry	25	General Business	Withdrew after first year
Nathan	19	Fine Art	Graduated
Ryan	32	Fine Art	Graduated
Natalie	23	Fine Art	Graduated
Kelly	23	Fashion Textiles Management	Withdrew after first year
Chloe	19	Fashion Textiles Management	Graduated
Octavia	19	Fashion Textiles Management	Graduated

Frances had decided on a degree because 'you needed a degree' to work for good companies. For Kelly too, a degree was important for advancement. She had a clearly identified goal of becoming a fashion buyer:

> [. . .] but for us in Korea [we need a] higher qualification if we want a higher position [. . .] especially for women, so you need a strong degree or work experience in a foreign country, so I chose this degree.

They all aspired to a 'good' degree, a minimum of a '2.1'. Martin was confident of a 'first'. Some students saw this degree as a step toward a 'necessary masters':

> I would like to further my education after my degree because you know how I said before how everyone sees a degree as the norm now [. . .] but I want to be a step further than that.
>
> (Kevin)

Several students had particular career/job expectations. For example, Martin wanted to be a stockbroker at Morgan Stanley, emulating relatives who he admired and saw as role models. Students on placement degrees indicated that the placement would improve their job prospects and some had already thought about where they would like their placement to be. Kevin and Martin in particular wanted to secure their own placements, get that sorted out early, and if possible work abroad.

Four had chosen teaching as their career and their degree reflected their personal interests and/or subject strengths. John had some work experience at his school, shadowing teachers which inspired him to want to teach. He had known that he wanted to teach since he was 14 years old.

[. . .] one of my English teachers [. . .] communicated in a way that everyone got along with and I think it's great for someone to be able to teach and make it fun and get results from it [. . .] it's vital for people to understand but enjoy a subject as well.

The remaining students, although they knew the area that they wanted to work in, were not specific about the role/job they wished to undertake and had chosen their degree with a view to maintaining flexibility. Frances expressed this view, 'because I don't want my, like, options shut'.

However, going to university was not all about employability. Some thought that it was the next natural step and that they were not yet ready to work.

I have always thought that everyone goes to university [. . .] and I wanted to keep learning, I did not want to go straight to work. I do not feel that I am ready for it yet.

(Chloe)

A major factor in the decision to attend this university was based on geography: it was close enough for the students to go home at the weekends but far enough away to live an independent life (although this did not apply to the international student).

There was a general vagueness about what university teaching and learning involved. Expectations about lectures and other classes seemed to be based on stereotypical conjecture rather than anything firmer. They all intended to work hard and do whatever it took to do well. They were equally vague about the nature of relationships with teaching staff. They expected lectures to be a passive experience and seminars to be active discussions. Some students had gathered the impression that attendance at class was obligatory, whereas others perceived that it was entirely optional.

The students studying Fine Art emphasized the opportunity working in the studio would give them, for example Ryan expected to spend much of his time there on self-study. In terms of studying outside class, the general view was that this would involve working alone, either at home or perhaps the library. This form of work is seen as hard and certainly not fun, but necessary in order to 'digest information in own time [. . .] let it sink in' (Frances).

This raises the issue of the role of the teacher. There was a broad range of views. At one end of the spectrum was Frances, who wanted one-to-one support from the teacher but was unsure how that would be delivered with such a lot of students. Others looked forward to much greater freedom. Kevin looked forward to a different relationship with teachers:

Yes [. . .] you could go to a teacher and talk about anything [. . .] you wouldn't even call them teacher you would call them by their first name whatever [. . .] that's what I think.

However, the overall sense of expectation about their courses and their studies was one of vagueness. There was little evidence that students had sought to investigate this area before they came. The sources of their rather half-formed expectations were friends, relatives and teachers (who had been to university many years before) or even TV soaps:

> I watch *Hollyoaks* and things like that. I discussed it with a friend, whether university will be like that, a seating area with a sofa and stuff, [but] we thought it was a bit unrealistic.
>
> (Octavia)

Among these students, there was sense of confidence and looking forward in a very positive way. Even if there were a few uncertainties, these were not very important at all to them at this stage. So after a few weeks they wanted to be settled in, and have some assurance that things were going well.

> [University] it's a big unknown, but I have positive attitude [. . .] I just want to take everything in my stride.
>
> (Terry)

The area of greatest uncertainly was the social dimension. Almost all of the students had 'settling in' as a key aim for their first days and weeks. Indeed, friendship groups were already forming at the time of arrival, while Martin had even used social networking prior to arriving and 'got a few replies and it was like "oh I know you"', when they met for the first time. The mix of anticipation, excitement and worry about meeting new people was clear. As John said; 'I am terrified and then the next minute really excited.'

With the exception of four students, who lived at home and commuted into university, the majority of the students were in halls of residence. But both groups expected to keep in touch with old friends. Frances was close enough to her hometown, 'so I can see them at weekends'.

In overview, initial personal projects were present, but generally fairly vague and not all that powerfully expressed. Even more vague were expectations about the academic dimension of the course. We can characterize this beginning phase as full of high hopes, and very positive. Ryan was the most relaxed of everyone; he had been to university before for a period: 'Expectations? There aren't any, I just want to take it as it comes and live it as I know I have the opportunity I have.' The most trepidatious was Kelly, who, although she had already spent two years at a Korean university and a further three months on a preparatory language course before this degree, was concerned about her lack of English language skills and ability 'to fit in'.

Early transitions

The students all survived the first semester. Some found the return after Christmas difficult, particularly Octavia (Ozga and Sukhnandan, 1998). This was because just when they had started to establish a sense of 'settling in' they went home and 'had to start again' when they returned, and felt a dislocation once more from friends and family. For most students the 'honeymoon period' was brief. They identified a number of alienating challenges about their courses:

- On General Business they detested one particular module on academic skills: 'boring, irrelevant and badly delivered', so they stopped attending it: 'We all know it's crap' (Trevor).
- They did not enjoy the passivity of lectures: 'They just read off the slides, what's the point?' (Frances).
- Lack of expected autonomy: 'dictatorial tutors who tell me how to live my life' (Kevin).
- Lack of challenge: 'It's a lot less than I expected' (Kevin); a lack of work to do and easy assessments; 'I went into the test, totally unprepared, but did OK' (Martin).
- Conversely, too much challenge, for Kelly: 'it's getting harder and harder'; too much work; 'I studied every day and weekends, but I'm lacking time.' For Ella it was 'mind boggling' and 'so long and boring'.
- Time management and struggling to keep focus between intense periods around deadlines and 'slack' periods in between; 'so much free time' (Martin).
- Dysfunctional group work due to freeloading and lack of collaboration: 'I'd be better off, like, doing it on my own' (Octavia).
- The downside of independence: 'people feel a bit lost sometimes. I don't know how much reading to do [. . .] how much to study' (Jack).

Another major domain of concern among the students was the weakness of relationships with staff. They found some staff were unwelcoming (Ella: 'Some tutors may not be as friendly as they could be') and unavailable (Natalie: 'It's a bit difficult to talk to him'). Few students had any dialogue and, far short of discourse, they got a brief response to an email at best. As Kevin put it, there was 'no opportunity to chat [. . .] you're quite far away to have a social conversation. At high school it was quite small so like you walk across the corridor, say hello basically.' Another problem was that feedback on assessment had not guided them on how to improve.

Nonetheless, these negative experiences were not experienced by all or even perceived in that light by all. There were also some features which they really appreciated. Ryan was reveling in being a student: 'I love it, absolutely living it.' He thought the tutors were 'superb', and he worked very hard and relished the 'challenge to think and justify yourself intellectually'. He was the only student to be confident enough to take risks and relished exploring new areas.

Ella struggled to motivate herself in 'traditional' modules, but found her integrated group project immensely enjoyable, 'running our own business'. Keith and John enjoyed the seminars in Humanities, with opportunities to engage in 'critical debate', and the requirement to research topics more deeply for assignments. Martin, due to gregariousness and confidence, seemed to get on well with the staff but this had a downside:

> [. . .] all the seminar tutors seem to love me [. . .] just because I can do the work and so they don't really have to pay that much attention to me until I ask a question and if I need something I'll ask them so I think that's the main reason why I'm quite popular with the tutors, but a lot of people in the class don't get on with them so I get quite a bit of stick for that [. . .] you get little whispers coming from the back and the classroom going 'oh why'. It's just pointless.

For the other students, relationships with their peers were generally a source of engagement. A few students had come to university with existing friends, and that was helpful, but the others rapidly found new friends at halls, via hobbies and on the course. By the end of year, they had all found a group of peers who they saw as compatible and a source of peer support and identity (Grosset, 1991). The General Business course, despite its size, had no social events and this contrasted with the smaller courses, where there was a much stronger sense of community. Frances, though, had found a good balance and found that living with girls who shared her strong work ethic and getting on well with her peers in seminars provided strong engagement to participate in class.

Indeed, social interaction in groups and classes was positive in the main, particularly when they got used to working together. Thus social integration into a learning setting was strongly engaging (Askham, 2008). The studio was a particularly good environment for this. Ryan said, 'I like to drift around the studio, just interact with others, have fun, just bouncing of ideas.' He was the only one to really feel part of a community of practice.

Two students withdrew at the end of the first year. Kelly found that all her worst fears were realized. She struggled to comprehend lectures, participate or gain anything from seminars or group work, and only made a very narrow circle of friends (nearly all fellow international students). Trying to keep up with the work and challenge made her physically ill. She did find a way of alleviating this in second semester, through the less than ideal method of reducing attendance and reducing her focus on academic work. She felt the staff gave her platitudes 'they keep telling me I am doing fine, but I am not fine'. Although she scraped through her assessments, she did not return for second year.

Terry was overwhelmingly positive about being a student in all his interviews in first year:

> It's great. I've learnt a lot throughout the year, I've learnt my weaknesses as a person, I've learnt my strengths as a person [. . .] I'm still fighting to be the best in what I do [. . .] I don't just want to get a 2.1 or a first. I just want to get more than I am supposed to get.

He became the senior first year course rep, attended every event he could and worked hard at getting to know the staff. So on one level he was very engaged and felt a strong sense of belonging, although he struggled to find friends as he was older 'and other students don't click with me'. However, despite all this, Terry found the academic challenge of the course really difficult. He never discussed this with staff and nobody spotted the risks this was creating. He failed almost every assignment, missing all the summative exams through illness and, sadly, then disappeared without trace from the university.

Thus, unfortunately, two of the students who brought the least cultural and academic capital to university were not well supported by the university and lost their way. For the others, first year was more of a social than academic transition. They all felt they had settled in well by the end of the first year. There was a general sense of belonging and integration. For each student the locus of that differed between peer groups (which varied considerably), the course and the broader university. So they had settled in socially and established a student identity (Kantanis, 2000), albeit, in the main, with weak relationships with staff. Their initial expectations appear to have had little impact on their experience. Only when the experience was strongly negative, as it was for Kelly, did a mismatch of expectations really matter. Previous studies (e.g. Lowe and Cook, 2003) have suggested that the mismatch of expectations from reality is a serious issue, but it was not here, except for Kelly. Ironically, she had had a very strong personal project at the outset but this did not, on its own, provide enough engagement for persistence.

There was little evidence that the students had developed intellectually in the first year. Some did indeed work as hard as they said they would, such as Ryan and Keith. The others struggled to motivate themselves to do so, sometimes because of a perceived lack of challenge, or a lack of intrinsic interest in the subject, or weak relationships with staff and peers on their course. These students, apart from Ryan, seemed to need a 'high trust' social relationship before they could have a constructive dialogue with staff, and they did not have that. It appeared that they all could pass by taking an 'absolute knowing' approach (Baxter Magolda, 1992). Only a handful had met Upcraft and Gardner's (1989) definition of full success in first year transition in terms of personal and educational development.

Second and third year ups and downs

The journeys the students took diverged after the first year. Although some shared the same course and other contexts, this did not mean they took the same path. We shall look at similar contexts first before considering cross-cutting themes.

Chloe and Octavia, on Fashion Textiles Management, both noted a continuing high workload. They found that easier to manage as their experience of doing so increased. Seminars started to provide a better source of support, as they felt they had better relationships with their peers (and a little more with tutors) so felt more relaxed and able to engage more in constructive discussion. They both lived with flatmates from their halls but grew away from them and closer to course-mates, choosing the latter to live with in final year. Chloe did her placement year in New York: 'it was really fun, and really nice to work and have a specific job, and go home and do what you wanted to do on the weekends'. Octavia found a placement in the UK in a different role from her original personal project, but enjoyed it so much that she accepted an offer to return after graduation. She relished the trust her manager put in her: 'I think when you get more responsibility it helps you develop as well.'

They both struggled to settle back into university in their final year. Chloe said: 'it's difficult going from a nine to six job to a nothing to nothing job'. Octavia was excited about being a student again, but the reality did not match up: 'once I actually started, I was like "oh, I can't wait for this to be over!"' They both found the workload in the final year particularly high but not stretching academically, with the exception of the dissertation. They found the dissertation a very good experience and the first time they had really got to know and trust a staff member: 'she seemed interested in my topic, she was really good' (Octavia); 'she's been so good. Really, really helpful, it's really nice to have some-one, who knows you by now' (Chloe).

The experiences of Ryan, Natalie and Nathan in Fine Art were much more contrasting. Nathan decided to come out over the summer before second year and this put his family relationships under some stress. He changed his medium to video and live performance and attached this to his emerging identity. This was quite stressful and induced panic attacks and a 'breakdown'. He overcame this and continued to build his own identity as a performing drag artist. He built up networks both with peers and outside the university, performing in the streets and, notably, in Berlin. This built up considerable confidence in his work and through gaining positive feedback. But in a course which was all assessed on project work this created a tension. Nathan struggled with writing and the academic provenance behind his creative ideas. Thus, despite improving dialogue with tutors, as the degree progressed ('I've got a like-minded tutor so she knows the subject'), Nathan struggled to find his ideas and work accepted by academic assessors. This made final year rather problematic, and made Nathan depressed at the mid-point of that. In the final semester, he decided to keep to his personal project as a performing artist that he had established, but found that others did not consider this to 'be proper art' or consider his 'research to be rigorous':

> I've never really had good feedback [. . .] certain tutors can be quite unkind [. . .] I'm gonna to do it, do what I gonna do, and keep going, develop it further, and kinda push it.

Nathan received a third class degree and was very disappointed and angry about that.

Natalie began second year with weak relationships with staff and course-mates. This did not really improve and she felt she had to be self-taught. She regretted her course choice:

> I keep thinking I should have picked a course that did have structure that
> I could just work to some parameters with 'cos there's no parameters. Just
> drop yourself in the ocean and swim about a bit.

Nonetheless, being forced to be independent did build her confidence. She had
early setbacks in final year with some personal problems and losing all her work
in a computer crash. However, by this time, she had gained the confidence to
regroup and produce an excellent final project and aspired to be a practicing artist
after graduation. She felt she had found her own voice, at last. Natalie never really
got very close to her course peers; she did not identify with them, other than to
draw some peer feedback. She relied on a network of friends outside the course.

Ryan moved in with 10 other Art students at the beginning of second year,
with a purpose of creating an art community with them. However, this disin-
tegrated rapidly ('too many egos') and, in Ryan's view, the other students had
too many parties. Apart from that, Ryan went from strength to strength. He felt
relationships with tutors were stronger and he found a kindred peer group where
they discussed art and their work in the studio all the time. His personal project
moved away from becoming a professional artist to a more academic focus, practicing and teaching art at university. He immersed himself in all the extra-curricular
activities around the course, participating in shows and exhibitions. He professed
a strong affinity to being part of a learning community. He found the freedom of
the course enabled him to give full range to his creativity but felt that he was in a
supported environment too. His work and its underpinning academic insights were
highly regarded by peers and staff, and he achieved a first class degree.

The paths of John and Keith on Humanities diverged sharply in second year.
John embraced the step up to being more critical in his academic work, 'because
you've proved yourself in the first year that you are capable'. His grades, which
already had been good, became even better. This was because he was not only
relaxed about putting in the effort but was also due to his growing sense of confidence in his independence. Therefore, he was assured in his ability to work on his
own, to be creative and give his own opinion when appropriate. He related more
to staff, when he felt this was useful, although he found some 'rather distant'
due to their focus on research rather than students. They were 'not accessible,
approachable, not there when I went to collect my essay for example'. His growing sense of independence encompassed the social domain too, and he relied less
on parental support while feeling part of a new group of peers. It was not all plain
sailing, but he coped with any blips without much problem.

John navigated the rest of his degree with assurance. By the middle of final
year he felt that, along with his peers, he was familiar with all the cultural rules
and thus could draw most benefit. So seminars now really were open discussions.
His dissertation was a piece of creative writing and he valued the structured peer
feedback sessions designed to provide constructive critique. He was now really
appreciating collaborative learning. His relationship with staff had progressed
from a situation of 'the teacher always knows more' to one where his and peers'

opinions were as important. He had changed his 'way of knowing' to 'independent' (Baxter Magolda, 1992). John observed that, in reality, nothing had changed with staff:

> There's no difference between now and the first year. But it's just having that [. . .] I don't really know what it's about because it's not like they never said 'we have office hours, come and see us'.

However, final-year students had gained the confidence to make use of this because they knew 'how things work'. John had reflected on his own personal project to become a teacher and was now considering alternative options more directly related to his development as a writer: 'screenplays, perhaps'. He comfortably achieved a 2.1 degree.

Keith found the second year altogether more problematic. He really struggled to stay motivated: more workload; too many close deadlines; more pressure; and continuing weak relationships with staff. He disliked his second subject in the joint degree and became disengaged with that subject. At the mid-point of the year, he nearly left: 'I just felt drained, isolated from everyone.' Fortunately, his good relationships with course peers were enough to turn this around: '[it is] especially important to have friends to help you through it [to] motivate each other, drag ourselves through'. Another major turnaround was starting his dissertation project early over the summer vacation and this re-established his motivation for study. At this point Keith thought:

> You can see the light at the end of the tunnel. Whereas in first year you're just walking into that, in second year, you're in the middle and you don't know where you are.

The final year was much better and central to that improvement was the dissertation. His relationship with the supervisor was one of 'mutual respect'. Keith said of his supervisor: 'he wants to learn about the subject as much as I do, [my findings] are new to him [. . .] he's finding it really interesting'. Relationships with other History staff had really improved too: 'I have a laugh with them.' Keith had formed an informal study group with peers, which he found was invaluable for support. His whole social network was one which he was very comfortable within and was in good balance with his studies. Like John, his personal project had become less certain, and he was not so enthusiastic about a teaching career. Although Keith had become much more self-assured over his degree, he still lacked personal confidence about his ability, doubting that he would get a good degree (he got a 2.1) and unwilling to take the risk of doing a Master's and pursuing his ideal aspiration, to become a military historian.

Ella nearly did not gain her in-company placement at all ('I can come across as girly [. . .] blonde bimbo kind of thing') but scraped in at the last moment. The job was a long way from home and forced her to reduce her reliance on family. A crisis arose early on, with a breakdown in relations where she was living, but moving in with her boyfriend's parents gave her a new form of family support that sustained her through all the challenges of a demanding role, studying at a distance and on her own. This was supplemented by the social network of her course peers that she maintained throughout. 'Practicing' business management was perfect for Ella, and gave her a level of understanding that started to translate through into much better academic grades. The guarantee of a job on graduation (if she got a 2.1) inspired her to work really hard: 'I am going to get a first.' It created '100% engagement' with the course and led her to taking leadership and responsibility of group projects. This sustained her all the way through the remainder of the degree 'because our course is all about on-the-job learning we learn ourselves, we learn through the companies we are in'. She too formed a trust relationship with her dissertation supervisor. However, she also had other staff 'role models', the colleagues in her company who made her feel part of a professional community. She sailed past the 2.1 boundary and continued working for the company after graduation. At that point, Ella noted that she was still 'blonde' but not a bimbo, describing herself as, 'not clever, clever but not stupid!'

The General Management students also had varied experiences. Jack had worked hard in his first year but was only semi-engaged with the course: 'I'm not that passionate about it [. . .] I don't feel attached to it particularly.' However, in the second year he began to specialize in a subject he preferred and one that was relevant to future plans. This meant a smaller cohort and closer contact with the same staff. One source of motivation was 'when your student loan receipt come[s] through, how much you owe, and you think "shouldn't mess this up!"' The second year went smoothly and he believed he had become a more independent learner and more confident.

But in his placement year, Jack learnt 'so much more than I have done in the whole university because you can't teach what you learn'. The company offered him a job after graduation, which he accepted. This led to him returning for final year 'totally refreshed'. He was disappointed with what he saw as some disorganized modules, lack of feedback, lack of relevance of subjects and poor relationships with staff:

> I hate the last year. It's, once you have been away and you come back, it's just boring [. . .] You're skint again and it's [. . .] yeah it's rubbish. It's just [...] it's you feel like you're being patronised all the time and having to jump through hoops [. . .] Well I don't think anything you learn in the classroom is particularly applicable because it's all just theory and academia that you learn about.

At the end of the four years, Jack came to hate university 'to be honest. It's just so money grabbing [. . .] they just don't care about you at all.' His personal project was no longer to start his own business. That had become a long term possibility, but he wanted to develop a solid professional career in accountancy before reconsidering that.

In second year, Kevin specialized in Marketing, his desired career on graduation. He became more involved in extra-curricular roles involving societies and sport. He felt he widened his circle of friends and felt part of the 'community of Nottingham'. His initial plans for a placement abroad did not work out, and he did not secure any placement at all. Instead, he took a year out, returning home to London and working part-time. Kevin was glad to be back at university and to focus on his studies as 'it's the final year and it kind of hits you, the realisation that this is it'. He specialized in Marketing and International Management which reflected his career ambitions, to enter an international business, 'maybe as a linguist in Europe and China'. He found International Management too 'low level' (as it seemed 'aimed at international students') but tutors in marketing pushed him to be more creative and use his initiative. The classes were small, with continual assessment and good feedback. Again, the dissertation proved engaging, as he was able to specialize in the subject of China and build a stronger relationship with his supervisor, much more so than other staff. Overall, Kevin felt that university had enabled him to mature and become independent. A factor that enabled this was becoming president of a society:

> I'm twenty-two now. I can work independently [. . .] and I realize the importance of extra activities, extra-curricular activities which is why I applied for the presidency, which is why I've took mentoring lessons and just simple things like that which help you improve.

Frances also focused on Marketing and continued with same strong work ethic she previously displayed. She continued to do well, except in group work where her peers were not as diligent: 'I don't like it when other people can influence my grade.' She put a lot of effort into finding a placement too, getting two offers well before most of her peers had seriously engaged with this process. Notably, she rejected the offer that was closest to her original personal project, opting instead for a broader, more responsible post. For Frances, relationships with staff remained weak: 'I wish I had a personal tutor.' Relations with her course-mates were not much stronger than that either. Her social support came from a group of friends she met in halls, which lasted through all four years of her degree. She found it 'refreshing' to spend her time out of class with a group who were studying quite different degrees to her. Frances seemed to develop incrementally and steadily over the course of the year. One particular source of gaining assurance and interpersonal skills was the experience of being a student associate teaching assistant in a local school.

She really enjoyed her placement, feeling well supported and socially at ease. She did not find the previous two years of study of much relevance to her role at all. Notably, she found her placement linked much better to her final-year curriculum and benefitted her, thus:

Just skills like time management, proactivity, initiative, I think you are a lot more determined to work harder and you can see the end goal by doing a work placement. You are a lot more proactive to do well in final year because for me I couldn't wait to get back to uni in a way because although I really loved placement it was hard and I wanted to enjoy final year and make the most of it.

Nonetheless, her personal project took another twist and she turned down the chance to work for her placement company. Instead, she reverted to a merchandising role in a large retailer, which was her original plan. Typical of Frances, she had secured this graduate position by February of final year.

An alienating element in final year was that Frances had carried forward an average from second year close to a first but was frustrated by more group assessments, which started to drag her marks down again. Moreover, tutors did not explain at all how to deliver the quality of work expected for a first on any module. She gave up hope of achieving that (and indeed got a 2.1). But Frances did enjoy final year despite having no time for socializing or extra-curricular activity (in her own words). The dissertation was not very engaging because she had chosen a topic based on safety rather than passion. She was supported by a group rather than individual supervision, so this did not enhance relations with her supervisor. However, she did build stronger relationships with some staff, but this was down to her own proactivity (similar to John). By the end of her degree, Frances was considerably more assured and open minded in her thinking. She was genuinely self-critical, Nicol's (2010) key graduate attribute:

Oh yeah, I think the university as a whole has opened up lots of opportunities and there is a lot more, obviously my eyes are open to a lot more things that are going on.

Martin had coasted through first year. He was very upbeat at the end of that year, feeling very much 'part of the whole Trent army thing'. But in the second year it all began to unravel. He became more and more disenchanted with the curriculum. He disliked all the modules he was doing, and was particularly offended by one: 'hard selling is immoral'. He contended that the curriculum and assessment were so prescriptive, giving him no freedom to express himself, forcing him to regurgitate what the marker wanted to see. Soon he fell behind and failed more and more assessments. Although he had closer (but not social) relationships with staff in first year, being taught by an array of different, and changing, staff in second year meant he lost this rapport. The policy of all-new seminar groupings in second year too meant that he lost contact with the friends he had made among his peers. Even someone as gregarious as Martin struggled to make any new friends at this stage.

Moreover, Martin's living arrangements went badly wrong when he fell out with his flatmates and could not extricate himself from his rental arrangement.

He was also under financial pressure. Martin felt increasingly isolated and fell ill with depression. His course, university and external social networks were much too weak to sustain him through this difficult period: 'I drift between friends.' Therefore, despite appearing to be the student with as strong a personal project as any other at the outset, apparent strong integration into the university community subsequently and some intellectual engagement with some of his subjects (a complete set of the factors identified by Dubet, 1994), Martin withdrew at the end of second year. A caveat is that Martin was always so ebullient in his interviews in first year that there was likely to be an element of illusion in his claims, although he was reflective and insightful too. He rejected the identity of 'being a student' and is now thriving in a business role, where he has been able to recover his former confidence.

Becoming and transforming

An element that was included in all the interviews was 'ways of knowing' (Baxter Magolda, 1992). Most students started in the position of 'absolute knowing', but there were some who were already in 'transitional knowing', most notably Ryan, Keith and John. Over the course of the degree, these three individuals moved on considerably into 'independent knowing', with Ryan starting to do that in first year, John in second year, and Keith catching up in third year. It was through strong engagement with the course and their studies that seemed to be the prerequisite for this to occur. However, we shall look at catalysts for this in more detail later. Others who made the jump to independent learning, albeit in different ways, were Ella and Frances, who had both begun very much more in the mode of 'right and wrong' answers. The other students did not seem to advance as much. They were neither sufficiently challenged nor engaged to get beyond a 'transitional knowing' stage. In General Business and Fashion Textiles Management, there seemed some potential for this to happen but the environment they were in was not conducive to engage them sufficiently, and it was quite possible to gain the desired 2.1 without going beyond reproduction or demonstrating criticality (Barnett, 2007). Fine Art allowed plenty of scope to challenge students but was unstructured and left students to tackle the course by themselves. Natalie and Nathan floundered in this setting in terms of academic progress and development, although Natalie found a suitable focus later on.

Two important elements in the model of relational engagement (Solomonides et al., 2012a) are sense of professional formation and sense of expertise in the discipline. Again, our students diverged in the extent that they perceived they had made progress over their degrees. For those that did a placement, they all gained much benefit from their immersion in the working world. This was particularly spectacular for Ella, with the nature of her placement-based degree suiting her own disposition so well, and by graduation she was very much a professional, and felt that too. Due to his taking out a year out rather than bona fide placement, Kevin did not gain the full experience of that. Ryan had developed strongly as a professional, by immersing himself in the world of art whilst studying, and having a clear (if changing) goal in doing so. Indeed, he started to identify with his own academic environment, and decided to pursue that as a professional career. Nathan embarked on a 'professional identity project' (Holmes, 1995) which began to clash with his academic studies, but he pursued that focus, at some cost to his degree result. This 'becoming a professional' very much connected to his changing personal identity.

The Humanities students, initially aiming to become teachers, had a professional vocation which was not connected directly to and within their studies. Notably, their aims started to change and to align more to their subject. John and Keith are good examples of individuals who embraced a growing expertise in their subjects of creative writing and History as elements of their identity as their degree progressed. Ryan too embraced a strong sense of discipline knowledge, as it aligned with his goals and interests. For the 'vocational degrees' it was less clear in regards to this territory, in part because the discipline tended to be an academic construct which does not mirror the 'practice' going on in the workplace. Indeed, some students rejected the academic 'sphere' in final year. They did enough to get the degree they needed for a graduate post but aligned themselves to the values of practice rather than academia.

Nonetheless, there are other aspects to becoming too. All the students that got through to the end of their degree gained self-assurance and confidence, which are of such importance. In large measure they felt themselves to be more independent, more capable of making their own decisions and more mature.

We can say with some confidence that all these graduates changed in a positive, developmental way and added value to themselves. That happened in spite of alienating forces, issues within their degrees and broader experiences which hindered rather than helped. So, what were the key catalysts behind these transformations?

Undertaking a placement was a transformational experience for the students. They felt they learned so much more there, arguably more (that they valued) than the rest of the degree. The opportunity to take responsibility and deliver achievements that they felt mattered was greater in the placement than in the curriculum. They all worked really hard while on placement, whereas sometimes they intended to study hard but did not deliver on that, or not at least until final year. There was a downside to placements: returning to study! Students commented that they were not re-inducted into study and found that hard. However, some returned feeling that the academic curriculum was irrelevant to their goals. They all said that the academic knowledge they had gained before they went on placement was not of particular use in undertaking their roles. Frances found her placement experience valuable to link to her academic understanding in final year. Conversely, Jack found the strictures and his perceived irrelevance of final year resulted in despising his last year at university. Ella seemed to have the best of all worlds, by doing a two-year placement while she studied at the same time. That worked well for her as she made connections between the two and valued the academic as well as the professional.

Some students gained essential confidence and developed graduate attributes by undertaking extra-curricular roles and interests. For example, Kevin connected his growing interest in China to learning Mandarin and becoming President of the Chinese Society, while Frances appreciated her role as teaching assistant. This may also be a source of social support during difficult times too, as it was for Keith and Natalie.

Social learning opportunities were a powerful source of engagement and thus a catalyst for transformation, not least because they provided opportunities for students to mix with good peer role models and engage in collaborative learning. A good example was the integrated project that Ella undertook and which sustained her in first year. This enabled her to bond with her peers, to link her academic subjects and to prepare her for practice. Group work clearly did not deliver the same good outcomes, and only started to do that if it was set up very carefully. Indeed, the disbenefits of group work tended to alienate. The studio environment in Fine Art was a good example of a learning community and proto-community of practice. The key beneficiary of that was Ryan, who fully embraced what it offered. Natalie and Nathan tended to remain very much at the periphery of the studio and thus did not realize its potential although Nathan had a small group of supportive peers, Natalie had none. However, that was not 'their fault', and showed that such environments may not be inclusive.

The dissertation proved to be a major catalyst for several students, notably Keith. The opportunity to choose your own topic, to research it and the autonomy it afforded was a source of strong engagement and ownership. At the same time, having a dedicated supervisor as support created the one and only trust relationship with a staff member that these students had on their degree. That trust relationship was very sustaining. Some students got less out of the dissertation, as they had adopted a 'safety first' choice or were part of group supervision arrangements. The final-year project may also have given rise to considerable stress and anxiety, such as in the case of Fine Art, as it was worth the entire final year. That may be less engaging.

Discussion

There is another complementary aspect to catalysts for engagement and transformation: that is the territory of sources of sustenance in hard times, the presence of which gives the student sufficient resilience to overcome moments of doubt and alienation. A crucial source for these students was having a supportive social network. Terry, Kelly and Martin all lacked that, whereas for Keith, Nathan and Ella there was such a network in place for when it was needed (but this was not provided by the university).

The second year can be a difficult time, as students start to question why they are studying a particular degree and/or not enjoying their student experience. This coincides with a time when they may be growing apart from friends made in halls and not have made many friends among their course peers. The latter seems to matter less in first year. Unfortunately for some of these students, there were no mechanisms within the course to nurture engagement or social relations at this point. This is more than a sophomore slump (Gump, 2007) and at its root was a complete lack of trust relationships between the students and staff. These relationships had not been established in first year and the conditions and culture in second year actually worked to diminish them further. The occasional e-mail exchange is not a substitute for a dialogue!

There was not a particular change of environment to create a stronger rapport between staff and students in final year. Three factors contributed here. It would appear that some staff are much more willing to engage with final-year students than those in earlier years, on the basis the students are now 'mature enough' to participate in an academic conversation. But as some students noted, it was not so much the staff that changed their attitudes and approaches, but the students. The students had gained the confidence (and, possibly, recognized the necessity) to seek staff out, for example to uncover the mysteries of assessment criteria. The third factor was the final-year project, where there was usually a 1:1 arrangement for supervision, a feature so lacking in every other module.

It is deeply problematic that it takes until final year before students really learned the 'rules' and had developed the assurance to move beyond, or even approach the boundary, of the course community. That is when most students in our study became comfortable enough to start to realize their potential and add most value to themselves. Much of the becoming and transformation really happened in final year, or in the placement year just before it, for those who had such an opportunity.

It is very easy to criticize the degrees the students were on, all of whom seem to have had some serious defects. That might be harsh, as these degree arrangements and their supporting mechanisms are fairly typical of similar degrees across the sector. This study only focused on relatively few students, so it is inappropriate to generalize too widely. Arguably, the students volunteered to take part in a project which demanded quite a lot of their time and energy, so they were likely to be quite engaged students in the first place. The point that at least three withdrew early, with little if any intervention by the university, is telling.

A detrimental feature of two of the bigger degrees was the way they kept students so busy in second and third year without really stretching or challenging them to think. There appeared to be so many assessments in final year that the students felt there was no time to socialize or engage in any extra-curricular activity. There was a general lack of co-curricular activity too, including too few efforts to weave 'practice' and more authentic tasks and projects into the curriculum, which have been found elsewhere to be so engaging to students (McCune, 2009). Such approaches might have served to keep engaged those who had returned from placements. It is ironic that as a consequence of an earlier study on student engagement (Bryson and Hand, 2007) the degree on which the General Management students in the current study were on, had been radically redesigned before they did it. That earlier study had identified that an incoherent curriculum with too much assessment led to students experiencing a 'joyless slog' (ibid.). It would appear that the principles that were developed to address that did not carry through into implementation. And it is abundantly clear that General Business desperately needed some more personal elements to break down the anonymity of such a large degree, for example, by initiating peer mentor and personal tutor schemes.

The in-company Applied Business degree appeared to offer much to address such problems, although one might note a year cohort of 40 against one of 500 plus on General Management and issues of scalability. Nonetheless, approaches such as integrated projects in the first year could be scaled up and introduced, as well as similar approaches based on undergraduate research and active, enquiry-based learning.

The Fine Art and Humanities degrees both seemed to be structured in such a way as to offer more engagement. There was more student autonomy and choice. Indeed, on Fine Art it was totally unstructured, too much so, from some students' perspectives. These degrees seemed to offer some opportunities for students to reflect. This was totally lacking on General Management. Frances had been asked to complete a reflective diary on placement, which she duly did in order to have this accredited, but the idea had been dropped by the time she returned and no staff even looked at it. The students commented that it was the interviews with us that gave them their only opportunity to reflect.

These findings present a real challenge to curriculum designers and to those responsible for enhancing the student experience. Before they tear everything up and start again, they should begin by asking the students what works. There do appear to be some interesting possibilities to discuss. Why not have projects and placements earlier in the degree (especially on vocational degrees)? Why not create far more opportunities to integrate and weave together the extra-curricular into the curriculum? We are well aware that since this study colleagues at Nottingham Trent have launched all sorts of initiatives for engagement, some of which are presented later in this volume.

Finally, what of the conceptual models and their value in analyzing these student narratives? The first problem to acknowledge is just how rich and complex these narratives are. It would take a chapter this length to present each student's journey properly in terms of all its twists and turns and all the issues that had some bearing on their engagement. Models tend to try to fit such complexity into neat boxes. Dubet's (1994) 'ways of being a student' has helped to structure the summarizing of our findings but by no means addresses all the relevant issues. Personal projects for individuals were subject to change, and what may have begun as a strong personal project for an individual can become diluted, or vice versa, or be amended, as the individual's perspectives and what they value and aspire to is reconstructed. Thus, this is not a great universal predictor of engagement and success. Integration into university covers a huge territory, taking place in diverse ways and can be much more fragile than appearances can convey. Opportunities for intellectual engagement with the subject seem to vary between and within degrees, so again this parameter is inappropriate to apply in a generic way. The relational engagement model (Solomonides et al., 2012a) offers some appropriate concepts and processes and the notion of 'sense of' that is explicit on the model captures the constructivist nature of engagement. Again, the evidence did not always fit too neatly although processes like transformation provided a good lens to examine how students had changed. Kahu's (2013) model appears elegant and comprehensive but it was beyond us how to apply it to these complex and diverse student journeys!

Chapter 3

The listening project

Physiotherapy students' narratives of their Higher Education experiences

Claire Hamshire and Christopher Wibberley

Introduction

This chapter examines physiotherapy students' stories of their undergraduate experiences. It presents findings gathered from a three-year longitudinal study in which the central aim was to listen to students' stories told in their own words over a series of interviews throughout their degree programme. But to begin with we will tell our own story of how the study arose.

Reading our own, and others' studies on student experiences, we were struck by the way in which most of these studies fragmented the experience of the student. This fragmentation took the form of only looking at a particular snapshot in time of the students' overall experience and/or targeting a particular aspect of that experience. To focus criticism on our own studies, we had targeted: becoming an autonomous learner (Hamshire, Cullen and Wibberley, 2009); student expectations (Hamshire, Willgoss and Wibberley, 2013a); student attrition (Hamshire, Willgoss and Wibberley, 2011); and retention (Hamshire, Willgoss and Wibberley, 2013b) – with each of these 'thematically splitting' the target of interest further. The studies followed agendas set by institutions, both providers and purchasers, and whilst we tried to value and honour the student voice as much as possible in these works, we felt the journey that students undertook, over their student career, was underplayed. In our defence, we will merely comment that we were far from alone in representing students in this way.

As we reflected on this, we were drawn to justifications of narrative enquiry such as 'within the narrative method "the interview or story is taken as a whole"' (Nettleton et al., 2005: 206) and 'unlike other qualitative methods the approach [of narrative analysis] does not fragment texts into thematic categories for coding purposes. The approach preserves the integrity of the narrative [. . .]' (Edvardsson et al., 2003: 379).

Additionally, it was not unusual in narrative studies for the researcher(s) to return to the participants a number of times to allow the narrative to develop over time (see for example Gubrium, 1993; Stamm et al., 2008). We were also struck by the way that stories were elicited from participants using a relatively open invitation for them to tell their story. We felt that the holistic nature of narrative enquiry would give students an opportunity to focus on key personal events and describe their experiences, rather than following an agenda set by the researcher, and would allow us to investigate students' experiences in all their complexity and richness (Webster and Mertova, 2007).

Thus, listening to students describe their experiences at a range of points within their studies was the main aim of this project. Each of the seven students who volunteered to be included in the study were interviewed on at least five occasions. At each interview they were encouraged with a narrative prompt to tell the stories of their experiences as a series of 'episodes' beginning and finishing wherever and however they felt was most appropriate. This narrative prompt provided an opportunity for the students to speak about themselves in relation to their experiences over time and convey, from their point of view, their learner experiences of Higher Education. At each subsequent interview the students were asked to tell the next 'episode' and the stories the students told allowed us to view holistically their learning experiences in all their complexity and richness.

This chapter presents some of this evidence and offers an insight into the individual lives of seven students, as they chose to represent them, as they navigated through the academic and practical discipline of an undergraduate physiotherapy degree.

The students' stories

Each of the stories portrayed the way in which individual students interpreted and narrated their experiences of being a student. There were varieties, variance and difference throughout the narratives, yet commonalities could also be identified. Both academic and personal dimensions could be seen to impact upon the students' experiences and these were initially used to construct narratives from across each student's interviews. Care in listening and re-listening to interviews, reading and re-reading the constructed narratives of the seven students subsequently identified that whilst individual experiences were multi-layered, 'being a student' was for each student dominated by a specific orientation: peer support, financial difficulties, learner self-direction or personal issues. Within each of these orientations we also recognized the uniqueness of each student's story.

There were some students that had hints of particular orientations within their narrative, whereas others had orientations that were substantial. Some at times combined orientations with diverse narrative linkages. However, we acknowledge that none of these orientations exclusively determined the students' experiences. For each student there were other on-going concerns and challenges and as texts of experiences the stories presented here will be incomplete. The stories were constructed and described by the interviewees to meet the circumstances of the occasioned telling and therefore each story may have multiple coherences on different occasions (Holstein and Gubrium, 2000).

Using the four orientations we will present each student's narrative as a story. The first of these is peer support, in which we depict two students (Alice and

Sara) who had a personal need for friendship and academic support in order to negotiate successfully their undergraduate studies and assessments. The second orientation relates to financial difficulties. We describe two mature male students (Oliver and Paul) who explored issues around how they managed to balance their academic commitments with the on-going need to undertake paid work. In the third orientation, students' development as self-directed learners, we consider how two of the young male students (Jack and Adnam) managed their personal learning transition as they adjusted to degree level working. Finally, within the personal difficulties orientation, we detail how one mature female student (Maria) negotiated her academic studies around the decline of her marriage and the subsequent emotional upheaval.

The importance of peer support: Alice and Sara

This narrative orientation presents some of the intricacies of peer-to-peer relations that impact upon students' engagement and academic achievement. Each of the seven students spoke about the peer networks they developed over the three years of their undergraduate studies, with peer support being a common and recurring subject. However, how alliances and friendships were formed and their relative importance varied across the seven students. For some it was a profoundly central issue and until new friendships were formed there was in essence a loss of personal identity and, subsequently, engagement. For other, perhaps more self-reliant students, peer support was a marginal issue that was only mentioned sporadically.

Alice and Sara, the two interviewees considered in this section, both included descriptions of supportive families and happy schooldays when they began their narratives. Both also made regular reference to strong friendships and parents with whom they had close, positive relationships several times within their interviews. Family and friendship were very much part of their identity and for both of these students developing new friendships at university was an important early goal.

Alice

Alice's narrative was that of a direct-entry student, studying close to home. Establishing a social network was important to Alice from the beginning of her transition to university. In her first interview she returned to the topic of friendships frequently. She believed that it was good to 'get to know' other students and wanted more social activities in the first weeks of term so 'we could get to know a lot more people'. Unfortunately, she initially struggled to make friends and there was also a clear indication in her narrative that she felt excluded from the main cohort that were living in shared accommodation together, saying 'they have their own little group of friends'. She expressed regret that she was not included within this group and she initially failed to make any lasting friendships with the other students on her programme. Although they made conversation during the taught sessions on campus, she rarely saw these students at evenings or weekends and she talked at length about how excluded she felt from the majority of her group:

> I wish I had been able to go to those halls of residence because I know that all the other students are there, so a lot of them know each other. They have their own little group of friends because they're always there which is why I wanted to go there initially.

Alice also felt isolated in the evenings, as she only saw her flatmate occasionally and they had not established a rapport:

> I only live with one flatmate and we don't see each other a lot. I'm on my own quite a lot at uni, I make an effort but she's not very sociable and I just think she wants to keep herself to herself really. I don't really see anyone to be honest.

Fortunately, in the second term of her first year Alice developed a peer support network with a group of mature students, following a group assessment, and this was pivotal in her engagement. She explained that one of the key aspects of these friendships was the peer support as they shared knowledge and revised together:

> Since the assessment I've started hanging around with them a lot more because I need to be doing stuff to learn. These girls are a lot older than I am, but I get on with them really well and we work together really well, we all email each other our work.

When Alice reflected on these friendships, she identified that the group had developed as they had a shared ethos and commitment to academic engagement:

> I think I get on with them better because they seem to work harder, whereas some of the younger students who are more my age don't. Sometimes in lessons they just don't pay attention they just want to be somewhere else. We're not in uni that often are we, so the times that I am in I'd rather be working and learning and concentrating on what I'm doing.

As Alice interacted with the older students in the cohort and developed a peer support group, she also had a greater degree of engagement with her studies and academic success (see Tinto, 1987). This peer support network that she developed was therefore crucial as it gave her an opportunity to build relationships that provided both academic support as well as a group of friends who supported her personally. Thus, essentially, they formed a group who had a similarity of purpose. This peer support network continued throughout the rest of Alice's undergraduate studies; there was a clear change in the tone of Alice's narrative and she was much more engaged with her studies. Alice's experience was an exemplar of the findings of Tinto (1987) who states that social integration can be a prerequisite for academic integration for some students. In the second year, she explained how the group worked together to support each other:

> Working as a group has helped me loads, things that sometimes I'm stuck on, they'll help, they'll explain it to me and put it in a way that I can understand it.

At the end of the three years, she credited this peer support group as being instrumental in her eventual academic success of achieving a 2.1:

> The work load is so intense without sharing it with my friends I would have struggled more, yeah that little triangle of friends was really good to be able to practice things, it really helped.

Sara

Sara joined the Physiotherapy programme after deferring entry to travel for a year and, initially, she struggled to adapt to her new environment and experiences, saying 'it was good to come here but as soon as I got here I didn't really want to be here anymore'. She was the student in this study who initially seemed the most unhappy during her initial transition and she particularly struggled during the first few weeks of term:

> The first week you have to go out; you are a wet blanket it you don't go out in that first week it's just like Fresher's week and you have to go out every night and I don't want to go out every night. I didn't enjoy the pressure of feeling like you had to go out. I did go out but it was the fact that everyone else felt they had to go out and no one stayed in so you were alone when you did stay in. My house mates are party animals.

Essentially, Sara felt isolated as she had few commonalities with the students that she shared university accommodation with and did not have a sense of 'belonging' to the institution as she described herself as 'not fitting in'. At the end of her first interview, her reluctance to commit to her undergraduate studies was clear as she emphasized her difficulties engaging with her peers and struggled to set any goals for the end of the academic year. Sara kept her temporal horizons close to the present: 'I don't have any massive goals just to be here is great to be honest just to have got this far.' It was apparent that at this time she did not see a distinctive future self, going forward into the academic year.

Towards the end of her first year, when Sara reflected back on her experiences, she admitted that she had seriously considered leaving several times, saying 'at the beginning, I hated it and just wanted to leave' which she attributed to a feeling of just 'not fitting in'. It was only after she developed friendships through a

Students' Union Society she had joined that she began to enjoy herself more and started to concentrate on her academic studies:

> Coming here and only having one group of friends was really odd for me. I didn't really like it but now I've branched out a lot, it's good to have friends and that's why I'm really glad I went on the Society trip as well.

Eventually, towards the end of her first year Sara effectively made a 'new home' and an emotional transition as she moved accommodation to share a flat with friends she made on the programme. From this point on, as the supportive friendships developed and the positives of peer support became a central focus of her narrative, she began to feel that she 'belonged' (see also Bryson and Hardy, 2012). It was a new beginning and the moment when her university experiences began to mirror the imagined future she had had; she began to look forward:

> I moved halls and now I am in her crowd of friends it's really good, it's really nice so I'm living with them next year as well.

In her second year, further friendships developed with a group of students within her tutor group and they formed a supportive peer network who shared revision tasks:

> The other day we had tons of work, you just could not do it all by yourself. I don't know how anyone on their own did it; we had enough to split it between us all, we all emailed each other the things that we had done which was really nice.

As Sara reflected on her learning experiences, she believed that working within a peer support group had significantly enhanced her academic performance and helped her establish a new way of learning:

> I think it is interesting actually because I have only just found out how to learn, everyone sits there writing notes and I don't learn a thing from doing that at all. I have got away from the writing of notes and started talking it out more because that is the only way I remember.

Sara graduated from the Physiotherapy programme with a first class honours degree; after her graduation she directly attributed her academic success to the close group of friends that she had worked with. In common with the findings of Bryson and Hardy (2012), she detailed how social integration had a positive impact on her academic engagement:

> Having a supportive network around you really helps; I don't think I would have been nearly as successful otherwise. We all helped each other all the time and it was nice just to have that support, we still keep in touch.

This statement is a clear indication of the importance of supportive peer friendships on Sara's learning experiences.

The impact of financial concerns: Oliver and Paul

This narrative orientation was concerned with conveying how some students struggled with financial difficulties during their studies and how, over time, this could have an impact on both academic engagement and achievement. The majority of the students commented on financial concerns over their three years of undergraduate studies. The dominant thread within five of those student narratives was always linked to academic achievement, whereas for both Oliver and Paul the dominant strand was always financial and they used words such as 'constantly insecure' and 'exhausting' to express their financial concerns.

Oliver and Paul were both mature students who had already completed first degrees. Oliver had completed his degree before working in an administrative position for three years. Paul had spent some time travelling and then completed the first year of another degree (his second), which he had subsequently left to start the Physiotherapy programme. Paul in particular struggled financially and worked a significant number of hours doing a number of poorly paid jobs, and several times during his degree this had a significant impact upon his studies. Oliver managed to get better paid, longer term, part-time jobs and successfully applied to the Access to Learning Fund. Financial difficulties prompted both students to consider leaving the programme.

Oliver

Oliver's narrative clearly depicted the on-going impact of his financial difficulties and he used emotive language to portray his financial anxieties. The significance of finances to his narrative was clearly disclosed as he stated that 'finance is a massive issue' and that 'finance dictates this university course'. Finances were always dominant and he frequently expressed how he felt lucky that he had managed to find paid employment. Although he was also focused on gaining a first class degree, finances and financial worries were forever connected to his academic achievements within his narrative.

Oliver was a highly motivated and confident 24 year old man who had a clear focus on a future profession as a physiotherapist. He was the most focused student within the study, and his narrative was dominated throughout by his unwavering focus on his financial circumstances which began as soon as he had accepted a place on the programme:

> I started drawing up budgets of how much money I was going to need, how many hours I was going to need to work and things like that, getting as much money together as I could.

His concern with managing his finances was paramount throughout his studies; he openly admitted that although he was academically successful, he would leave the programme if he could not find part-time work:

> If I couldn't get work I'd have to drop out of the course, it doesn't make financial sense to accumulate three years of debt to come out of it to have uncertainty of getting a job and having a huge debt behind you.

As the first year progressed, Oliver managed to find employment but only on short-term contracts; his anxiety about managing financially was always evident within his narrative:

> I'd like to maybe have some more financial stability, I'd like not to work but you know it would be impossible to do that really. My goals are pretty much to do with stability and security really, I'll feel happy if I get the grade that I want I'll feel secure in the course, I'll feel safe. I need the money obviously to allow me enough time to study to get the grades that I want.

At the end of the first year, as his full-time work placements were approaching, Oliver was concerned with earning enough money over the summer break so that he could manage financially whilst he was unable to work part-time:

> My plan is to work full-time all summer and save up as much money as possible, leave in February to do my placements and then I suppose start again looking for something else. I would like to study more but I think that's the realization that I need to work to use half of my wages for living and the other half to put away for the placements.

At the start of the third year when Oliver had successfully completed his placements, he was delighted to have found a well-paid part-time job that fitted in with his study requirements. He was optimistic about managing his finances in the third year and attributed this to his secure employment:

> If I had said to you this time last year if you had asked me how I was going to get through my placements I would have said I don't know. Probably at some point, I would have had to get a loan or something that would have messed me up for when I finished the course. I couldn't be more grateful for the job I think if it wasn't for that, I might not be here today. I am managing time, money and study, I am not falling behind.

I spoke to Oliver shortly after he graduated with a first and asked him to reflect back on his studies. He said:

Money always was a key influence and fortunately I always seem to land on my feet when it came to work, if I hadn't have got the work when I did, things could have been very different. I feel lucky that I always managed to have a steady income and maintained a balance between studying and working.

Paul

For Paul, financial difficulties peaked when he was studying on his placements. Financial challenges can become particularly significant during extended and inflexible placement hours (Hamshire et al., 2013b), and this was apparent within Paul's narrative as he had to work night shifts and weekends whilst he was on placement. The ultimate effect of placement working and part-time work was depicted as a sub-theme of a chaotic life within Paul's narrative. At times he seemed on the edge of control as his extended work commitments and subsequent fatigue meant that he forgot to hand assessments in, overlooked assessment deadlines and missed taught sessions as he had arranged to work.

Initially, at the start of his first year, Paul was looking forward to the programme, a new life in Manchester and he was determined to do well academically:

I want to feel part of this university. I'd like to know the staff and be comfortable completely with fellow students in the class. I think I just want to have achieved. I'd like to get at least a 2:1 after my first year and if I don't do too well in the first assignments then I'm going to work harder in the next. I think it helps to get off on a good start from the beginning try and work hard to get good grades in the beginning.

Unfortunately, when he got his first assessment back he was disappointed with the results, although he acknowledged that he had had little time for studying and preparation due to his work commitments:

The exam was OK, I wasn't. I didn't think I was as prepared as I should've been for it. I mean I still passed the exams but kind of mediocre not as well as I thought I would do but I think I was working a lot at that time. It was the run up to Christmas and I was kind of over-exerting myself, just working part-time jobs and doing university at the same time [. . .] I wasn't giving myself enough time because I was more worried about finances towards the end of the term. I think I was just burning the candle at both ends really, working late at night and then coming into class in the morning.

At the start of the second year, as Paul reflected back on his first-year experiences, he was pragmatic about his performance. Although he had initially engaged with the programme and wanted to succeed academically, he had had to devote a significant amount of time to work, and he believed that this had affected his academic performance:

> I think with work and finances and stuff it has been difficult. It sometimes gets to you with regards to having to do uni work and stuff and being tired in uni but I think that is just the way it is isn't it?

When I spoke to Paul in the second year just before he started his work placements, he articulated his frustration that although he believed that he was able to obtain a good grade, he was underachieving because of his work commitments:

> I was thinking to myself I know that I am clever enough it's just applying myself to get excellent grades, cutting down on work etc. and putting in more hours at university.

By the start of his third year, Paul was less optimistic about his chances of academic success:

> I want to feel confident about finishing my degree because at the moment I don't know for sure how anything is going to turn out. I would like to know what is going to happen for third year.

Paul graduated with a 2.2. He was somewhat disappointed and believed that he could have done better:

> I was a wee bit disappointed but to be honest, sometimes I think I was kidding myself. I was working so much and then with uni at the same time, when I was on placement I was seven days a week, so I was just shattered really. I scraped my way through in the end I suppose, I think and I just found juggling jobs, working and lifestyle and uni all at the same time all quite difficult.

Development as a self-directed learner: Jack and Adnam

Learning development was a common strand across the student narratives as they talked about their personal adaptation to the particular requirements of studying for the Physiotherapy programme. However, whilst the other students detailed how they had changed and adapted as learners, the storytellers within this orientation were young men who essentially had an on-going struggle adjusting to a new way of learning after prior teacher-led experiences.

Jack and Adnam, the two interviewees considered in this section, had both recently completed their A-levels within a didactic teaching environment before they came to university. They both separately pronounced their learning experiences as 'spoon-feeding' repeatedly during their interviews and explained how they had subsequently struggled during their transition to independent learning. They expressed a desire for greater direction and support from the academic team, which would necessitate less effort from them, whilst still acknowledging the positives of autonomous learning. Throughout their interviews they described how they struggled to engage with the programme, get started on assessments and were easily distracted from their studies.

Jack

Jack's dominant orientation was his development as a learner and his narrative revealed that struggling to engage with assessments was a theme throughout his educational studies: 'I struggled with the step from GCSE to AS but then the step to A2 was even greater.' At times he desired a greater level of support from the academic team but was also aware that he needed to develop as a learner:

> I suppose in a way it's good doing self-learning and stuff but umm, I don't know, it might be nice to have a wee bit more, a bit more of a helping hand.

As the first year progressed, Jack struggled to concentrate during the long days on campus and found it difficult to work independently at home:

> The lectures I find a bit more difficult to concentrate in just because there's so many people. It can be difficult to keep concentrating and I like having those two days off; they're not days off, they're for studying, but it's good having that. This course has moved so quickly. It was a lot of work, a lot of work and I definitely didn't do enough of it.

It is important therefore to consider whether Jack's 'willingness to engage', as described by McCune (2009) in a study exploring Biosciences students' experiences, was influenced by his perceptions of his Higher Education learning experiences or whether it was a mind-set that had developed over his previous educational experiences that he had brought with him to university. Jack's narrative revealed that he had struggled to fully engage with his studies and assessments for a number of years and he was aware that this was particularly apparent around planning and writing assessments:

> I'm not really a big fan of assignments. I don't really know why [laughs]. I'm kind of starting to work a bit harder on it but I'll be last minute.

As Jack's narrative progressed into the second and third years, his engagement and interest in his academic studies increased, particularly when he was studying on his clinical placements. Analyzing Jack's narrative identified that two factors contributed to this. He repeatedly stated that he preferred practical work to academic sessions, and essentially, placement education enabled practical application of knowledge introduced in taught sessions:

> Like, placement is where you properly learn like and it'll kind of stick in my head.

Secondly, on each of his placements he got one-to-one supervision from a clinical tutor: 'my educator was really good, giving me support'. Other studies have already identified that easily accessible support systems, particularly from personal tutors, are highly valued by students (Brown and Edelmann, 2000) and this is essentially what Jack got on placement: a readily available dedicated member of staff committed to facilitating his learning development. As the second and third year marks were largely dependent on placement grades, Jack graduated with a first class degree.

Adnam

In a number of ways, Adnam's narrative closely mirrored Jack's. He clearly articulated a mismatch between his academic preparedness and his learning experiences during the first year:

> With A-levels they told you everything that you needed to know about your studies [. . .] while here mostly your studies are new materials it's really different.

Adnam also acknowledged that at times he did not put in the maximum effort:

> I've got a lazy personality. I'll do anything but not do the work basically, anything [. . .] but not do the work.

At the start of his second year when he reflected back on his first-year learning experiences, he explained how towards the end of the first year he had struggled to engage as he felt overwhelmed by the workload:

> I've learned my lesson. I just couldn't get out of that frame of mind of just not doing anything all the time. I just got lazy to be honest and it just carried on. I did do some of the work but I'm just too relaxed and couldn't do much. The whole term was a bit heavy for me.

Adnam also preferred the practical learning experiences of the placement environment and tended to get slightly better grades for his placements, but his reasons for this were slightly different to Jack's. On campus, in taught sessions, Adnam tended to be distracted by his friends 'messing about' and therefore believed that the staff and other students consider his group of friends to be 'slackers'.

He therefore acknowledged that he would have to make more effort within the clinical environment:

> We do tend to mess about and stuff but it's totally different when you get out there [. . .] I think I'm definitely going to have to be a lot more mature in the practice placement area. I think it is a lot easier doing it in person than having to actually learn everything from a book and stuff.

Adnam enjoyed his placements and as he developed as a self-directed learner, he began to improve his grades. Unfortunately, due to marks from the second year he graduated with a 2.2. He believed that this was not a true reflection of his abilities:

> If I am left to do stuff on my own I am probably not as reliable as when I have to do stuff or be somewhere at a set time. But when it comes to giving me a bit more free will I am a little bit more lazy to be honest but that has improved over the three years. You can't rely on others the whole time, you have to do it yourself in the second and third year; I know I didn't do anywhere near enough work.

The impact of personal difficulties: Maria

Many of the students alluded to personal difficulties during their narratives of their undergraduate experiences. There were various narrative threads of relationship breakups, family disagreements and discord amongst friendship groups. However, although these issues were personally significant for each student at the time they occurred, they tended to recede into unimportance over time, never to be mentioned again. For one student in this study there was a special circumstance to the orientation of her narrative: the emotional journey of the breakdown of her relationship. Maria was initially happy and optimistic at the start of the programme but her on-going narrative detailed worry and unhappiness, eventually leading to separation and divorce. This emotional journey was so central to her narrative that it overshadowed all other orientations. She is considered here to recognize that some students bring with them lives that contain domestic upheaval and unhappiness that impact significantly on their engagement.

In Maria's story, it is not easy to separate her own individual transition from that of connected others and in particular from her relationship with her partner. Her personal history and relationship clearly influenced her emotional, social and academic adaptation during her undergraduate studies. The analysis of her narrative revealed a challenging story of achievements and disappointments, detailing the emotional dimensions of learning that were on-going throughout her undergraduate studies. A comment she made at the start of our second meeting, 'University was exciting at first and then it got a bit overwhelming and then it went easy again', probably sums up her experience, as she conveyed the roller coaster ride of her transition. It was a statement indicative of some of the joys and successes but also of the difficulties that she had encountered.

Maria's main focus throughout the first year was academic achievement and she set herself the goal of achieving a first. She struggled initially, as she was returning to education after working, but she was determined to try hard and succeed:

> I found the course very structured, very good, fast paced, a bit more than expected and a bit more self-learning than I expected. In a way I was a bit disappointed but then I realized that it's actually better for me to go and look for the information, not that I didn't do that already. I'm the type of person that likes to find out for myself. I wouldn't say the course is exactly how I expected it to be but it's turning out to be better than I expected and I'm adapting really well.

Her social and personal developments were to a great extent secondary to this goal. Although she developed a social network consisting of mature and international students amongst her peers, this was as a means of supporting her academic progression and she rarely spent time with these people off-campus. She spent most of her free time studying, saying:

> In terms of my private life outside of the university life, I've found myself so into studying I wasn't giving my husband enough time to talk to, relax or even myself time to relax. I can prioritize things and leave other things behind quite easily. I don't know if that is good, but if you leave your husband behind it is not nice, you know what I mean, it's not [. . .] in a bad way.

While she was concerned with doing well academically, the overriding story in Maria's narrative was one of a relationship breakdown. As the study continued, she began to elaborate on the subject of her relationship and eventually this was the narrative linkage around which the rest of her story fitted. The couple subsequently separated and Maria talked at length about how this had impacted upon her academic achievements. In the second and third years she described herself as just pleased to be passing her assessments:

> I have had a hard time but I am pleased to pass. I would say I had a difficult final two years; but emotionally I am back to normal now I would say.

McGivney (2003) has suggested that non-academic reasons are the primary cause of withdrawal of mature students from courses and at times Maria considered suspending her studies. In the end she decided that as her future was so uncertain, persisting with the programme gave her a needed focus and a 'constant' in her life. Looking to the future, Maria also recognized that she would need a professional qualification to gain employment. As she eventually graduated with a 2.2, she was not sure if she had made the right decision:

> I think what I went through emotionally had a big impact in a sense that my confidence now is not where it should be because in the last two years I feel like I have missed something. Even though I did learn, I feel like I have missed something and sometimes I wonder whether I should have taken a year break and let everything cool down and then come back to it, or whether I did the right thing of going through at the same time as everything was happening.

Discussion

The students in this study talked at length about their Higher Education experiences and analysis of their narratives identified four significant orientations that impacted upon their engagement: peer support, finances, learner development and personal circumstances.

Peer support

Peer support is a multifaceted and dynamic concept that is underpinned and influenced by individual expectations and a sense of identity. It has different meanings and interpretations that are profoundly individual and specific to time. As the two students considered within the orientation were both young women in their teens, perhaps this orientation can therefore be seen as focusing on the complexities of young women's relationships with their friends rather than on student peer relations. However, numerous previous studies have highlighted that social integration is a key aspect of a successful transition to university for all students, for example, in the seminal work of Tinto (1987). Other authors concur and suggest that students who fail to develop social networks and do not fit in, are more likely to struggle academically and withdraw early (Thomas, 2002). Social networks have also been identified as important to sustain students during times of doubt and uncertainty (Bryson and Hardy, 2012) and friendship, or more importantly the lack of it, is one of the key factors that has been recognized as influencing students' decisions to leave (Thomas, 2002).

Financial concerns

Identifying financial difficulties within the narratives was not unexpected, as debt concerns amongst students are not uncommon and were identified by half of the healthcare students in Hamshire et al.'s (2013b) study. Several previous studies of students on healthcare programmes have also identified finances as one of the biggest challenges faced by some students (for example Steele et al., 2005 and Brown and Edelmann, 2000). However, what the narratives clearly depicted was the on-going impact of the financial difficulties, as Oliver in particular repeatedly used emotive language to portray his financial anxieties. In accord with the findings of Brown and Edelmann (2000), Paul's financial circumstances played a pivotal role in his learning experiences as he struggled to find time for his studies and assessment. Eventually, the ultimate impact was his graduation with a 2.2 and when I spoke to Paul after graduation there was a sense of dissatisfaction as he reflected back over his experiences and declared that he was 'a bit disappointed to be honest'.

The wider implications of these narratives are important to note, as undoubtedly these two students were not alone in experiencing financial difficulties. Whilst finances have already been acknowledged as being a factor that contributes towards student dissatisfaction and attrition, there is less evidence that explores the on-going impact on students' academic achievements and personal well-being. Higher Education is currently undergoing unprecedented change and universities must adjust to meet the evolving needs of students and other stakeholders, within a competitive market and under a new student finance scheme. Although the eventual impact of these initiatives is as yet unknown, the potential effect on finances for future students could be considerable.

Learner self-direction

Students may engage differently with various spheres of their Higher Education experiences and the narratives of both Jack and Adnam demonstrate this. They engaged with social aspects and some academic aspects but at times struggled to develop as independent learners. Both the storytellers within this orientation were young men essentially adjusting to a new way of learning after prior experiences of teacher-led learning and struggling at times as they adapted. Both students revealed complex contradictions within their narratives as they told of starting work on assessments at the last minute, not trying their utmost to succeed academically and being satisfied with 'good enough', whilst also wanting to be academically successful. There also seemed to be a notion of ambivalence, as they described themselves as just 'getting by' at times in both narratives, particularly in the first year when both seemed uncertain at times whether to fully engage with their studies or whether to aim for the minimum pass mark.

These two narratives, in essence, extend beyond the local and personal and bring in broader questions about students' readiness for degree-level working. Academic integration is a broad term that includes students' engagement with academic staff, their peers and their attendance at timetabled sessions (Tinto, 1987). Two factors combine to influence academic integration: an individual student's level of academic preparedness and the experience of the academic programme that they are studying (Thomas, 2002). Academic preparedness encompasses students' past educational experiences, their individual expectations, academic capabilities and personal autonomy, which combine to give students a 'state of readiness' for studying at Higher Education. The academic experience provided by an institution is heavily influenced by the values and practices of an institution (Thomas, 2002) as well as the teaching and learning strategies and relationships with staff on a particular programme. Previous research has indicated that if there is a 'match' between academic preparedness of an individual and the academic experience, the student is more likely to engage with the programme (for example Tinto, 1987; Thomas, 2002). Individual expectations can also have a profound impact upon students' perceptions of their learning experiences (Ecclestone et al., 2010) and neither Adnam nor Jack believed that they had been particularly academically prepared for the UK Higher Education system by their previous educational experiences, as they both clearly articulate their struggles to adapt during their narratives of their on-going process of adjustment. It must be acknowledged though that whilst accepting that they were poorly prepared, they were both at times rather reluctant to take personal responsibility for their own academic difficulties.

Personal circumstances

As a mature student, Maria's narrative is complex and atypical of the majority of the students in the cohort, focusing on a relationship breakdown. Yet it details the personal and academic challenges that can constitute a Higher Education experience, as personal history and expectations have a varying degree of influence on an individual's transition (Ecclestone et al., 2010).

Previous studies have already identified that students' initial transitions to university can be an emotional journey, as they manage both academic and social transformation during a time of considerable adjustment (Yorke, 2000; Thomas, 2002). It is also noted that the transition to Higher Education is not just an individual experience, as family and friends will play a role and give a particular context (Holdsworth and Morgan, 2005). Steele et al. (2005) highlighted difficulties of the work–study–life balance among mature nursing students; in particular, they found balancing academic life with family commitments was problematic, with the cumulative and additive nature of such problems compounding the difficulties that the students experienced.

Conclusion

The use of narrative enquiry within this study allowed an insight into the complex, individual experiences of these seven students and we have attempted to tell their stories through common orientations, presenting a text that demonstrates the multifaceted nature of undergraduate students' journeys. A holistic view of student experiences and engagement needs to take into account each of these four orientations and the impact upon students' academic achievements and sense of belonging to an institution. Students' engagement varies over time as personal and social factors impact upon experiences; projects that aim to promote student engagement need to be sensitive to these factors and take into account the entirety of students' on-going experiences.

Chapter 4

Engagement as dynamic and relational

Students' accounts and achievements over time

Julie Wintrup

When those who have the power to name and to socially construct reality choose not to see you or hear you, whether you are dark-skinned, old, disabled, female or speak with a different accent than theirs, when someone with the authority of a teacher, say, describes the world and you are not in it, there is a moment of psychic disequilibrium, as if you looked into a mirror and saw nothing.

(Adrienne Rich, 1986)

Introduction

This chapter draws on research with 357 mature, part-time and working health-care students over a period of six years, who entered Higher Education (HE) through a Foundation degree. Findings are drawn from extensive demographic, longitudinal and qualitative data; 39 also participated in interviews over two or three years. Progression statistics show that despite setbacks, this diverse, experienced group with their vocational, work-based entry qualifications persisted and succeeded in significant numbers. Many continued their education beyond the Foundation degree, subsequently doing well in competitive professional programmes.

Personal accounts described immense pride and excitement as new career possibilities opened up. But they also detailed hurdles, crisis points and (at times) overwhelming stressors. In part, these related to academic work. But even after coming to terms with the new demands, poor communication, inadequate use of systems and bureaucratic failings caused high levels of stress and frustration. For some participants this was alienating and led them to question whether they really belonged to the University community.

Difficult transitions were described during the second year and were only made bearable by the support and encouragement of fellow students. All reported, in different ways, the development of a heightened sense of awareness, criticality and collectivity. Themes reflect and reinforce earlier research: that is, although valued and transformative, HE can be experienced as an emotional roller coaster for some working, mature students.

Background

Two strands of research from the same case study are presented and discussed here together for the first time. Each has been published separately, one as a qualitative study (Wintrup et al., 2012) and the other as a longitudinal study of educational outcomes (Wintrup et al., 2013). The aim of the research was to understand more about, and to improve, the progression opportunities in HE for working students in healthcare. Viewing the strands as parts of a whole has offered scope to revisit findings and pose new questions for future research. For example, is the importance to students of social and peer support, and the all-important sense of belonging, inculcated through our processes and cultures? Are achievements, as perceived by students, recognized and used to develop an evidence base, or is attention primarily on organizational strategies to prevent 'attrition'?

The students who participated in the research were generally new to academia, entering HE for the first time in significant numbers as a result of New Labour's 'Foundation degree' initiative. The Secretary of State for Education, David Blunkett, introduced this new, diploma-equivalent qualification to the United Kingdom (UK) in 2000, to bridge a workforce skills gap *and* widen participation to HE (DfEE, 2000). Concerns were voiced that the two agendas were not complementary (Brain et al., 2004); without labour market pull, Foundation degrees would simply become a stepping-stone to Honours degrees (Little, 2005). Foundation degrees were nonetheless ideally placed to facilitate employer-led, work-based learning and to promote employability, particularly in vocational areas with skill shortages (HEFCE, 2000).

The Foundation degree was designed as a first-wave prototype, incorporating access routes to Honours programmes (in Physiotherapy, Occupational Therapy, Audiology, Nursing, Social Work, Health Sciences and Podiatry) and work-related roles (in children's services, long term conditions and rehabilitation). The degree was used as a case study of good practice by Skills for Health (the sector skills council) for some years. A sense of expectation, that existing barriers to professions and career progression were being breached, informed and infused the new programmes.

To support the widening access agenda, the Higher Education Funding Council England (HEFCE) funded regional collaborations (Lifelong Learning Networks or LLNs) of HE providers, Further Education Colleges (FECs) and employers to promote inclusion and progression (HEFCE, 2010a). Some LLNs promoted research and it was through this route that the project was funded.

Literature

It is well established in the literature that mature, working, part-time learners are at high risk of early departure (Yorke, 1999; Yorke and Longden, 2008). Dropout, or 'attrition', has been associated with a lack of integration and involvement in HE since Tinto's (1975 and 1987) seminal research. His subsequent model of persistence/withdrawal identified 'involvement' – in various aspects of University and College life – as a powerful indicator of future completion (Tinto, 1987, 2006). Yorke and Longden (2008) concluded from a mixed method study that while engagement is multifaceted and interconnected, Higher Education Institutions (HEIs) have only limited influence; while they might be able to improve students' prospects through learning and teaching strategies and practices, they have little influence over the many other aspects of students' lives and earlier educational experiences.

Foundation degree research

During the planning of the study, little published research into Foundation degrees was available. However, early concerns about attrition were apparent. The first decade showed high levels of attrition: 31 per cent in FECs and 20 per cent in HEIs (HEFCE, 2010b). Differences emerged between groups: full-time students completed more quickly and in greater numbers than part-time students, yet part-time students generally continued to a full-time degree (National Audit Office, 2007). Around 50 per cent of all graduates progressed immediately to Honours degree programmes although completion data is not available (HEFCE, 2010b).

Subsequently summarized and critiqued by Harvey (2009), what early research there was showed clear themes across different subject areas. For example, qualitative research into Early Years Foundation degree students' experiences identified transition problems from Further Education to HE, which were found to be stressful due to less time and support from lecturers (Greenbank, 2007). Similarly, Knight et al. (2006: 6) found second years to feel 'abandoned' when tutors took a more 'hands-off' approach. Students reported facing workplace impediments to study and feeling unable to cope with demands, combined with a lack of support from the institution, tutors and peers (Knight et al., 2006).

Widening participation and diversity research

Much of the research into widening participation is large cohort data, which elicits patterns or trends generally associated with personal characteristics (such as age and gender), across time. Some trends are resilient; for example, students from less affluent family backgrounds remain under-represented (DfEE, 1998; BIS, 2010). Others show changes, as more women than men participate and there are increasing numbers of UK students from minority ethnic groups (UUK, 2011). A complex picture shows that while no single groups are under-represented, Chinese, Black-African and Indian students are represented most strongly, although almost half study in newer London universities: 'Minority ethnic students make up over 60 per cent of the full time undergraduate population at modern universities in London, compared to 36 per cent of the total at old Universities' (Bhattacharyya et al., 2003). A more recent Universities UK (UUK, 2011) study reflects this finding. Men remain most likely to drop out early (Johnes and McNabb, 2004; HEPI,

2009) although mature students (aged over 21 on entry) were found to comprise almost a third of all undergraduates (Million+, NUS, 2012).

Since the introduction of higher tuition fees and other funding changes in the UK, this latter group has dropped dramatically (HEFCE, 2013). Long seen as a marginalized group whose primary duty is to work, Sissel et al. (2001) go further, describing mature learners as exploited by a system which reifies younger students as 'future leaders'. A different perspective is offered by Bowl (2001) who reported the experiences of three mature women; despite motivation and encouragement, their progress was frustrated by trauma, isolation and an absence of meaningful information and guidance.

Healthcare education research

Factors unique to healthcare education emerge from research into nursing, the largest of the professional groups. Funded by Government, programmes have for many years been commissioned and monitored by the Department of Health (UUK, 2012). Attrition has been seen as problematic in both human and financial terms, as contracts include penalties. Coakley (1997) reported a high of 60 per cent attrition in the first year of mental health nursing in the 1960s. More recently, attrition of 20 per cent was discovered in a longitudinal analysis of nursing cohorts, with men and younger students being most likely to leave early (Mulholland et al., 2008). To investigate the experience of male student nurses, Stott (2006) used interviews and diaries; their descriptions of both clinical and academic settings included feeling isolated and excluded. The importance of belonging emerged clearly in the work of Levett-Jones et al. (2007) who found mentors to be key to creating a sense of welcome amongst student nurses in clinical placement. Echoing Hockings' (2010) research, students reported feeling alienated by an unwelcoming environment and a mismatch in values, which in turn impeded their learning and created distress, detachment and disengagement.

Literature suggested then that a new group of working, largely part-time healthcare entrants to HE would experience just as many stresses as other students, along with the complications of combining study, personal lives and work. They would also be less likely to have the networks or connections possessed by more established groups and individuals entering HE. However, as a group with career ambitions, they could be seen to bring a sense of direction and purpose born of experience. For many, local knowledge, work and contacts meant areas of stability and security, for those fortunate to have such networks. Not all students were so fortunate; the health and care workforce is very diverse and increasingly casualized. Several interviewees described managing considerable insecurities.

The study aims

The research sought to understand more about the progression, journeys and experiences of this group of students, new to HE, and to discover any impediments they encountered. Appreciation of the contextual, social and relational factors impacting on their education was sought so that attention might be paid to the plurality of student perspectives.

Methodology

Study design

Using a case study approach defined by Stake (1995), a boundary was drawn around related people, processes and events occurring within a defined place and time period: that is, entry, progression and exit profiles of students entering one HEI's Health and Social Care Foundation degree, and accounts given by volunteers through interviews, over a total period of six years. Data gathered included:

1   semi-structured interviews with 39 student volunteers over a period of three and a half years, spanning cohort groups from 2007 to 2011, reported in Wintrup et al. (2012);
2   analysis of anonymized, coded whole cohort institutional data including demographic, entry, progress and exit data, spanning 2005–2011, reported in Wintrup et al. (2013).

Ethical approval was gained through the University Ethics Committee. There were limits on what could be discovered despite permission to access data, such as:

1   the flexible programme meant it was not possible to capture movement between modes of study;
2   entry routes (school, work, Further Education) were not reliably or consistently identified;
3   self-reported details had gaps and 48 per cent declined to classify themselves in terms of socio-economic occupational class;
4   postcode details confirmed entrants were mostly local but only large areas were identified;
5   'reasons for leaving' were rarely given.

Each year, different ways of categorizing previous educational achievements meant this component of data was largely unreliable and therefore excluded.

Interviews: data collection and analysis

All students who entered the Foundation degree between 2007 and 2010 were invited to take part in the study, one strand being semi-structured interviews lasting between one and two hours. They were advised that volunteers would be sought each year while they attended University. Students were recruited each year, many participating in second and third interviews. Sixty-five interviews were conducted altogether, with 39 students. Only words from those who undertook two or three interviews were used for this analysis, meaning that words from a potential 20 participants were drawn from 48 separate interviews over either two or three years.

Entry, progression and exit statistics: data collection and analysis

Anonymized cohort data from the University's central planning team included all entrants who had enrolled and registered on the programme over six years. Forms of analysis were determined by usable categories of information given on enrolment, including age, gender, disability and ethnicity. Breakdowns included early leavers with no qualification, those exiting with a Certificate in Higher Education (CertHE) or Foundation degree, and those continuing to other qualifications within the university during the study period.

This enabled a descriptive analysis of *all* entrants and their award status on exit, including: early leavers with no qualifications or a CertHE, Foundation degree graduates, and those who graduated from or continuing on other Honours degree programmes within the same University, again during the study period. Four demographic features accessed through central planning were considered reliable: ethnicity, age, gender and disability.

Findings

For the purposes of this chapter, a synopsis of findings from both strands of the study is offered, given the aim of discussing them for the first time in relation to each other. Fuller analyses are available elsewhere.

Descriptive statistical data

Entry and progression data showed that during the academic years 2005/6 and 2010/11, 357 people enrolled on the Foundation degree, in cohorts of around 60 per year. Characteristics included:

- ages ranged from 18–66 years old, with 75 per cent being over the age of 21 on commencement of the programme;
- their average age (mean and median) was 34 years. Reflecting the gendered care workforce, men were in a minority of 12 per cent (or 1:7);
- of those who selected a category, 68 people (19 per cent) identified with one of the following: Black, Asian, Chinese, Mixed or Other. Seven people left the section blank and the remainder identified as White;
- disability was identified by 15 per cent of entrants, ranging from dyslexia to a wide range of physical and mental health issues.

Each intake showed a broadly similar occurrence of all these characteristics, with minor variations across years.

Characteristics and early departure

During the six-year study period, 69 people (19 per cent of all entrants) left the programme and did not return to the University, reflecting HEFCE's (2010b) finding of 20 per cent attrition for Foundation degrees in HEIs. No obvious 'peak' was evident through the year. Another 11 people, 3 per cent, left with a CertHE. Academic failure of the first year necessitated some departures, but others used exit questionnaires to communicate their choice to transfer to another University (a CertHE was accepted at several Universities as evidence of recent study so enabled access directly to professional degree programmes). Reflecting existing research, men and younger students left in larger proportions than women and mature students.

Characteristics and progression

Of those students who could have continued beyond the Foundation degree, 30 per cent progressed to Honours or Diploma programmes in the shortest time possible. Central data showed that Foundation degree graduates went on to study not only Honours degrees with formal progression pathways – Physiotherapy, Occupational Therapy, Social Work, Nursing, Health and Social Care and Podiatry – but also audiology, sports studies, mathematics and education (with Qualified Teacher Status), achieving a normal distribution of degree classifications.

Interview themes, year one: expectations, a sense of the possible and the formation of friendships

Interviews conducted during the first year often described a lack of information and some very different expectations. Some felt unprepared for the academic aspect of the degree. One asserted: 'I didn't come on the course to learn about theories.' Another compared learning approaches: 'I don't think we fully realized how much emphasis there would be on self-directed study [. . .] it's so different in Further Education.'

The stimulation of learning was viewed positively. Several expressed pride, anticipation and new career possibilities: 'once I finish this and have got over the stresses of it, I'll be looking for the next thing I can do and I think it will carry on for a long time', and 'it's opening up areas which I wouldn't even have considered at the beginning of the year, because I didn't know they were out there'.

A sense of optimism and a problem-solving mentality permeated first-year interviews. People described being supported by the development of close friendships and study groups: 'we all supported each other. We used to thrash things out. Outside of work, in our own time', and 'it's nice because if ever you feel you are falling back, or you miss something, you know someone else is going to be there to help you and bring you back up'.

Previous poor experiences, particularly at school, were very common: 'I remember being written off quite early [. . .] I think that stays with you.'

So first-year interviews showed that several interviewees felt ill-prepared for HE and many doubted their ability, but pride and a sense of having achieved an important first step was a motivating factor, as were supportive social relationships. However, making pathway choices for year two were experienced as stressful.

Interview themes, year two: choices, complications and difficult transitions

Planning second-year options was difficult and too early for one: 'I didn't want to enrol on something I would be stuck on.' For another, it brought back fears of inadequacy: 'I wasn't sure I was capable of doing it, or had the intelligence to do it.' Another remembered: 'a lecturer [. . .] told us what the course was, what the essays were, statistics [. . .] which I was very scared and worried about'.

For *all* interviewees, the second year was much more difficult. Several described considerable stress to the point of wanting to leave. Different pathways and options meant that close-knit first-year groups found themselves split apart with different timetables, routines and academic demands. There was quite a lot of unhappiness at the start of year two.

> The second year [. . .] was hard. Stressful, because I was still working, and the assignments I found, were much more in-depth, and the memories I have first and foremost, being in tears most of the time, saying *I can't do this*.

One described 'adapting' to new lecturers, saying 'you had to learn about what their expectations were' and 'in a large group [the lecturer] didn't relate very well'. She thought a more 'student friendly' teaching approach was needed: 'particularly for students who are quite scared of academics'.

Feedback was important: '[. . .] the lecturer had written: "it is obvious you find this very difficult to write, and you will make a very good [professional]." So I'm trying to hold on to these bits, to get me through.' The same person felt her work placement feedback helped in difficult times: '[. . .] certainly, if I hadn't had those two placements, and with that recommendation from the [professional] in that school [. . .] I would have given up by now'.

Timetable and room changes were found to be highly stressful. 'I could have insisted, I could have stood there and said "I'm not going until I get a timetable"', although this student later says, 'I didn't have it in me to insist.' Another was also worn down:

> Three of us, we've had to really fight for it [. . .] just to get from lectures to seminars to everything else [. . .] and we've had to fight for everything [. . .] it was so annoying, it was so, that, I nearly gave up.

A more grimly determined narrative replaced the earlier optimism:

> I didn't want to, you know, pack it in halfway through the course because I would have felt as if I'd failed again. I had to do it; it's proving it to myself again. So that's what kept me going.

Another asserted 'I'm here for the long haul.' Seeing the end in sight made achievement seem real for a student determined to become a registered nurse: 'I really want it so badly.'

Interview themes, year three: reflections on the social, collective nature of higher education and future goals

The third year could be a lonelier period, as some were completing more slowly than others or had entered new programmes:

> In my class everybody was nice to me, but I think when you are from the minority ethnic you always feel as though there is a wall between you and other people [. . .] in the end I am thinking 'it's me only, I am on my own, I have to do it'.

Another missed earlier social contact: 'I have no friends and nobody else in the group to talk to, or say "what was your understanding of that [topic]".'

Stereotypes were annoying: 'they assume everyone's 19 and lives on campus [. . .] I found that really frustrating', and on-going organizational issues were also wearing: 'probably about this time last year, I'd got so fed up with the admin problems and timetabling issues, I actually said, I don't want to do this anymore'.

Yet all third-year interviewees commented on the opportunity presented by the new qualification: 'the Foundation degree lets down a ladder that you can climb up'. Descriptions of personal development were communicated: 'it's broadened and deepened my perspective on society and how things work – on the big picture really'. Another felt it had 'opened her eyes' and made her question things.

> I don't just want to know the surface, and know my job, I want to know underneath why I'm doing that, where does that come from, who said we had to do it like that.

> It's made me angry about things as well [. . .] but maybe that's a good thing, I don't know.

The goal of achieving a degree or professional qualification acted as a powerful motivator for staying the course. Of those who talked very seriously of contemplating giving up their studies, support from and for each other emerged as the single most important feature of deciding to continue:

I spend more time away from campus [. . .] but [. . .] we've been really supportive of each other, because it's been really, really tough; we've kind of bonded together.

Another student describes determinedly supporting others: 'a couple of people on my course were going "I don't want to do this anymore, I'm going to give up" [enacts] "oh no you don't give up! You're not!" and you sort of help them out there.'

Unusually a student describes seeking assistance from a tutor when family problems become overwhelming:

I didn't say much to tutors or anything until it got a little bit too bad, and then it was quite obvious all was not right, and I spoke to [the lecturer] and she was brilliant, she just said 'take time out, take as much as you need [. . .] you need a break, just go and we'll sort things out'.

One person who described struggling with workload remembered: 'there was one point, around February or March in the second year, I thought "I'm never going to get through this"'. Duties as a course representative compounded her own burden, but also provided a way through the problems:

As the course rep I contacted course leaders and said 'Look this is just. . .' I was getting phone calls from other people saying, 'I can't cope with this, there's too many things all due in at the same time' [. . .] so we did get an extension for one of them, it was a big help.

Again when advice was sought from tutors, she concludes: 'to be fair, when there was a problem, the lecturers were very understanding'.

A lack of clarity in an assignment brief provided another opportunity for speaking out:

We felt bewildered at the beginning. And then we all started realizing that actually we had voices. So when we all decided to say something – it was brushed under the carpet at first – and then suddenly, it was recognized and apologies were made, and that was appreciated. That was really appreciated. And then we seemed all right again. We seemed to be okay again.

So, in the face of real problems, participants described peer support as their first source of help, followed by their course representative, then individual tutors and finally the module or programme leader.

Discussion

The purpose of the study was to improve the education and work progression opportunities of new entrants to one HEI by understanding the nature of opportunities for, and barriers to, progress from the students' perspectives and, where possible, developing strategies to overcome them. The programme itself was subsequently discontinued, due to a change of strategic direction internally, and local/political drivers externally, but a number of insights led to considerable learning about and from students.

In addition, assumptions about the likely success of Foundation degree graduates were challenged by their *actual* achievements. As Fuller (2001) and others had predicted, many students were not prepared to 'step off' the education ladder with their Foundation degree. While this might have understandably been disappointing for employers, who hoped to see a better-educated staff member return with new ideas and skills, it is more than understandable. Few of the promised 'new roles' had materialized, yet registered professions continued to have status and a little more security than support-worker posts.

Students can be seen to have negotiated an ambitious, problematic new programme, with new pathway transitions created at critical points. By developing these alternative routes, the programme challenged more traditional A-level routes into professions.

The political origins of the Foundation degree, and of the new roles graduates were supposed to take up on graduation, challenged established professional and academic norms and practices. There had been no evolution, no sense of ownership from within, so there were no chances to 'prove' its value to established members of the academy, something Prentice (1999) identifies as a major risk for innovations in education.

Nonetheless, students were not only attracted to the programme but made it their own, finding ways around problems, pushing for more pathways, creating their own where none existed and leaving to go to other universities when no other option was available to them. The accounts of persisting, problem solving and balancing competing demands will surely be music to the ears of future employers. They generated their *own* form of social capital, developing intense bonds and effective networks – with each other in preference to staff – and normally communicated through friendship and study groups using social media outside formal university time, systems or virtual platforms.

Such high attrition is unlikely to have been accepted so matter-of-factly on a traditional Honours programme and would have been a major problem in a commissioned health or social work degree. While the experimental and collaborative nature of the Foundation degree made some early attrition probable, it is interesting to question its apparent acceptance, even at a national level.

Central data revealed retention by the institution, if not the programme. Students who moved on to other programmes were thought to have dropped out yet many went on to succeed in very different programmes. In these instances, the Foundation degree appears to have been simply a way into the University. Possibly lower expectations (of the new student group, the new programme, or of the sometimes tricky collaborations with providers) may unwittingly have led to fewer questions being asked of either the university processes (such as exit interviews or questionnaires) or of the individuals themselves, possibly during the phases of withdrawal which precede departure.

Conclusion

In the introduction, the following questions were posed:

- Is the importance to students of social and peer support, and the all-important concepts of belonging, inculcated through our processes and cultures?
- Are achievements, as perceived by students, recognized and used to develop an evidence base, or is attention primarily on organizational strategies to prevent 'attrition'?

The renewed emphasis in the UK on further widening of HE access to the most socially and economically deprived groups might usefully be accompanied by research which learns *from and about* those very students and alumni, if HEIs are to learn from the Foundation degree experiment. In particular, students who have overcome setbacks are well placed to offer insights to institutions wishing to develop a welcoming and caring reputation.

Whether systems and processes in HE are inculcating a sense of belonging, or supporting students' own attempts to persist, is equally difficult to discover without actually asking students and understanding the growing place of social media in their lives. Social networks, and the sense of collectivism they offer in the face of problems, are not amenable to reproduction within the formal curriculum. However, their importance could be made explicit and conditions created to engender and promote such relationships and ambitions. While mature or part-time students might be seen to lack the kind of cultural capital readily recognized by lecturers in HE, interviewees clearly generated horizontal networks; they created effective learning communities which offered and reinforced a sense of themselves as mutually dependent social subjects (Bernstein, 2006). These structures and relationships were clearly sustaining and highly effective sources of information and active support; they were, in interviewees' accounts, pivotal to developing persistence. Relying only on representative structures and vertical 'reporting' forms of communication risks missing the very voices we need to hear.

Persistence, if construed as an individual attribute, can be seen as a feature of being securely attached, whether to other people, or to study routines and purposes, or to some other feature of the educational experience, such as the driving passion to become a nurse. But when understood as a more radical concept – a set of capabilities, interactions and responses, performed in social settings – then access to resources, accurate and timely information, and supportive relationships must be part of the broader context (Tinto, 1998).

The will to learn is evident in students' accounts but, as Barnett (2007) describes, it is fragile, becoming only slightly more robust over time and is contingent upon friendships and the all-important sense of belonging. Rather than wonder at their ability to become critical thinkers and beings, it is important to ask: what was it about their encounter with HE that contributed to such low confidence and so many passive forms of coping?

Colley (2006) describes the 'unwritten curricula' that requires the cost of 'emotional labour' to be borne quietly and 'correctly'. If caring can be confused with self-sacrifice, then educators in health professions have a responsibility to invite and scaffold a critical take on care within its political and societal context. Caring work, still a largely female domain, needs more than ever such a questioning and confident stance.

A sense of the agentic self – as a valued member of a learning community, intellectually capable, with a unique, valued contribution and the ability to make a difference – is developed and reinforced through relationships. Being seen, being heard and being listened to is a basic tenet of belonging; like looking into that mirror and seeing yourself.

The final question asks whether achievements, other than degree classifications or employer-directed curriculum vitae activities, are routinely recognized and used to develop an evidence base. It is easy to assume that such 'evidence' as interviewees provided (of altruism, persistence and collectivism) is intangible, suited only to memories or reunion stories. Without the careful seeking out, questioning, recording and analysis of both words and educational achievements, this evidence would not be known or shared here. Yet such concepts as graduate attributes or students as agents of change (Fielding, 2001) recognize HE as a source of radicalization and transformative learning, reduced and commodified by a set of final results or a classification. Learning is described by interviewees as a series of crisis points, of shared realizations and 'light-bulb' moments, of thresholds crossed alone and with others, in workplaces, with patients or colleagues, at home with families or at midnight on Facebook. Hearing from them has enabled a different understanding of how to build an evidence base.

Part II

Students engaging

Perspectives from students

Chapter 5

Experiences of engagement

The successes and issues from a student perspective

*Ruth Furlonger, Daniel Johnson
and Beth Parker*

Introduction

As Combined Honours (CH) students, we face unique challenges which have an impact on our engagement. In a multi-disciplinary degree with a choice of 26 subjects and countless modules, each student navigates a unique path through their degree. Students face the logistical challenges of organizing timetables and becoming accustomed to varying administrative and assessment practices in the different schools where they are taught. In this context, it is difficult to make friends and integrate within the CH community. Students have no assigned class time with fellow combiners and are likely to belong to more than one school; therefore, forming an identity is problematic. It is fundamentally difficult to achieve cohesion on a degree where there are no obvious spaces to get involved and this has been reflected through student feedback, which has reported a sense of isolation.

Within the last four years, there have been large-scale changes in the way students are supported in an attempt to address these challenges and allow them opportunities to engage. The overall success of this work, and the schemes which have resulted from it, is reflected in a vastly improved National Student Survey (NSS) score between these two periods (from 73 per cent overall satisfaction in 2008, the lowest of all programmes at Newcastle, to 96 per cent in 2011, one of the highest in the sector). This chapter will describe the important elements of each scheme within CH: the Student Staff Committee (SSC), mentoring, Peer-Assisted Study Support (PASS) and the Combined Honours Society (CHS). Following this, we will present our own engagement journeys as three students who have taken on leadership responsibilities within the different schemes. Finally, we will use this, and further reflection, to consider the challenges faced in our efforts to promote engagement.

Student representation and the SCC

Student representation, specifically the SSC, has been instrumental in implementing changes to CH. The SSC operates with the understanding that in order for schemes to be valuable, staff must listen to the needs of students and enable them to be actively involved in delivering changes. Therefore, the SSC is a student-led and student-chaired committee with a ratio of 16 student representatives to one staff facilitator, in order to give the reps confidence to deliver their own voices in meetings. Working groups, made up of the reps, are also established each year to make positive changes to the degree. Particular successes coming out of this scheme have included:

- 'CH Week': a careers week providing opportunities to integrate and think about options after graduation.
- The Independent Studies module: an innovative final-year module, designed as an alternative to a dissertation. This permits students to combine their subjects and do something more creative than a traditional essay.
- Induction and first-year mentoring: to improve transition for greater integration and support, the SSC set up what is now a flagship mentoring scheme.

Student mentoring

The mentoring scheme focuses on the social integration of first years into university life and the CH degree specifically. It has become a student-led scheme, with students responsible for recruitment, selection, training and management, with staff purely in a supportive role. Mentors are second- and third-year students who take responsibility for a group of five to seven mentees, grouped according to subjects studied. Communication is initiated by the mentor before the first-year students arrive at Newcastle, meaning that the first point of call for a new student is within CH.

Mentors plan and deliver activities on Induction Day within their mentor groups, helping to create cohesion and friendships among mentees. Throughout the academic year, mentors hold informal meetings which cover practical issues relevant to new students. However, the most important aim of these meetings is to create a sense of community within the degree programme.

The scheme has been hugely successful; on some occasions, mentors have been instrumental in preventing a student from leaving the University. Students often report feeling like they 'belong' to the degree as a result of interactions with their mentor groups and many lasting friendships have grown out of this. Crucially, surveys confirm a sense of community has become more prevalent since the introduction of the scheme.

The PASS scheme

The predominant focus on students' social integration in our scheme means mentors often feel uneasy about fulfilling mentees demands for academic advice. Due to the nature of the CH degree, students frequently miss out on academic skills modules studied by their single honours counterparts, as they do not have sufficient credits to undertake them. However, previous efforts to fill this gap have not been well received; mentor workshops and a skills module run by CH were both unpopular and unsuccessful.

The creation of the PASS scheme, based on Peer-Assisted Learning models, tries to combat these issues. PASS aims to support the development of CH students' academic writing skills; however, support is generic to all subjects and has no connection to any specific curriculum. Like the SSC and mentoring, PASS is coordinated by students and supported by staff. Students run the application and selection processes and successful applicants are selected based on their ability to effectively relate to other students rather than academic talent. PASS leaders are trained by staff to provide solely structural and technical advice on assignments. This is then delivered on a one-to-one basis with students that attend the sessions. It is mainly marketed as an informal drop-in service, but meetings on request are also available. Although fewer students actively engage with PASS, compared, for example, to mentoring, those that do utilize the scheme become repeat visitors and the help they received has been reflected through their improved grades.

The CHS

Unlike the schemes already described, the CHS is unique in the sense that it is completely run by the students rather than in partnership with staff. The overriding focus of the society is to provide opportunities for students to socially integrate away from the academic university setting. This allows groups of students that are reluctant to engage with staff-inclusive schemes a different route into the combined community.

Though mentoring goes a long way to encouraging this type of social integration, it is limited to the first-year cohort. The society gives students a chance to meet combiners across the four years and, where possible, links up with other schemes to appeal to the wider combined population. Once a small group of friends, the CHS has grown into a large and vibrant society exceeding membership to over one hundred people in just a five-year period. Ticket sales for our most recent event, a summer ball boat cruise, reached a record high of 90 participants and featured the 'CH Awards'. With both student and staff-chosen winners, these awards give members an opportunity to see fellow students recognized and rewarded for their outstanding contributions as an engaged combiner.

These schemes have encouraged students to participate and engage with Combined – forming a community, providing opportunities and giving students a voice. We now turn to our own narratives to highlight the outcomes for those who take up these opportunities.

Beth

When I first applied to university, CH wasn't even on my application. I wanted to do English Literature and I was really disappointed when I had to apply again, this time to do English Literature with Sociology in Combined. I came to university after having had a gap year, where I was employed full-time, and decided to stay working full-time when I started my course. I hadn't done much research into the CH programme at Newcastle and had no idea what I wanted out of it other than a degree at the end. I saw university as simply something I had to go through to get a decent job, and had no expectations of the social or extra-curricular aspects.

I decided to become a mentor after an uneventful first semester in which, with hindsight, I don't think I'd integrated socially very well at all. However, at the time I wasn't really aware of this; as a home student, I still had my family and friends from school and work, so I didn't really notice a lack of social relationships at university in the same way as a traditional student might. So although becoming involved in a role within CH eventually changed this, I can't say it was a factor which motivated me to apply to be a mentor in the first place.

Instead I felt, to some extent, prompted by a need to enhance my CV. I knew that in a competitive job market, having extra-curricular activities would make me seem a more rounded graduate. The fact that the mentor scheme was student-led also appealed to me. My own mentor hadn't been completely successful and I liked knowing I would have the chance to use my initiative to make the mentoring system work better for new students. At this point I had never taken on a leadership role and knew that in order to develop leadership skills I would also need to work on interpersonal communication. I knew that mentoring would give me the opportunity to improve in these areas, and that was a big draw for me.

Leading group meetings was far more challenging than I had expected, as some of my mentees were quite introverted and one in particular was initially very withdrawn. To overcome this, I was aware that I'd need to build trust relationships with each of my mentees, so a few weeks in I decided to depart from the traditional group meeting and arranged individual meetings with each of them to get to know them better. Though this was slightly risky as it took time away from creating cohesion and friendships within the group, I was free to use my own judgement and decided this would be worthwhile. I'm naturally quite cautious when it comes to risk-taking and so this was incredibly daunting at first. However, the trust placed in me by staff gave me faith in my ability and a little more willingness to step out of my comfort zone.

These individual meetings were a massive test of my interpersonal skills, especially in the meeting with the disengaged student. Despite my best efforts, this mentee seemed determined to give one-word answers and was completely closed off. As I'm quite shy and eager to avoid confrontation, it would have been easy to just end the meeting and give up. In this case though, my role as mentor meant I had a responsibility to my mentee; I knew it was important to overcome my discomfort and persevere in case she did have a problem. Eventually my mentee did confide in me about her problems settling into university. Once I understood what was bothering her, I could give her appropriate advice and she became visibly more relaxed and willing to talk. After our meeting, she sent me a text saying how grateful she was for my help and that she felt much better after our conversation. It was hugely satisfying to know I'd not only made a difference to someone's experience at university, but changed the way I interacted to be more dynamic and constructive.

The positive outcome of this meeting gave me a huge boost of confidence and faith in my own decision-making abilities. I'm also a lot more wary of letting my natural shyness dictate the way I handle situations and interact with others. I also went on to become a mentor leader, which required me to lead a team of five mentors and be far more assertive than I normally would. Being a leader and confidently expressing my opinions and making decisions is something I can now achieve quite comfortably.

For me, this is why student-led schemes are so valuable; the opportunity to take risks and use initiative is hardly ever present in academic work to the same degree. It's also vital in challenging the notion that students are passive recipients of their university education, which is really all I had expected when I started my course. Being seen as a partner to staff within these schemes has given me enough confidence in my own judgements to challenge staff in other schools who don't have this attitude. Having encouragement to use my initiative and take responsibility for my decisions has completely changed the way I approach challenges and new situations, and that's something difficult to teach within an academic curriculum. Knowing that staff support my decisions and listen to my opinions has given me the confidence to take calculated risks and step outside my comfort zone, which were skills I didn't have before but which I can't imagine being without now. In particular, these new skills were invaluable to me when completing an independent project in the final year. I was able to challenge supervisory advice, take a big risk, and create a project I felt passionate about. These risks paid off, I got my highest mark for any assignment and was voted as the winner of Best Short Paper when I presented my project at the CH Conference.

Therefore, my initial expectation that I would improve my confidence and leadership and communication skills through becoming a mentor has definitely been met, but what I have actually gained is so much more. That earlier issue I mentioned of being a home student who worked full-time made it really difficult, initially, for me to integrate into the CH community. When I arrived at university my course-mates had already formed friendship groups in their halls of residence, and my socializing opportunities outside classes were much more limited. Being so busy outside university, I didn't even realize how much I was missing out on until I got involved. Becoming a mentor gave me the chance to gain a new circle of friends on my course and I finally felt I had become part of a community at university. So for me, mentoring not only involved socially integrating first years into university life, but also helped me to integrate myself and gain a network of support (staff and students) who all helped to build my confidence. In the final year I participated in most of the CH social events and in lots of other activities and events in the degree. For example, I have been very involved in promoting CH to new applicants and presented at no less than four conferences, including doing keynotes to large audiences. This was still scary, but would have been totally unthinkable three years ago. Winning the title 'Role Model of the Year' at our annual CH awards recently really made me feel I'd made a difference to others on my degree too, which is so personally rewarding.

So while at first I was disappointed to have had to apply to Combined, now I know it was the best thing that could have happened. Now, I can be confident that I'm graduating with far more than I expected at first. Not just a degree, but confidence, skills and life-long friends.

Daniel

In September 2009, I began a Business Management degree. I felt I had a natural aptitude for the subject and it was a 'safe bet' for a relatively well paid job upon graduation. More than the subject, it was the promise of 'university life' which motivated me to enter Higher Education: the opportunity to make friends, experience something exciting, and become independent.

'Fitting in' was particularly difficult in the first few weeks, mostly due to my aversion to clubbing, not ideal in the 'party city' of the UK. Struggling to adapt to the student culture or connect to my peers, I looked to my course to keep me inspired, but teaching too failed to engage me. There were no attempts made by staff to engage us and we were treated with indifference. Nobody, including my personal tutor, seemed bothered about how I was settling in. There seemed to be a collective feeling that all that mattered was a degree certificate. Ultimately I felt lost; this was not what I had worked towards. Lacking in confidence, I did not attend society events and two-hour gaps in my timetable left enough time to go back to halls. By the end of the year, I had made firm friends with my flatmates, one of whom was studying on CH. Still uninspired by my course, I began to consider an alternative career path and opted to change onto the CH programme. Frustrated by my lack of integration, I also felt a change would provide opportunities and spaces to get involved which suited me.

I joined CH at the start of the next academic year. Feeling relatively settled, I was determined to find extra-curricular opportunities that would make me more employable and reflected my academic interests practically, i.e. working with people. I signed up to volunteer with the Samaritans and Nightline, which was, essentially, a Samaritans for Newcastle students, and felt excited about the potential to make a difference. During my course induction, a much more friendly and student-led event than the two-hour lecture I'd received the previous year, I heard about student representation. Course reps had designed the day and created our student mentoring scheme. I'd never been involved in any such work before but decided, thinking back to my previous experience, that any course which cared about, and empowered, its students was worth being involved with. Being a student rep meant being involved in decision making, but also presented an opportunity to get to know people and be truly active in implementing changes. I set up a careers week in my introductory year and went on to lead the committee, a role I've had for the last two years.

Being given the opportunity to lead felt like my capabilities were being recognized and I've been enthusiastic to meet these, and my own, expectations and do a good job. Being invited to conferences, liaising with staff and chairing formal meetings initially felt like intimidating tasks beyond what it meant to be an undergraduate. But, through encouragement from my degree director to view staff as colleagues, I've come to be more enterprising in my approach to meeting staff and giving confident talks. I've been made to feel that I have something of tremendous value to contribute as a student; not just my voice but my capacity, through lobbying etc., to make something happen and this has really enhanced my self-belief. I hope that as a professional I will be given similar space to follow my own ideas, to work on behalf of others and have their words and my voice heard when it matters.

Taking on chairing duties as well as co-ordinating Nightline has required managing a variety of people and doing a lot of work. At times the workload is a little overwhelming, particularly when you impose pressure on yourself to deliver something of quality, and I have often reflected back on a week and realized I've only made time for extra-curricular work. This though, above the academic work, has given me a richer university experience and an opportunity to develop my professionalism (not least with time management). I don't think all students have this opportunity to develop but I feel, through proactively pursuing opportunities, I have.

On my previous degree I struggled to make friends and my self-esteem was knocked. The support of mentoring introduced me to a group of people who I could call friends relatively instantly. Getting more involved through the SSC and Nightline has only helped further and, along with all the other benefits, I've had a reason to speak to students who I otherwise wouldn't have come in to contact with. I recognize that I am shy in approaching people in the first instance (the idea of networking still terrifies me) but over the last three years, as my confidence has grown in other areas, I've encouraged myself to ultimately make a great group of friends who have, in turn, made my experience so much better; they've encouraged me to go to socials (my aversion to clubbing is no longer so strong) and made me realize my self-esteem once more.

In the end my 'journey' is one of extremes, from complete disengagement to being 'super-engaged', responsible for the representation of other students and running a student service, as well as being an author in this book. I've achieved this by running with opportunities and trying to get things done. The experience I'd wanted at the very beginning followed. I have matured and grown in the way of feeling capable and confident, had my politics and values reinforced, particularly those around supporting and listening to people in need, made great friends and I've had fun! I feel immensely privileged to have been given the space, time, encouragement and opportunities to have and do all that.

Studying at university, I've found, isn't about having better job prospects simply by virtue of having a certificate and skills to succeed but provides an opportunity to become an individual who is more assured and equipped to make a quality contribution to wider society. To me, universities and Students' Unions should be aiming to foster this transformative outcome for all, irrespective, but mindful, of circumstance.

Ruth

My journey into Higher Education was relatively traditional. I had always loved the educational environment and knew from an early stage that I wanted to combine my two favourite subjects in order to keep my options post-university as open as possible. The problematic decision came when I had to choose which institution to attend after being lucky enough to receive five offers. Newcastle had never been my favourite; I had originally set out applying for joint degrees and it was only included due to limited courses with my chosen combination of subjects. Nevertheless, at my mother's request I attended the post-application open day. As much of a cliché as it must sound given the nature of this book, the promotion by student speakers about the schemes of engagement within the CH department did for me something no other university open day had managed – achieved a feeling of community. It reflected an attitude of partnership and integration, something I had always assumed would end at college given the independent nature of a degree. The strong relationships amongst the combined students, and crucially between staff and students, which I felt were a direct result of this ethos, made up my mind that Newcastle was the right place for me.

One would assume that the chance to get involved in these schemes, which had seemingly attracted me, would have been high on my priorities upon arriving at Newcastle. However, opportunities to get involved as first years were limited; most roles were allocated prior to the end of the academic year so prospective students were automatically excluded. Instead of actively seeking out the few that were available, the influence from my peers to party as much as possible was too hard to resist. Therefore, for me, the campus became a place purely connected to academic work, where I only ventured for lectures.

By the end of semester one I was extremely happy. I had formed strong friendships with my flatmates and loved the freedom university life brought. However, this meant I felt no pressure to integrate myself into the CH community and, as a result, I knew no one on the course itself. Unfortunately, the two meetings my mentor had set up in the first month were poorly attended and as a result she quickly gave up, leaving me feeling like I had missed out. So when the chance to become a mentor arose at the start of my second semester, although I was mainly motivated by the opportunity to enhance my CV, I also wanted the chance to improve on my own experience by persevering to support a scheme I knew had the potential to be of real value. It was in the undertaking of this role that my journey toward becoming an engaged student kicked in with full effect.

Becoming a mentor led to a wealth of opportunities and I regretted not taking advantage of these beneficial chances sooner. My mentor interview, carried out by staff and students in partnership, reminded me of the original appeal of the department and gave me a renewed sense that the CH community was worth becoming part of. Team building exercises during mentor training soon made me feel like I was integrated amongst my fellow engaged students and had a space within the CH common room, the power of which is not to be underestimated. The campus now became a place where I was both socially and academically integrated. Into my second year I had made a number of strong friendships with combiners across all four years and felt much more confident in myself. I knew I always had people behind me if I encountered any issues on the course and, most importantly, I felt like I belonged somewhere within the university setting.

I had also seemingly made a good impression in my mentor interview and as a result was asked to represent the department at a conference. Although this seemed like a frightening prospect, I felt compelled to say yes, as not only had I been asked directly by my head of department, but I had nothing extra-curricular to show for my time at university at this point. It gave me the opportunity to exercise my public speaking, something I had some practice in before university but had not done for a long time. I have since presented our schemes of engagement to audiences of increased sizes at both conferences and open days, and along with two fellow students was given the opportunity to completely design and present our own paper. While a massive responsibility, it was a great privilege to be trusted and formed part of the assessment in 'Developing Graduate Attributes', a module aimed at identifying how these responsibilities have developed my graduate skills. As a consequence of this presentation, my outlook on student life changed; for the first time I felt staff listened to my advice on improving schemes and, more than that, they valued it.

By third year, I had moved from being an engaged to a 'super-engaged' student. After a challenging, yet positive experience as a mentor, I took on numerous roles. Through helping one of my mentees overcome some very complex issues, and ultimately playing a part in her decision to remain at university, I was assured that my hard work mattered and improved not only my own student experience, but that of other students too. In addition, the 'Developing Graduate Attributes' module, which I chose in connection with my mentor role, highlighted how I could apply the skills I used in my extra-curricular positions onto my academic work. For the first time I saw how the two sides of university, academic and extra-curricular, worked together, increasing my confidence and academic achievement. So, in an effort to further enhance the student experience and encourage others to engage, I stood for President of the CHS and was elected in by my fellow students. Simultaneously, I took on the task of being a mentor leader, which involved taking responsibility for a group of six mentors and providing them with encouragement, advice and feedback in order to enable them to fulfil their role to its highest potential. I am confident from positive feedback and increased attendance levels at CHS events that I, and the teams I have led, have made a wider impact on engaging students who otherwise would have remained distant from Combined.

Becoming an integral part in the CH team has shown me that all students have a voice and when they use them it can bring about massive changes. When starting university I thought the staff–student relationship would be a replica of high school, where staff opinions largely come first. Instead, CH has shown me that schemes run in partnership not only improve the student experience for those that choose to engage but crucially improve our all-round employability. The students and staff in CH have helped shaped me into the person I am today, confident to step into the wider world.

Tensions and barriers

We feel very positive about our experiences as CH students and know that the students around us feel a similar sense of appreciation towards the degree. CH has achieved a sense of community and provides opportunities to all students who want to take a proactive role within it. However, there are still a number of barriers to be explored and resolved, if possible, in order to reach even more of the student body.

While we have all achieved success in the various schemes we are involved with, the opportunities we offer are not always taken up by large numbers of CH students. For instance, although mentoring reaches everyone on the degree (as all first years are allocated a mentor) there have been many instances where mentors and mentor leaders have spent a lot of time planning meetings and organizing events which nobody attended. The main purpose of mentoring is to create cohesion among students. This becomes impossible when students don't attend. This is not only frustrating and demoralizing as a mentor and mentor leader, but inhibits the success of the scheme as it relies on the participation of other students.

The problem with this is that we cannot always rely on other students to be as proactive as we need them to be. This is especially problematic for PASS leaders. Students often have not finished their assignments in time to attend a PASS session, leaving it until the day of the deadline. SSC reps also often find it difficult to obtain responses and input from their constituents, whether this is in terms of attending focus groups or answering emails.

Students give us many reasons why they do not always make use of the schemes. For us, one of the most frustrating explanations from students is a lack of awareness. Many claim to be unaware of the various schemes and give this as a reason for not using them. This kind of response occurs consistently, despite our continual efforts to promote the schemes in emails, posters and events, such as CH Week.

One way this kind of student resistance can be explained is a belief amongst some of the cohort that their peers are incapable of fulfilling the level of support and advice our schemes provide. This is particularly true of PASS, where PASS leaders are considered under-qualified to provide academic support. In surveys, many students say they prefer to utilize staff-led alternatives because the staff are thought to have 'experience and authority'. Similarly, SSC reps can be seen to lack the authority necessary to make real or tangible changes. This is apparent in students not taking up opportunities to provide their voice or, in the case of PASS, have their work proofread. While this is less of a problem for mentors (they are seen as having authority, having come from similar experiences themselves in the recent past), mentor leaders have also struggled to instil a sense of authority among the mentors they support. Meetings with mentor leaders were less well-attended than those led by staff, suggesting that mentors felt less compelled to attend meetings led by their peers.

In our experience, we know all the schemes are useful and that students are capable of delivering great results (whether through empowerment, extensive training, etc.) but it is frustrating that others do not see this value and trust their peers, not least as it means student volunteers are not utilized.

In order to run these schemes successfully a group of student volunteers are required to take leading roles. The three of us have chosen to take on these leadership roles, partly due to our previous experiences within the various schemes, but mainly because we feel a sense of attachment to our CH community. Arguably, our achievement as leaders and continued engagement means the three of us could be categorized as 'star performers', at least in the view of staff and peers, because we play such a prominent part. Our enthusiasm means we are often the first to volunteer and, consequently, we are in the same group of students that are repeatedly offered opportunities from staff. However, this creates a potential problem as the staff come to rely on the small group of students that are perceived to be the 'star performers'.

Although, as our stories demonstrate, our overall experiences as student leaders are overwhelmingly positive, there are still several tensions remaining. Our passion to improve not only our own student experience, but also that of the students around us, often leads to a huge level of frustration, when despite efforts to promote schemes they are underused and undervalued by our fellow students. Already under huge pressure to simultaneously deliver in these roles and our degrees, it puts us under further pressure to try and solve these issues so that the other students involved feel appreciated.

We believe that student-led schemes are such an important part of engaging the wider body of students. However, we would never have taken on leadership roles without the support and encouragement of CH staff. Despite feeling pressured to fulfil staff expectations and provide role model examples in the hope of encouraging staff outside CH to place more trust in their students, these opportunities have, more importantly, given us confidence to achieve our ambitions and take on multiple roles. The schemes cannot run effectively without these star performers at the forefront and we hope that our hard work encourages other students to take up the opportunities on offer to them and perceive us as role models.

Conclusions

The personal accounts and barriers sections above draw attention to a number of pertinent questions. While we hesitate to suggest any ultimate answers to these (or even that any exist), there are certain insights we can offer from our perspective as 'super-engaged' students.

Firstly, it is clear from our personal accounts that taking on leadership roles within the schemes has been transformative, vital in building skills and confidence for all of us. With over 400 students on the degree, there simply is not room for all students to take on these roles; there are only six PASS leaders needed to cover the current level of participation, for example. However, every effort is made to provide a role for those students who are proactive about getting involved.

Similarly, the frustration around low participation from other students requires us to consider whether it is realistic to aim for 100 per cent take up of the schemes. Is it even desirable, given the pressure this would put on the 'star performers'? For us, it seems to be enough to offer the opportunities, even if they are not always actively used by students. Particularly in the case of mentoring, students report that even if they have not 'used' their mentor much, they appreciated knowing peer support was there if they needed it.

Finally, there remains the issue of who must assume ultimate responsibility for the success of these schemes. While there is a danger of expecting too much of the students in the roles (bearing in mind that they are simultaneously studying, usually full-time), the ethos of partnership with staff does make us feel responsible for achieving success within the schemes. However, for us, it seems to be the process of *trying* to make the schemes work which is most important. None of us would claim that every single thing we have tried has been 100 per cent successful. However, the process has always been valuable, both personally for our own development, and in terms of 'trial and error' with regards to knowing what works for the schemes.

Chapter 6

Music to listen to while writing
Ludovico Einaudi or amazing piano music

Susan Lund

Introduction

This chapter explores my experiences as a student embarking, with four others, on a collaborative project on transition into Higher Education (HE) with one of our academic tutors. The transition project began its journey towards the end of our first year at university. In this first stage, ten students participated, taking part in one-to-one interview discussions which explored why they decided to enter the HE system. The second part of the project gave students the opportunity to create videos which captured our unique and individual experience of transition into HE. We had complete freedom about what we included in our videos. Carol, our lecturer, arranged for an e-learning support lecturer with expertise of creating videos to come along on the day of shooting our videos to help us master the important basics of operating the equipment. The support lecturer stayed the whole day, offering invaluable advice on composition techniques. This included the use of lighting to create a sense of air and movement, and how to work out portions when doing a self-interview for those of us brave enough to go in front of the camera. In addition, he taught us the art of editing and enhancing our videos. Without this guidance and support while making the video, I believe my video would not have been as effective at giving me my voice. The next part of the project involved showing our videos to an audience of 16–17-year-old sixth-form Psychology students at a local sixth-form college in a deprived area with the aim of raising their aspirations. We also talked to them about our individual journeys to HE and discussed aspects of university life with them.

At this point several students left the project, resulting in five or six students continuing to dedicate time to the project. It seemed to us that there was something extraordinary and worthwhile about taking this project forward and we talked with the tutor about new ways to drive this project on. For example, after the video-making process and talking to students in the local college, we did presentations within the university to fellow students, faculty staff and academics, some of whom were already involved in similar student engagement projects. At the end of our first year we presented at a national conference about such academic educational research. The two lecturers presented with us (three students), enabling us to demonstrate our enthusiasm for the project and to answer any questions about the project from a student's perspective. I was thrilled to be one of only three students to get this opportunity to speak to a distinguished audience about the project, but also terrified of not being able to answer their questions or not living up to my tutors' expectations. However, it went exceptionally well and to take part in this experience was an honour and privilege that could not be missed.

Staff–student presentations gave us all a valuable insight into the benefits of such collaborations and enhanced the student experience because as students we feel valued and that our voice is heard.

Working alongside Carol on the project could prove challenging at times. We all had different agendas and as a student, my main priority was to successfully complete my academic studies to gain the highest degree classification possible. This meant that working on the project was always put on hold until the end of the second semester of each academic year. I feel that Carol's main aim in doing this was because she didn't want the project to distract us too much from our studies. Carol's agenda was governed by her teaching commitment and workload as a Senior Lecturer in education. As students, I feel that we were as much a driving force behind the project as Carol. We were all eager to explore new and interesting ways to take the project to greater heights, such as doing the videos and creating the poems. I myself wanted to do something extraordinary, something which not all other students get the opportunity to do, which would make me stand out in a crowded market later, either moving onto a post-graduate course or in finding employment. Many of the major decisions were made by Carol, due to her expertise in the field of student engagement. However, Carol would take our thoughts and ideas into consideration when making her final decision. If this was not feasible, Carol would always try to critically feedback her rationale. Some of the reasons why we were unable to do certain things was due to time constraints or financial reasons. This illustrates the power dynamics which are involved with academic and student engagement projects, which can cause problems, as some students may feel their contribution is treated in a tokenistic manner. I think that staff members who offer the opportunity to work in partnership with students can gain a greater knowledge of the reality of what student life can be like, for instance, how complex it can be living away from home for the first time, as captured in fellow student's poem. It can also bring about much improved student and academic communication, allowing for more understanding of each other's roles and responsibilities. Moreover, I feel that many academics gain a sense of pride watching young adults develop a range of invaluable life skills, some of which are transferable, such as negotiation skills or how to deliver a confident presentation to a mixture of audiences. Moreover, staff can get a glimpse into how the student can widen their knowledge of how an HE institution works and how they become much more independent and reflectively aware of their own learning capabilities.

Towards the end of the second year of academic teaching, the project was given some financial assistance to develop it further by running a creative writing workshop. The aim was to create something collaborative with the aid of the academic tutor to guide us. This was also an exciting opportunity for us to have the potential to write an article for publication which would illustrate students' experiences of transition into HE and our journey so far. Getting it to this point was a real challenge. During our final year of study there was very little time for us or lecturer to work on the project and eventually the student element of the project finished due to many of us gaining employment or moving onto new opportunities.

Having introduced the project and given an overview of its structure and stages, in this chapter I want to focus on the video, which was created at the end of the first year of university, and the Transition Poem, which I wrote in the creative writing workshop at the end of the second year. I am concentrating on these two elements of the project because both are innovative methods through which I have learned to express myself in an original way using my own voice, while at the same time developing skills I never had before. Additionally, both elements are exceptionally reflective of my journey through the transition process into the educational institution.

Creative representations of transition: video and poetry

The discussion in the rest of this chapter will provide insights which enable readers to step into my student world and illustrate my personal transition into HE. It does this through the creativity of video and poetry as alternative forms of discourse. These unusual approaches go against many of the norms and conventions which could be seen as more traditionally 'academic'. First of all, I will analyze my video which I created in the first year when I was experiencing many diverse emotions, from fear of failure to exhilaration of passing all my assignments with very high grades, which I thought would never happen. It explores the way in which music and visual images create atmosphere and mystique about the person behind the camera. I then move onto articulating how transition feels using poetry, after gaining the opportunity to undergo the three day creative writing course which I referred to above. The poem unravels intriguing insights which have been hidden in my subconscious, which I was unaware of until critical analysis.

What I have tried to do is portray my story of a student engagement project from my perspective as an undergraduate. As such, it is a contribution to knowledge which gives a heartfelt insight into how students from a working class background may feel about being out of their depth and unsure about their abilities when going through the transition into HE. The chapter illuminates how determined I have had to be in overcoming adversity, and how I succeeded in realizing my potential in order to complete my degree studies. Moreover, it illustrates how academics that use creative approaches can help students to become more critically reflective, identify how far they have come from the beginning of their journey, along with how much they have evolved and accomplished as scholars. I believe my insights are particularly useful in highlighting the benefits of collaborative student engagement projects between academics and students. I also want to put forward the view that such approaches will be even more beneficial in the new 'marketized' climate in HE when Higher Education Institutions will be looking to find new ways to enhance the student experience.

The beginning to becoming

My video depicts the beginning of the long, emotional and personal roller coaster journey of my first year at Sheffield Hallam University. The aim was to give the audience access to images shot through the lens of my own eyes and glimpses into what, where and who were meaningful to me at that pivotal stage in my academic life.

Initially, I was supposed to be working with some friends on the video. However, due to us not being able to reach an agreement about what to do, Carol placed a camcorder into my hands and told me to go film something. I went off alone, filled with fear and horrified at the thought that I had to create my own video. In addition, I had no prior knowledge or experience of film making and no real clear direction of what to do. I didn't have a plan!

After getting over the shock of going it alone, I felt more in control and even got enthusiastic about this chance to explore my creativity and produce something original which could illustrate my personal journey and experiences, which could be beneficial to other students experiencing something similar. Images of university spaces and places, and of other people, were my preferred method to communicate with my audience and were used throughout. I myself am too shy to expose both myself and my emotions on camera. As a result, I used music as a technique to build feelings in my audience of those who know me and my story, while enabling those who didn't know me to build up their own image of me as an individual.

My video journey begins with the poem called *What If?* by the former Poet Laureate Sir Andrew Motion, written down the side of the Owen building. Figure 6.1 displays the poem.

Not only is this building one of the tallest in Sheffield, it is also on the main walkway up from the railway station, which means that it is a landmark for all rail visitors coming to the city. However, this building is also significant to me personally for another reason, as it is where most of my lectures took place in the first year and in the subsequent two years of my degree. This poem is significant due to its power to hold my gaze while I read each sentence word for word while trying to uncover its meaning. Uncovering meanings of things by analyzing issues, becoming a scholar and giving me a better start in life: these were all part of my rationale for coming to university and taking on all the opportunities it had to offer, such as this project, in the first place. All of the aforementioned were denied and restricted to me when I was younger due to my disability. When I edited my

Figure 6.1 The poem *What If?*, written by former Poet Laureate Sir Andrew Motion, on the side of Sheffield Hallam University's Owen Building

video, I included as a backing track Snow Patrol's song 'Take Back the City' at this point to exemplify this hidden meaning of injustice. It was also to show those who I felt had denied me earlier opportunities that I was intelligent enough for HE and could rise to its challenges.

The video then includes shots of the Owen Building's atrium and shots panning around the café area. I wanted to demonstrate the sheer scale of the building, while also viewing the spaces where I would take study breaks. Panning up to the glass ceiling of the atrium, its strong glass and steel structure illustrated how I see myself as penetrating the 'academic elite ceiling', one which every student could look up to and aspire to be. However, many are told that only the brightest students would penetrate through it to achieve the highest grades and degree classifications. I was always told I would never break through this 'academic elite ceiling' because I was 'not good enough'. However, putting this image of the glass ceiling into my video worked perfectly to show where I was going to catapult myself; with blood, sweat, tears, hard work and determination. No one or nothing was ever going to hold me back. I used the Kings of Leon track 'Use Somebody' to symbolize me using the power of knowledge to attend university and build a more prosperous future for myself.

The library became my friend and surrogate academic home for large parts of my time while studying. It is here where I learned to think analytically about issues, do my research and write some of my most successful pieces of work. I chose to film what seemed like millions of abandoned desks, which would normally be jammed packed with noisy student bodies, mulling around busily trying to complete work or revise. I panned the camera down the never-ending isles of bookcases, encompassing a wealth of knowledge hidden on their shelves for the students to unravel. There was little evidence of student life, only a handful of Malaysian students who were here for the summer. The atmosphere in the library felt surreal without the presence of the students, as if it had gone into hibernation; it brought back the memories of how overwhelmingly lonely and isolated you could get while you were studying for long periods of time at night. I captured one of the TV screens which depicted a soft toy monkey, which was supposed to represent a student at a desk with all their work spread out, looking tired and exhausted. This image made me laugh and reflect on how I was like this creature, needing someone to take care of me after a long study session. I used Snow Patrol's song 'Shut the Shutters' over these images, as this represents me having to shut most of the outside world and its distractions out of my mind in order to focus on my studies and complete assignments. It was like I had to 'shut the shutters' down and barricade myself inside the library or there was a possibility I would fail, an option I was not willing to accept. Shutting myself away proved challenging at times but I had to convince myself that this was not going to be for forever and would be worth it in the long run. All of these feelings felt very unique to me at this time in my life; there was little room for other peoples' feelings as these could be distractions from my work at hand.

Taking part in the student experience project and the making of this video enabled me to critically reflect upon my first academic year and see my personal transformation up to that point. It unlocked memories of when I wanted to give up because something was very challenging, and it brought to mind how my loved ones were completely supportive of me, even when they themselves had never experienced going to university and knew nothing of its intensity. It also made me think of my lecturers and personal tutors who believed in my aptitude to achieve things, which I never thought possible.

New windows on transition

The creative writing workshop took place in a conference room within a church in Sheffield. Carol, our lecturer who was the leader on the transition project, had invited a fellow academic, Liz, who had years of experience of successfully writing poetry. Liz's role was to help inspire us while preparing our minds for the art of writing creatively, as many of us were unaccustomed to any style of writing other than academic writing. In order to get us started, Liz went around the table and asked everyone to think about concrete images of what transition could 'look' like if we could see it, touch it, smell it or taste it. These concrete images gave us visual cues to work from. All of these visuals cues were written on a flipchart and collaboratively rearranged into a group poem about transition. This collaborative effort formed the basis for our own individual sonnet, which Liz invited us to create in just five minutes shortly afterwards. We were encouraged to use elements from the group poem to write our own poem of what transition 'meant' to us as individuals. When we had finished, our task was to read our poems aloud to the rest of the group to gain critical feedback on individual style, mood, movement and use of language to express ourselves.

Below is my interpretation of my poem of what transition into HE means to me. I have included the full text of my poem first. This is then followed by an analysis of my poem. Here, each individual line of the poem is in italics, followed by a short analytical account underneath which unlocks the hidden 'snapshots' of meaning behind how I was feeling while writing the poem and how I had felt up until that point. Writing this poem in such a short timescale felt pressured and nerve-wracking; this experience was out of my comfort zone as I had not written any kind of poetry since secondary school.

Reflective Windows through Transition

It's a speed camera on over drive
It makes me cry the closer I get to the finish line
It's the bank statement that states there's nothing there
It's the empty purse when I could do with my cup of tea
It's the car alarm that I just want to ditch
It's the computer that's lost the will to live
It's the locked door I am trying to escape
It's the child who refuses to give in
It's my mum when I am desperate for a hug
It's the cunning fox who has lured me to its den
It's the thief who stole my identity
It's the home where it all starts and ends
It's the seminar presentation I just love to hate.

The meaning of my poem

It's a speed camera on over drive

This portrays the constant pace in which the degree is travelling and permanent logging of all the progress I am making with my studies. This includes my ever growing confidence in my ability to express myself analytically in academic debates. The camera is producing photographic evidence while keeping a close check of all the excellent grades on my 'educational record' which will form my final degree classification for eternity.

It makes me cry the closer I get to the finish line

These tears are not of unhappiness but of that of joy with all that I have achieved, for instance being able to make new friends from different backgrounds. This is while still knowing that at some point the people who I have studied alongside and have grown fond of might soon leave to chase their dreams and we may never again get the chance to share such moments.

It's the bank statement that states there's nothing there

This represents my learning and understanding of deferred gratification, about accepting my financial situation, which is similar to other students. However, this problem will only last for a short while and afterwards I will be free to apply for more stimulating jobs, enabling me to work with more like-minded people.

It's the empty purse when I could do with my cup of tea

This reiterates what it's like to have no money when you want to buy some basic refreshments. It's also about wanting the comfort of home and the ordinary things in life, such as a cup of tea, which are important to me.

It's the car alarm that I just want to ditch

The image of the car alarm going off is a continuous reminder of all the assignments and deadlines which are seemingly never-ending. The constant battle of trying not to feel guilty for having some 'me time' to enjoy, without having my studies linger in the back of my mind.

It's the computer that's lost the will to live

The computer is a metaphor for my own brain and the way it has to process so much written information, which is needed to be put into my assignments. It represents when you are trying to scrape that last bit of emotional, mental and physical effort out of every corner of your brain to complete that assignment which you have been up all night trying to finish.

It's the locked door I am trying to escape

This is linked to me wanting to change my life for the better and to get away from my old job which I was no longer happy with. However, I have entered another locked door at Sheffield Hallam University, as I have to concentrate and study before I can be given the key that enables me to unlock the door to a whole new world of fresh and exciting opportunities.

It's the child who refuses to give in

This symbolizes all the times when someone has said 'no, you will not or cannot achieve [something]' but I still keep fighting because I will not accept that I am simply not bright enough. It represents all the challenges I have had to overcome when I have been against the ropes, only to become the champion.

It's my mum when I am desperate for a hug

My mum is a key figure in my academic achievement as without her support I would have given up on my dreams years ago. She's the reassuring voice who always knows what to do or say at various stages of doubt to put me back on the right path to success.

It's the cunning fox who has lured me to its den

The cunning fox represents the university itself, with the bold black and cream flower feature on its city building wall, along with its striking poem running down the side that drew my gaze towards it. It represented and promised a new life, a new start, everything I wanted. But, like a cunning fox, it didn't scream back the amount of hard work or time I would have to put in to achieve all I desired.

It's the thief who stole my identity

Going through the first year of uni, I didn't really know if I belonged there, if this was my academic home. I felt like a 'fish out of water' or like Julie Walters' titular character in *Educating Rita*. I didn't fit in with my old life and friends but didn't fit in with the university environment either. Going to university made me question who I was and what I wanted out of life. It made me question whether going to university was the right decision. Ultimately, I found that the university didn't steal my identity, it just enhanced it greatly, enabling me to see more clearly what I wanted from life. It opened up a world of opportunities which would have remained off-limits otherwise.

It's the home where it all starts and ends

Sheffield Hallam University is where I started a new chapter in my life, a new adventure of looking for a direction which would bring me job satisfaction, not necessarily more money. This journey still continues now as I work as part of the disability team within the university. Therefore, my chapter will continue to unfold for the world to witness.

It's the seminar presentation I just love to hate

This symbolizes the dread I had when giving any type of presentation in front of my peers in first year. It's the stumbling and mumbling of getting my words out, the feelings of sheer nervousness which is so bad that I want to be sick. However, doing presentations with the project helped me overcome many of these issues with practice, which enabled my confidence to develop.

The whole process of going to university, taking part in the student engagement project and the writing of this chapter has opened a door to many new and exciting possibilities and has helped me develop forms of 'cultural capital' which would have remained off-limits if I had not come here. I have acquired a new found confidence in my own ability to take on new and complex challenges. It has allowed me to see diverse arguments from numerous different perspectives, while allowing me to think outside the box and create new forms of discourse through film and poetry. Doing my degree in education has given me a purpose and direction in life. I now know that I want to work within the HE sector, enabling others who are disabled to reach their full potential. Now I can see that I am a positive role model, not just of what we can achieve while at university but also after university, especially in a world where many graduates leave university without being able to find employment. If I had never come to university my life would be very different. Given where I came from, my working class background and the limited range of opportunities open to me, I would be doing a potentially soul-destroying job. I certainly would not be reaching my full potential.

Writing this chapter has been exhausting and exhilarating. Trying to get my experiences out of my head and onto the page has been a real struggle. In fact, it's been like scraping your favourite flavoured jam out of the bottom of the jam jar and scraping it over your toast. So I have to say thank you to the music of Ludovico Einaudi for helping me to write this chapter.

Chapter 7

Autoethnographic writing and student engagement practices

A personal and critical reflection

Zoë Sarah Baker

Introduction

This chapter provides a personal, reflective and critical account of my experience as an undergraduate BA (Hons) Education and Sociology student taking part in a module which aimed to put into practice a different approach to knowledge production and student engagement. This was achieved by the use of autoethnographic approaches to research and through students' participation in the production of an article for a web journal. I will reflect on how the use of autoethnographic methods incorporated personal forms of writing and visual methods and how this challenged conceptions of 'academic' research and writing. In addition, I will consider how the module was structured in ways which enabled students to develop greater control over their own learning and engagement. The chapter includes a discussion of the autoethnographic materials I produced and the theories drawn on to analyze these materials. I review how this module engaged students in ways which contrasted significantly with other 'typical' Higher Education (HE) modules we had studied, which were more based on a 'transmission' model of teaching and learning. The chapter will end by highlighting some of the potential implications of new approaches to student engagement which contest the current employability-focused discourses surrounding HE.

The module

The module, entitled 'Knowledge in the Postmodern World', was studied in the final year of my BA (Hons) in Education Studies and Sociology. Its main aim was to introduce students to the concept of autoethnography as a mode of research and knowledge production. Given the 'newness' of its use in HE, I will begin with a brief explanation of what autoethnography is. First of all, it is important to note that autoethnography can 'mean different things depending on how it is applied' (Hesse-Biber and Leavy, 2011: 211) and different approaches and practical exemplars of autoethnography can be found (Ellis and Bochner, 2000). My final completed journal article contained some features of 'analytical' (Anderson, 2006) and 'evocative' (Ellis, 2004) autoethnography, and was based on an original narrative text and visual images. Analytical autoethnography is described as an approach in which:

> [. . .] the researcher is (1) a full member in the research group or setting, (2) visible as such a member in the researcher's published texts, and (3) [. . .] focused on improving theoretical understandings of broader social phenomena.
>
> (Anderson, 2006: 375)

Ellis (2004: 19) defines autoethnography as 'research, writing and method that connect the personal to the cultural and social'. This view describes the autoethnography that I produced: I connected personal experience to 'cultural and social' factors, in that I chose to base my article on some critical incidents of my personal experiences of being a financially independent student required to balance full-time study with employment. I analyzed these through the theoretical lens of social identity theory, before relating this to the role of visual images and their importance in postmodernity. I see this aspect of my research and writing, then, as 'analytical autoethnography', in that I explored the usefulness of the 'social phenomena' of social identity theory. By contrast, evocative autoethnography 'involves primarily a description of what goes on in an individual's life or social environment and seeks to evoke emotion from the reader' (Hays and Singh 2012: 62). It is also an approach in which the writer analyzes the self to address personal experience (Mascia-Lees, 2011). In my autoethnography, I disclosed some key aspects of my personal experience in order to communicate my emotions and give the reader a 'felt sense' of my experiences.

The module was structured to assist students' understanding of autoethnography as a research genre. In the early stages of the module we explored different types and forms of autoethnographic materials, such as articles detailing visual, sensory approaches and personal narratives. In addition, we also engaged with writings that described and evaluated modernist and postmodernist perspectives of theories of knowledge production. These two approaches provided us with a broad and complex foundation of understanding to produce our own autoethnography. On a weekly basis, we would complete readings and nominate ourselves to deliver a summary of these to the group to act as a basis for discussion. This was an important part of the student-led nature of the module. The role of the tutor was to act as a guide for the group to stimulate further exploration of materials from our responses. This resulted in seminars based upon us sharing knowledge and engaging with one another's learning.

In keeping with the 'Education Studies' aspect of the degree course, the personal element of the autoethnography focused on a recollection of an educational experience. The 'academic' content consisted of the sociological theories or ideas that could be applied and used to appraise the personal elements of our autoethnography. We collectively explored and suggested ways in which these experiences could be conveyed. Many different ideas of ways to accomplish this emerged, including poetry writing, narrative accounts and photographs. These could then be linked to ideas previously studied which emerged from the readings, and could be used as a basis for considering different forms of knowledge production. The tutor would join in the discussion rather than lead it. Although other modules during the degree had elements of student-led discussion, these were often used alongside tutor-led elements. This module therefore demonstrated a marked shift of control to students. Admittedly, at the time this was received with some confusion due to the contrast between teaching and learning practices with previous modules. Our sense of being unsettled by this module was increased by the tutor's view that we had the freedom to choose any critical incidents, as long as we could explain and demonstrate their relevance in the article by using theory. I felt it took time for us to realize that we were in fact participating in an approach to learning and research which enabled us to construct knowledge and develop our understanding independently. Given that so much learning on the degree had been directly transmitted, it is not surprising that this module initially caused some considerable anxieties.

As part of the drafting process of producing our autoethnographic articles, we engaged in a peer review process. This gave each of us the opportunity to provide anonymous feedback to two of our peers and then for each of us to make judgements about how we incorporated that feedback in the development of our final articles. This process meant that we participated in an authentic experience of a formal research review process in ways which simulated the journal article production process in the 'real' world. As a class, we decided on the criteria that would be used to evaluate each other's articles. We made decisions about the tone and style of the feedback in order to emphasize our aim to be constructively critical, developmental and respectful of each other's feelings. After completing our articles, we uploaded them to an online web journal, collectively decided on the format details for the articles to be presented in and had an input into the design of the finished journal. This exemplifies the significant level of control that the students in this module possessed over both the 'content' and the 'process' of learning. Reviewing drafts and guidelines for how academic work is presented is a task typically carried out by tutors. Yet, the way in which we carried this out democratically as a group provided us with a sense of being effective contributors to each other's learning. In all of these ways the module provided the space for collective learning, acknowledgement of the social and cultural aspects of individual's learning, and enabled a high degree of student engagement in contrast with other, more typical forms of HE learning which are private and individualized.

As the module progressed, students worked out for themselves, and in discussion with the tutor, how to deal with and manage this more 'fluid' style of teaching and learning. In the beginning of the module, the tutor did provide us with some reading materials as a starting point to gain adequate knowledge of autoethnography. During the peer review process, the tutor coordinated the discussion of peer review criteria and guidance in order to provide effective and constructive feedback but she did not lead the discussion. She contributed ideas about peer review criteria but as part of the class, rather than its 'leader' or 'teacher'. The tutor's role in the peer review process was to act as a facilitator to learning, providing the students with code names in order to keep the peer review process anonymous, and managing the online submission process. This description indicates the extent to which the teaching and learning was student-centred and designed to promote student engagement.

The module tutor's role as facilitator also encouraged us to make key decisions about our learning. In terms of assessment, the tutor provided guidance which emphasized the 'openness' and flexibility of the assignment content. For example, the requirements of passing the module revolved around submitting a piece of work that included a personal voice, relating this to theoretical concepts on autoethnography and knowledge and engaging in a peer review process with fellow students. As a personal voice and the evaluation of this through a theoretical lens are the foundation of the autoethnographic approach, it became clear that the assessment criteria were there to enable, not constrain, individual students' choice of what and how to write their autoethnographic article. Meeting the assessment criteria seemed to become integrated into the learning in that the criteria acted as a guide to produce writing that complied with, but also interpreted, 'autoethnography' in a broad way. Assessment on this module was not about 'jumping through hoops' but about expressing ourselves creatively and analytically, although it took a while for the class to realize this.

Participating in the module provided me with a new perspective on student engagement. The strong personal element of the autoethnographic approach provided students with enhanced levels of control. The loose assessment criteria and the personal element of the autoethnographic approach meant that we had an unlimited scope of possibility as to what experiences to explore, and how we wanted to explore them. This level of freedom, combined with the peer review process, provided a clear sense of ownership in facilitating our own, and each other's, production of knowledge. It gave me an opportunity to reflect on and analyze some essential aspects of my identity, as I now go on to explain.

My autoethnography focused on my experiences of being a self-supporting student throughout my post-compulsory education, enabling me to speak personally of the multiple impacts this had on my identity. Within this, I focused on the conflicts I experienced in being a student and an employee simultaneously. I explored my personal narrative through identity theory in order to combine personal and theoretical elements which fitted into 'analytical' and 'evocative' autoethnography. Below, I have included three extracts of the autoethnography that I produced for the module. These particular extracts have been chosen to demonstrate the way autoethnography helps combine the 'personal' and the theoretical, as previously discussed. The first extract is a narrative section called 'Education first' which describes my personal experiences. The second extract contains photographic images I took, which provide a visual representation of the conflict in identity described in my personal narrative account. These images were significant in enabling me to apply theoretical concepts to my experience, while also highlighting the role of images in postmodern knowledge production. My third extract is a theoretical analysis of the links I drew between my own experience and social identity theory. In my full journal article I expanded on the importance of images but I have not included this here, as I wanted to focus primarily on my autoethnographic writing.

First extract: education first

I always feared having to support myself solely. Despite being deemed an 'independent' student even before progressing to university, I was always dependent on others that I shared my home(s) with. Splitting costs and sharing company with the wide array of people that I have shared home settings with over the past nearly five years made me feel independent yet dependent at the same time.

Even whilst moving frequently and not having the most comfortable living conditions, I always ensured that my education came first. I would rifle through text books for hours, read course materials and make sure my work was always up to date. In retrospect, I feel that this was the start of my self-driven obsession with education. I felt unsettled if I ever neglected my work. I rarely missed any college lessons even though events in my personal life seemed to be constantly intervening.

I was determined never to let external factors outside my education influence my studies or my progress. It took a lot of personal determination and strength to do this, and I had to take a very self-disciplined approach. I kept thinking that, as long as I struggled on through and progressed as far as I could in my education, it would not be like this forever.

During my gap year before university, I worked long hours in a busy call centre and volunteered for an emotional support charity. During this time I lived with a partner until I was due to progress onto my final year of university. This gave me the chance to build up a stable home life, providing me with little interferences with my education. Although I worked hard in employment and continued to engage in volunteer work for my first two years of university, I didn't feel as though I had to battle with any 'outer education' dilemmas. However, prior to progressing to my final year of university, circumstances changed and I had to live alone. Unable to split costs, this led to me having to take up a more demanding job for a higher income so I could survive financially. My main fear was that this would interfere with my studies. Could I even continue university? Yet I dismissed this thought. My education meant everything to me and I couldn't imagine what I would be without it. How would I see myself? I couldn't conceive being just an 'employee' without my 'student' identity.

Whilst this first extract is a narrative account of the journey through my personal concerns and conflicts between 'student' and 'employee' identity, my second extract is a visual representation of this experience and I use a number of photographic visual images to convey the concept of 'multiple identity' theory visually (Burke and Stets, 2009; Stryker and Burke, 2000). I have also included a short written explanation for the images.

Second extract: personal identity, social identity and 'the visual'

Figure 7.1 conveys my two identities and I use objects to represent my participation in these roles. Books related to my studies are used to connote my role as a student and an object related to my role as an employee (a staff identification card) are both merged into the same image. The second image (Figure 7.2) is split into four sections. Three of these consist of objects that are typical to my student role (folders, files and highlighter pens). The image in the upper left is a suit jacket which I wear at work whilst carrying out my role as an employee. This particular area of the image contrasts with the bright colours in the other three sections. This was to show, through visual technique, that my 'student identity' is more prominent than my 'employee identity', by making it much more striking with colour.

Figure 7.1 Merged photographic images representing two sides of student identity

Figure 7.2 Objects and clothing related to student and employee identity

Third extract: viewing my educational experience through the lens of social identity theory

Stryker and Burke (2000: 290) explain multiple identities as follows: 'persons typically are embedded in multiple role relationships in multiple groups and they hold multiple identities'. Thus, multiple identities stem from an individual taking part in 'multiple roles'. In my case, I am involved in carrying out roles within education, providing me with a 'student' identity, but also in the workplace, providing me with an additional identity as an 'employee'. My identity as a student involves me attending seminars and lectures, communicating with other students and tutors and involvement in university related social events. By contrast, my identity as an employee involves communication with colleagues, clients and carrying out my tasks in the environment in which I work. Therefore I can identify myself as having 'multiple identities', which I have suggested symbolically in my chosen images.

Saussure's notion of 'semiotics' (Chandler, 2007; North, 1995; Sanders, 2004) is also useful in analyzing these images. Semiotics was traditionally focused on linguistics (Frawley, 2003; Kress, 2003; Lechte, 2008) and incorporates the idea of Structuralism which can be described as:

[. . .] an analytical method which has been employed by many semioticians and which is based on Saussure's linguistic model [. . .] They engage in a search for 'deep structures' underlying the 'surface features' of phenomena.

(Chandler, 2007)

With regard to my selected images, at first glance, Figure 7.1 shows books which are related to my chosen discipline: Education Studies and Sociology. In our culture, books have numerous implications. When looking beyond the 'surface features', as Chandler (2007) said we should, books may conjure up relationships to education, study and knowledge. I intentionally chose them as a visual representation of my participation in HE, and the role I play as a student. Yet, the image contains an object in the background which is significant to my job: a staff identification card. I associate this object with my role as an employee as I am required to have this object on my person whilst in the building. Just as the books are used to convey my student identity, the object which is used to identify me as a member of staff portrays my 'employee' identity.

I used a 'transparent' photo editing effect between these two sets of objects. This resulted in the books being more clearly seen than those objects that are significant to my employment. This was intentional, as from a personal perspective I prioritize my education more so than my job. According to Butler (1997: 95) 'work is not the essence of life anymore [. . .] it is, rather, a necessity enabling us to get resources for other activities'. Butler's suggestion is that employment is no longer a dominant aspect of our lives. In contemporary society, employment may solely be considered as a means of funding 'other activities', such as hobbies and leisure activities. Butler's proposition that employment acts solely as a means of accessing other activities is applicable to my own personal experience. Partaking in HE could be viewed as a hobby. After all, I, like other students, have decided to invest time, effort and money into a course that is of interest to me and that I would like to gain a qualification in. Subsequently, my employment is giving me access to this activity, by providing me with the funds to manage my day to day life, making my participation in my role as a student possible. Figure 7.2 can be said to offer a similar meaning. Objects that I associate with study dominate the image, whilst the suit jacket that I associate with employment is comparatively insignificant.

My inclusion of connotations of my employment in my visual images could in fact imply that I regard this as a significant part of my identity. If an individual has multiple identities, why have I chosen only education and work? Other images could have been used to portray alternative 'identities' or rather 'roles' that I hold. To answer this question I turned to identity theory literature which indicates that we present ourselves how we would like others to see us (Goffman, 1959). According to Lemert and Branaman (1997), Goffman (1959: 96) suggests that we do this by playing particular roles, and that 'it is in these roles that we know each other; it is in these roles that we know ourselves'. In taking Goffman's view into consideration, I am presenting myself as I wish to be perceived by others. This could explain why my images are substantially weighted by representations of my role as a student; I stated in my evocative account that I could not imagine myself being an employee without also identifying as a student. Yet this is not necessarily just an act. This mask develops who we are and 'our conception of our role becomes second nature and an integral part of our personality' (Goffman 1959: 30). The role as an employee and also student are forming my own personality and identity, becoming 'second nature' to me. Therefore, both of these roles construct the person that I am. The reason that I prefer to be identified as a student rather than employee may just be an 'integral part' of my personality.

Woodward (2004: 8) raises a noteworthy point which helps me reflect on my two identities: 'The concept of identity encompasses some notion of human agency; an idea that we can have some control in constructing our own identities.' This makes it clear that I have a preference for my student role over my engagement as an employee throughout this article. However, the fact that I have focused on my role as an employee makes it apparent that even though I highly favour another aspect of my identity, this still constructs part of the whole. Woodward (2004: 8) goes onto explain how our individual agency can be limited by other factors: 'constraints which may lie in the external world, where material and societal factors may limit the degree of agency which individuals may have'.

I have engaged in a role as an employee due to influences in the 'external world', such as the need for income to live. Drawing on Butler's (1997) perception of employment makes me realize that I partake in this role to help fund my education. Yet, I recognize that this conflicts with my role as a student and vice versa. Despite having a personal preference to portray my student identity as the most prominent amongst my 'multiple identities', this appraisal establishes that even though human agency allows us to form identities for ourselves, society places restrictions on us. As a result, this produces limitations in what identities we choose to construct for ourselves.

Looking back on my article

On reflection, I felt the student-centred aspects of the module were incredibly useful for a number of reasons. Firstly, the use of autoethnography provided a new lens in which to view research, as well as being able to experience a different approach to writing. Prior to this module, I had not written about my own experiences in an academic piece. Indeed, it initially felt unusual to comprehend the idea of combining personal and academic elements into one piece of writing. Although I found this challenging at the outset, I believe that taking part in this module helped open my mind to other forms of research that do not necessarily comply with traditional methods. Participating in autoethnography also raised my awareness of some important methodological issues about researcher positionality, values and beliefs, all of which are part of our identity. Secondly, the way the module was constructed was beneficial, particularly the peer review process. Even though this was completed by fellow students, it was anonymous and provided a glimpse of a formal research process. The web publishing aspect was also interesting, as it provided the opportunity to view the autoethnographies produced by peers, which typically does not occur. I felt these reasons collectively formed an enriching experience.

Student perceptions

As I noted earlier, initially students found the purpose and style of the module difficult to grasp. This was mainly due to its open-ended nature, the freedom to write about personal experiences and the assessment criteria. This amount of freedom was initially quite foreign to us and even quite frightening.

I believe this reaction illuminates the nature of the teaching and learning principles and practices deemed as the 'norm' in our experiences of HE up to this point. My peers voiced concerns that the assessment criteria were not as rigid as other modules, that autoethnography as an approach to research was 'odd' and 'unfamiliar' and they found it challenging at first to combine the personal with the academic. This was partly because we had not encountered this before, but it was also due to our familiarity with modules which are structured to provide us with materials which directly comply with assessment criteria. Personally, the uncertainty that was present at the beginning of the module was largely due to the stark contrast that this module displayed in relation to other modules during our degree course. It seemed to throw us off balance at the beginning of our final and most important year, which contributed to our anxieties about 'getting it right'. Yet I believe it succeeded in its aims as it progressed. This experience has given me an insight into some of the difficulties in incorporating new modes of student engagement in learning, teaching and assessment. Students' experiences and understandings of such innovative student-centred modules appear to be seen in relation to those previously studied, in which 'transmission' modes of learning are given a high priority. Perhaps what my experience has shown is that degree modules which do not follow familiar formats may offer significant opportunities to enhance student engagement, though students may initially experience them as challenging. A potential solution would be for modules at all levels of undergraduate degrees to incorporate many different forms of teaching, learning and assessment. That way, even more radical forms of student engagement practices can be attempted in the future.

Student engagement in the current HE context: a personal view

Students' familiarity with certain types of module structure and delivery may not be the only obstacle in engaging students in different forms of learning experiences. One key concern is that the new climate being introduced by recent policy changes may hinder lecturers in finding space to experiment with new approaches to student engagement.

The proposals outlined in the government White Paper 'Students at the Heart of the System' (BIS, 2011) aim to alter the HE learning landscape. The White Paper emphasizes 'value for money' (BIS, 2011: 5) for students, and promotes the importance of student choices in relation to Higher Education Institutions (HEIs) and courses. To accommodate student choice, the white paper introduced 'Key Information Sets' (KIS) which are available collectively online (Unistats, 2012). These present information on courses based on results of the National Student Survey (NSS) and the Destination of Leavers from Higher Education survey (DLHE). Cost, time spent in lectures, and how 'satisfied' students are with teaching and resources are some of the areas in which statistics are provided. Potential students are encouraged to compare and contrast courses with the website containing a 'shortlist' function, similar to that of a market comparison website, which allows comparisons of courses based on these statistics. The KIS data also emphasizes employability and it is likely that students will see a future degree as valuable only in relation to graduate destinations and potential future salaries. This may lead students to be dissatisfied with any modules which they perceive as not enabling them directly to attain the requirements to progress onto their desired career. The changes to HE I have briefly described accentuate HEIs as market-orientated service providers and students as consumers. As a result, lecturers may feel apprehensive about risk-taking in terms of module content and structures. This may lead them into producing modules and degrees which are less rich in terms of learning opportunities because they think modules which are not so clearly aligned with students' assessments and future careers may be badly received and consequently reflected in the NSS. The autoethnography module I have discussed indirectly highlighted some of these issues, as students felt initially anxious as a result of the high level of control provided to us over our learning and assessment, rather than this being transmitted to us by the tutor.

From my own point of view and reflecting on the module retrospectively, I believe investigating and critically using different forms of knowledge, as well as relating knowledge to personal experience, is beneficial both in self-development and employment terms. The ability to draw together the personal with the academic, making connections between real life scenarios, sociological theory and the critical evaluation of these helps develop critical thinking. This in turn promotes an engagement with a deeper understanding of the world around us. Degree modules that encompass these aspects are useful in multiple ways and develop skills and ways of knowing that are important not just for a student's future employment, but for their future in general.

Chapter 8

People can make or break student engagement

Emma Chadwick

Introduction

I recently completed a Physiotherapy degree at Manchester Metropolitan University and graduated in July 2012 with a 2.1 degree. On completion I was invited to write this chapter, which prompted me to reflect on the teaching and learning of the three years of my undergraduate studies. Overall my experience was positive; the staff were enthusiastic and they provided the help and guidance I needed. The taught sessions were useful and the work-based placements excellent in providing me with the experience I required in order to achieve my first job upon graduation. What stands out to me now as being pivotal in my learning was the one-to-one support and encouragement that I got from the clinical staff, which supported my studying during work-based learning, and the peer support I received from my close friends.

Perceptions of engagement between students who progress onto university varies greatly. Gazing around lecture theatres showed a distinct difference in the attitudes of students; those playing on phones and those who don't bother to turn up on a regular basis evidently had a reduced engagement in their studies. My previous learning experiences provided me with the knowledge that, in order to succeed, I was required to work hard and that it is crucial to have an interest in what you are learning. An example from my personal experience of this would be taking Chemistry as an AS-level. During this course, I found that I had a limited interest in Chemistry which reduced my engagement in the subject. This was particularly true when I found parts of the course extremely difficult to understand. This subject then took up a lot of my valuable time and I was putting in a lot of hard work to only receive average grades. I decided to drop the subject in order to focus on my other A-level courses, which I had a greater interest in and was receiving higher grades.

My past experience had taught me that I needed to persevere, as I was not expecting to find my degree a walk in the park. Throughout the whole of my education, I have been a very hardworking and conscientious pupil; during primary school I was lucky enough to be classed as gifted and talented. However, while progressing through my education I found it very demanding to meet the grades at the top of the class. Progressing through to college and university, I found it increasingly difficult to stay engaged in my education, especially when I received grades which were less than I would have expected for the time and effort that I had put into the course. I also knew that when starting my degree it would take me a while to understand the new examination process and style, as this had previously happened in transition from my GCSEs to A-levels. Despite initially receiving low grades, I was encouraged to stay engaged, as I knew what to expect. Without this previous experience I would have become completely disengaged with my education very quickly, and would have wanted to drop out of university at a very early stage.

There are many factors which have affected both my own and other students' engagement during university. Distractions such as social networking, part-time working and invites to go out and meet friends seem much more appealing than a 2000 word essay, which can always be done tomorrow or the day after. Going to university is a new stage in anybody's life, particularly as for many students it is the first time they have lived independently away from home, cooked meals, washed clothes and travelled to their place of education every day on their own accord, including waking up and getting yourself out of bed. For university students, the choice is simple and their own: you both engage and embrace the choice in education you have chosen or you don't. Luckily, I was able to ignore most of the distractions around me, allowing me to concentrate on my studies, particularly when I received low grades and was working very hard.

Peer support

The support I received from my friends over the three years was particularly influential to my development. Initially, I struggled. However, the friendships which I built in my second year supported me throughout the rest of my degree. On being accepted into university, I was extremely excited about the first time I was living away from home and looking forward to meeting lots of new people. The only accommodation available to me at university was very small, with only two bedrooms and one flatmate. During my first week at university, I got on extremely well with my new flatmate, going out together and introducing each other to new friends we had made on our courses. However, as time passed by our friendship became more and more distant until eventually we didn't speak. Although I was disappointed, I saw this as an opportunity for no distractions and to throw myself into my studies. I never understood how my flatmate felt, as she was the one who stopped all interaction between us, but I know she saw the opportunity very differently to me. She threw lots of parties, which really disappointed me as she showed no consideration for my studies. This period was quite difficult for me and left me feeling quite lonely. I missed home a lot, so as soon I could I returned home every weekend. Whilst staying at university, I spent a lot of the time working but the rest of the time I would spend doing things that I enjoyed to counteract the loneliness I felt. This included social networking, going out and staying in contact with friends who had also moved away to university. Although I feel that I was still working very hard at this point, this time was very distracting for me as I continually wanted to be in the company of other people and not sat in my room alone and doing coursework. My engagement in my studies had greatly reduced. I didn't feel interested in what I was learning and only looked forward to the weekends and going home.

I feel that this in turn led to some of the lower grades which I received in my first year whilst living away at university. Receiving the grades for marked assignments I had submitted would sometimes make me feel very disappointed, as they were less than I had expected for the time and effort I had put into each particular piece of work. On one particular assignment, after reading the examination question and spending time to try and work out the answer, I was still unsure about what the question was actually asking me to write. I spent prolonged periods of time both working independently and talking to my tutors at university, to make sure that I was answering the question. On handing in my assignment, I then felt reassured that the answer I had written included the correct information in order to receive a good mark. On receiving a low mark for my assignment, I was very frustrated and upset, particularly because the marker had disagreed with the answer which I had written and they felt that I had not answered the question, which was one of my fears.

Receiving this low mark affected the motivation I had to complete any other university work; I had become completely disengaged from my studies as I felt that I was no longer getting the grades that I hoped to achieve. I always wanted to be able to obtain a first class degree; receiving low marks was making my dreams seem much more distant. This time of disengagement from my studies was also made more difficult through knowing that other students were not completing the tasks set for teaching groups with no repercussions. This was particularly true of periods where I had large amounts of work to complete alongside assignments. This made me feel like I wanted to abandon the work I needed to complete. I felt like there were other priorities, such as spending more time completing and perfecting assignments, or doing activities I found pleasurable, to counteract the loneliness I was experiencing. In these situations I knew that I needed to complete the work, because if it came up in an examination and I didn't know it, I would only have myself to blame. Reflecting on the lower grades which I had received, I decided to meet with the marking tutor of my assignment to gain further feedback and avoid making the same mistake again. By doing this, it allowed me to understand the reasons why I had been given a low mark; this helped to rebuild my confidence, as I was assured I wouldn't make the same mistake twice. Having such a poor relationship with my flatmate, I feel, had impacted heavily on my engagement of my degree by having a negative effect on the grades which I received.

At this point in my Higher Education career, my aspirations were severely reduced and I was unsure whether or not I wanted to continue with the course. I even questioned whether or not I had the determination to complete the course. The support the tutors at university provided was invaluable in helping me to find the motivation and belief in myself, so that I could complete the course. The tutors spent time looking through my assignments, explaining the feedback I had been given and helping to guide me in the right direction when writing my next assignment. Whilst planning future assignments, I made sure that I spent as much time as I possibly could on each essay, resulting in improved grades and greater engagement in my studies. After a short period of feeling poorly motivated, I knew that I needed to take a positive from this experience and not let it ruin all the hard work and commitment I had put into my degree.

During my second year at university I decided to live at home, following my unhappiness of living away at university with my flatmate in my first year. Commuting to university every day made working days at university much longer and increasingly tiring; however, by being at home I was surrounded by the love and support of my family. Typically, after a long and tiring day at university, I would not want to begin studying on returning home in the evening. However, commuting to university did have its positives, as the peer support from the new group of friends I made had a huge impact on my future engagement at university. Within my academic year group there tended to be quite a divide between students, particularly between those who commuted and those who lived away at university. Now living at home and being classed as a 'commuter', I had gained a whole new group of friends. This group of friends became a highly important aspect of me completing my second and final years at university. We all worked extremely well together, providing each other with the help and support that we required in order to stay engaged in our studies, particularly when we were finding times tough.

One of the girls in my friendship group lived locally to me, and we therefore both used this to our advantage by meeting up on our non-university days. We encouraged and motivated each other to study on the days that we weren't required to go into university. Working within a group of friends allowed us to assist each other with our studies. For example, if one member of our friendship group was struggling and required help, it was likely that another member of the group knew the answer and they would be able to explain it. Working together helped us as we were able to split and share the workload, therefore allowing us to produce quality work by having a greater length of time available to spend completing each piece.

Although working with my new friendship group increased my engagement in my degree, I also sometimes found it difficult to work alongside my peers. As we all worked so closely together on helping to complete assignments, in particular I found it very difficult when one member of the group received a lower mark. If I was the one to receive the lower grade, I felt slightly disheartened, as we all worked equally as hard to gain the best possible marks in our work. When one of the members of the group received the low mark, I would feel responsible, as we would read each other's work and provide them with any feedback we thought was necessary. Working as part of this friendship group impacted on my studies in the complete opposite way to the lone working which I endured during my first year at university, overall encouraging me to engage positively and allowed me to achieve the final grade I graduated with.

Work-based learning

Another aspect in particular which I feel was pertinent in encouraging engagement in my chosen degree was my participation in the work-based learning, which was included in my course during my second and third year at university. The clinical staff that I worked with inspired and encouraged me, but at the same time they challenged me. When I first began each placement, I developed a learning plan with the team which guided my learning. The inclusion of practical, work-based learning was one of the main reasons that I chose to complete this particular university course. Being a practical learner, the hands-on aspect worked very well for me and I felt much more confident within this area of my degree, compared to academic writing. During my second year at university, we completed the start of our work-based learning, which I was extremely nervous about. This was the first time that I had ever worked as a professional and with members of the public. Even though we had received all the theory at university and been provided with the appropriate training, moving into the working world still appeared very daunting. I was particularly aware that the skills and information that I had learnt from university was only the tip of the iceberg, in terms of the range and variety of problems that I could be faced with during my work-based learning. I looked forward to starting my work-based learning in my second year at university, as I knew that this type of learning and experience would be of great value in increasing my knowledge and skills to prepare me for my chosen career.

On my first work-based learning placement I was unsure about what to expect from the team which I was based within, and equally what the team would expect from me. I felt anxious initially that I would not meet their expectations and that in turn this would affect the grades which I would go on to receive. On my arrival, the team were very welcoming and my clinical leader assured me that I had nothing to worry about. At the end of each period I was marked and provided with feedback on a whole range of areas regarding the way in which I had worked. Initially, I received an extremely high grade which really boosted my confidence and encouraged me to continue to work hard and engage in my studies. This removed any concerns that I had in my first year during university, when I was receiving grades which were lower than expected, focusing my attention on my course once again. Clinical supervisors who guided me during this period passed on their knowledge and previous experience, which I feel was invaluable to me doing so well and gaining such high marks in my placement.

As part of the course, it was also expected that half way through each period the clinical staff would provide me with feedback. On one occasion, I received marks and feedback from the clinical staff, which I did not feel was appropriate and had not reflected the hard work I was putting in. This was critical to my final grades and I initially felt very disappointed and became disengaged briefly with my studies, as I wasn't sure how much harder I could work. I decided that it would be sensible to talk to the clinical staff to discuss this. They worked with me to set goals, so that I would be able to achieve the highest marks possible at the end of my work-based learning period. This was vital to my continued engagement, as this was the area of my university course which I felt confident in. The information and confidence in my chosen career which the work-based learning provided I feel are skills that you would never be able to learn from a textbook or lecture whilst in university. The positive influence on my studies, future engagement and the experience I gained was invaluable to prepare me for the world of work on graduation.

During my time at university, I also held a part-time job which I feel impacted on my engagement in the opposite way to work-based learning. However, it also provided me with skills that I could transfer into my chosen career. It was necessary for me to hold a part-time job alongside my studies, in order to provide myself with as much extra money as possible. The job supported my studies by allowing me to provide myself with any extra learning materials I required, such as books and equipment. My employer was very understanding and whilst completing my placements they knew that I was only able to carry out work at weekend as I was on placement during the week. However, to wake up on a Saturday morning knowing you have a full day of work does not encourage you to get out of bed. Working part-time became increasingly difficult when I had assignments to complete for a specific deadline. The only free time I had to complete the essays was at weekends when I needed to work. I felt that this sometimes reduced the engagement I had in my education, as finding time to complete work did become increasingly difficult the further I progressed through my course.

Although I only saw my part-time job as a necessity and a distraction, working with the public as a waitress allowed me to develop my communication skills. I feel these skills were transferable to the professional career that I had chosen. For example, in my part-time job I was often required to deal with customers who complained and in some circumstances were quite angry and short-tempered. In these situations it was essential for me to remain professional; this skill is transferable to treating patients, particularly when they are presenting a great deal of pain. Another skill that I was able to transfer from my part-time job as a waitress to my job as a physiotherapist was my organizational skills. Being a waitress in a very busy restaurant, I needed to be organized in order to provide the best service to each paying customer. This skill was also transferable to being a physiotherapist, particularly in an outpatient setting, where it is possible that you may be expected to see a new patient every 20 minutes. Although at the time my part-time job felt like a chore and reduced the amount of time I was able to spend studying, it helped me to broaden and improve the skills I already had and helped me develop a professional attitude.

Conclusion

Passing through state education before deciding to take up the opportunity to go to university, I had many friends and knew fellow pupils who presented a huge difference in attitude towards engagement in education compared to me. In primary school, there are pupils in your classroom that don't want to learn and will find many ways to distract both themselves and others. Guidance from both teachers and lecturers can sometimes be passed on to help those who find it difficult to engage. However, many students ignore the help they provide. Whilst at primary and secondary school, there were rewards and incentives to encourage pupils to be engaged in their learning, for example reward trips, certificates and prizes. At university these incentives do not exist and you either choose to work diligently on your own, or you can choose to fail. My past experiences in education prepared me for the working world and I feel that in the future I will be ready to continue my education to further my career. As I progressed through education and the harder my studies became, the more I felt I had to push myself in order to engage. Passing through Higher Education, I feel that, as an individual, my attitude towards my own learning and engagement changed dramatically. The beliefs and perceptions that I had about the workload/social life balance whilst at university very quickly changed, particularly enrolling onto a course with such a high demand in workload.

My motivations for achieving my personal goals have always been based around the grades that I received for tests and assignments. I have always used this as a personal indicator to identify how well I am doing in a particular course. Receiving good grades has always boosted my confidence and encouraged me to stay focused on my education. Reflecting on my experiences of Higher Education, I feel that I changed and developed dramatically from a student into a mature adult. Without those experiences at university I would not have become the professional I am today. Being alone in my first year at university required me to push myself in order to succeed and continue with my studies. My assumptions of the attitudes of other students at university completely changed, after being extremely let down by my flatmate in my first year. However, my faith was restored when I met my wonderful group of friends. As discussed above, there are many different factors which can influence student engagement both positively and negatively. However, being motivated and hardworking I was able to stay focused and achieve the right goals for me.

Chapter 9

Students as researchers

Personal reflections by students of their engagement in a research project

Viola Borsos, Christopher Demirjian, Ji Kim, Nga Wun Mok, Oliver Worsley, Christine Hardy and Sean Prince

Introduction

In December 2011, funding was gained from the Higher Education Academy to employ five students for fifteen months to become full members of a research team investigating the development of student intercultural competencies in the international classroom. The project commenced in January 2012 with the recruitment of five students: four international and one home. The students were all first years from the BA (Hons) Fashion Design course at Nottingham Trent University and came from the UK, Cyprus, China, South Korea and Hungary. Two other members of the team were academics: one working on the course, the other working for the School of Art and Design.

The project was set up to examine student perspectives of Internationalization at Home through examination of the curriculum itself and relationships between staff/students and students/students, to enable students to generate their own ideas for creating an inclusive learning environment through the development of curricular and extra-curricular activities, in order to engage all students with the internationalization agenda.

Students were directly engaged as active participants in the following ways:

- All student researchers received bursaries to work on the project and were part of a team with experience of undertaking student engagement research projects and experience of internationalization, including teaching in our international partner institutions in Hong Kong.
- Students were actively engaged in the whole research process and were required to develop appropriate research strategies and use a range of research methods to acquire the necessary data. They were supervised by the academics within the team and attended training workshops and regular team meetings.
- All students have been involved in the collection and analysis of data and information, which has included leading focus groups, interviewing academics working within the department and undertaking literature reviews.

- Students were given the opportunity to co-author publications and to be part of conference presentations as co-presenters. To date, one student has presented at the Researching, Advancing and Inspiring Student Engagement (RAISE) conference in 2012 and been a co-author on a journal paper, while all have been co-authors of a book chapter.

The project is on-going and although the period of paid engagement has finished, all students are continuing with the project with the expectation that they will be involved in writing and designing a range of materials for fellow students and recommendations for curricular design based on the results of the research. They are also very keen to evaluate any materials produced, as well as the project itself. In this chapter, the students reflect on their experiences on being involved in the project, with a working title of 'the journey of exploration', specifically:

- Who they are and why they are studying in the UK and why they chose to be involved in this project.
- Reflections on the formation of the group: pre-conceived ideas about what they thought it would be about, the development activities, getting to know each other, research and questions for focus groups. Their involvement and how they felt about it.
- Their experiences of the actual project.
- Their changing behaviours/perceptions.
- What they have learnt, how they now feel about internationalization and how they have changed (if at all) their next moves – what they are going to do in the future.

What follows are the students' reflections in their own words. The grammar has been corrected in some instances, but not the content.

Viola Borsos

Many an object is not seen, though if falls within our range of visual ray, because it doesn't come within the range of our intellectual ray, i.e. we are not looking for it. So, in the largest sense, we find only the world we look for.

(Thoreau, 1857)

What determines our 'intellectual ray'? Can we change it? How can we become interested in things we don't yet see? Do we really need to 'expand' our intellectual ray? But most importantly why? Is it really worth it?

My answer is yes. It is possible and it is worth it. My own curiosity and desire to try to constantly expand my own 'intellectual ray' has driven me to travel and work in different countries, as well as to return to education as a mature student: to study Fashion Design in the UK. It is my interest in foreign languages and cultures that motivated me to work in education, assessment and be a volunteer in a Bosnian refugee camp and a brain injury rehabilitation centre. I speak seven languages at levels ranging from A2 to C2. I have previously worked with international students and, being one myself, I have had first-hand experience of the joys and sorrows of being both. It was the challenges that kept me interested in how to function in an intercultural environment: how to be sensitive yet inquisitive, how to learn, but also how to share the knowledge and experience. I am a believer in learning opportunities 'off the beaten track'; I appreciate the chance to learn from people I work with whenever possible. I also think that educational establishments should encourage it. We need to have our 'intellectual ray' fine-tuned.

It is my fascination with different cultures, languages and learning styles that fuelled my motivation to be part of something so exciting: the chance to research how the importance of internationalization, and that of intercultural competencies, is perceived by students and staff at Nottingham Trent; whether it needs to be part of the curriculum and if so, how and why; whether it is considered to be mutually beneficial for both home and international students. Is it a skill that is equally important in the global creative industry, where goods are designed, manufactured and distributed across the globe? Does the curriculum reflect the need for students to be interculturally competent? Is their journey of becoming successful at working in culturally diverse environments facilitated enough?

These are some of the questions we tried to answer and I was very happy to become part of the team. The initial work was enjoyable and beneficial: the team building activities, learning about research methods, brainstorming and hypothesizing about possible scenarios and outcomes, drafting the focus group questionnaires. It was interesting to learn about each other not only in terms of personal journeys, but the different views on the topic drawing on previous and current experience. It was a very promising start.

As anticipated, getting volunteers for the focus group was very difficult for a number of reasons, such as clashing timetables or a lack of interest at times, and so a lot of help was needed from staff. However, it worked out and it proved to be a very interesting experience for a number of reasons: to learn more about the views of students, their perceptions and their suggestions. I was at times surprised by their sometimes contradictory views in terms of varying levels of interest and engagement regarding collaborations both with home and international students. While both parties seemed to see the benefits and value of internationalizing the curriculum in theory, they saw no or very little value in working with international students and vice versa. Interestingly enough, the chance to work in a culturally diverse group isn't always perceived as a learning opportunity to develop intercultural competencies. There is seemingly a lot of mutual respect but limited cooperation/collaboration when the opportunity arises. Students also emphasized the importance of international collaborations: visiting lecturers, further exploration of existing partnerships with universities and awareness raising workshops to improve intercultural competencies, for example different learning styles, different cultures, study trips and more exchanges. However, it was interesting to hear that whilst it was suggested to have more opportunities to welcome exchange students and take part in exchanges, a stereotypical view of 'abroad' and 'international' exchange students emerged, i.e. abroad being perceived as the USA and Australia. The rest of the world seems to be ignored due to a lack of language proficiency. I was surprised that the language barrier had been brought up as the main hindrance in the way of intercultural cooperation with fellow students, be it home or international. It would be interesting to see what the situation is if the language barrier is not an issue.

My perception and beliefs regarding internationalization and the importance of intercultural competencies hasn't changed during the research, but I think I feel stronger about the need to do more in terms of internationalizing the curriculum to develop intercultural competencies whilst at university. They are just as important as business skills or pattern cutting. The conversation needs to start possibly earlier than university, but definitely at university at the latest. The awareness needs to be raised. If the intellectual ray is fine-tuned, the rest comes naturally: the rich source of inspiration and knowledge that other cultures represent, the worlds that languages offer the access to are just the tip of the iceberg.

The limits of my language means the limits of my world.

(Wittgenstein, 2007)

Christopher Demirjian

I believe the universities in the UK are more recognized by the industry and in general across the globe. Personally, people back home have the idea that when a student stays to study in Cyprus then they tend to become teachers or work in the government, while students who choose to study abroad are meant to achieve greater things.

I chose to study Fashion Design because I love fashion and I am interested to learn the method of designing and making fashion. Moreover, I believe that if you create a good portfolio during your studies then you may have a lot of opportunities to find a job and succeed in the industry. This is one of the reasons why I chose to study in the UK.

Internationalization at home was perceived by me as a way of sharing my thoughts and experiences as an international student. Coming for the very first time to the UK all alone was very frightening. Being now a second year student, I could really feel and sense every international student's fear, whether it is being homesick etc. Moreover, I considered myself as an international even back home at school, since my parents are not Cypriots.

Therefore, I thought that this project would be a very interesting way in trying to improve any aspect of internationalization that could exist in the university, specifically in the course of Fashion Design, whether that concerns the curriculum or the students. It is important for all of the students, international or home, to learn from each other. Giving the opportunity for a home student to learn from the culture, way of living or language, etc. of an international student or vice versa, is very important as the fashion industry is based on internationalization itself; being a fashion designer means that you would have to work within a team made up of many nationalities.

In the initial phase of the project, I can say that I was very excited in meeting and getting to know students from different countries. I was even more excited to meet the tutors that we would work with and hear their opinions on what internationalization at home could be.

When it came to the moment of interviewing students in focus groups, I have to admit that I felt a bit panicked. I thought that I could handle the situation and feel more familiarized in interviewing international students and believed that I would struggle in trying to interview the home focus group, whether that would be because of the language barrier or due to being the only international student in the room. I even felt safer when I interviewed the groups with the help of a fellow colleague.

However, I realized during the interviews that my fears of handling the groups were not very important due to the fact that I had to deal with other significant issues. I realized that it was very difficult trying to get them to interact with each other or even trying to get them to speak. I found out that home students were eager to express and share their thoughts and opinions, while the international group needed a lot of encouragement to speak. In both cases, I have learned that each group, home, international or even mixed, require an appropriate approach. Moreover, we received many useful tips and suggestions of how the course could focus more on internationalization in order to gain more competencies.

I felt that our university has not neglected the fact that the Fashion Design should be taught at an international basis and many modifications are made to make it even better. Of course, there is always some room for improvement. In my opinion, I believe that the curriculum of Fashion Design can be improved by introducing international lecturers, or organizing more trips to fashion capitals. To conclude, I have changed my method of thinking. Before applying for this project I used to think of how I could gain benefits of knowledge from home students, in order to gain more competencies. I thought that I came to the UK to learn only from their culture, heritage and way of living. Nonetheless, now I give equal importance in trying to learn from the international students as well. My next moves are to try to incorporate as much as I have learned into my designs and to try to gain as many competencies as possible, as they play a major role in our future careers.

Ji Kim

To make a decision to study in a foreign country was big challenge for me. However, there was nothing to be lost as I wanted to learn Fashion in an environment in which free thought and free expression is evident. Korea, where I was born and lived for 19 years, has quite a different curriculum from the British one. I learnt to be polite to tutors and elders since my early years as it is part of the Korean culture, so I always felt it was difficult to ask for something from the tutors. This traditional thinking made me conform rather than recognizing diversity. After graduating from high school, I wanted to rid myself of the Korean curriculum and my ideas which seemed to be a barrier to having ideas. Eventually, I chose to study in UK. England is the best place to learn what I wanted to study, because I thought that English will be important in the fashion world or an undefined future. Additionally, I wanted to learn lots of things which were not limited to fashion. So I came to the UK with great expectations, though it was hard to adapt from one culture to another. The first barrier was the language. When I arrived in the UK, I never understood what the British said. Even though there were English classes in each year in Korea, we just learned grammar or reading skills, not speaking. Naturally, my speaking and listening ability is getting better over time but the English language was always an obstacle to doing something in the UK. I thought that my self-confidence was disappearing; I felt fearful to speak with other people as well. Moreover, I knew of no one to discuss my difficulty with; I struggled to solve it by myself.

Meanwhile, one of my tutors told me about the internationalization research project. I thought it would be a good opportunity to talk about my difficulties as an international student in the UK. There are many international students in the University, but there is no place where international students can speak about their distresses directly. I thought if I participated in this project, I could help with other international students' difficulties. Therefore, I decided to get involved with this project. When we met for the first time, all of the members were of a different nationality. Five members of the group and the two tutors didn't know each other well, even though we are from the same year and course. However, we had an open mind to each other; we were trying to understand our different cultures and languages through conversation and activities, which explored our different backgrounds. In the first meeting, we started by introducing ourselves such as 'who I am and what background I have'. It was an interesting beginning, which does not usually happen in the University because we usually have no time to get to know each other in class. Although I felt there was a language barrier, it was not difficult to understand each other. After that, we discussed the direction of the research group and organized what we could do about internationalization.

Our main method of research was the interview. I had not tried interviewing before, even in Korean, so on the one hand I was really nervous that I would be interviewing someone in English but on the other, I was excited to have the chance to listen and think about internationalization with other international and home students. My first focus group was with first year international students. I had not heard about their thinking or difficulties as international students in a UK university, so it was interesting to listen to what they were thinking. Their struggles were quite similar to what I felt; it was mainly the English and culture barriers produced with people from different backgrounds. I was worried when I interviewed the home students; I was afraid that we would not be able to understand each other's languages. The interview was such an informal atmosphere, however, that we interviewed without great difficulty. To be honest, the interview with home students changed my thinking about them. I had such a prejudice towards home students but I have changed what I thought through the interviews and am more able to approach my British classmates with improved ways of thinking.

I have learnt many things about groups and personally through the research project. I seem to have changed the way I treat international students and home students. After listening to their opinions about internationalization, I had the opportunity to compare them with my opinions and understand all students with a different perspective.

I really enjoyed this project; it was interesting to understand the different ways of thinking between home students and international students in the same situation. When this project ends, I will never forget what I felt from the research project. It will help me to communicate with people from different cultures with good effect.

Nga Wun Mok

My name is Nga Wun Mok, or Kitty. I came from Macau, China, and have been studying in the UK for four years. My mother sent me to an English school when I was eight since she thinks that English is a worldwide international language that people use in many places. When I was twelve, she gave me an opportunity to go on study trips to foreign countries such as Australia, the UK, France, the Netherlands and Germany. She wants me to be open-minded and independent. These study trips were my first experience of going outside my country by myself. Although it was a tough experience for a twelve-year-old girl, I enjoyed the trips and loved to study in foreign countries, as well as learning about their culture. I learned to be brave and independent. That was a really memorable experience for me. Because of that experience, I started to think about studying in a foreign country for my university degree. I chose to study in the UK because I had a wonderful trip to the UK previously and it is an artistic country with lots of inspiration.

When I came to study in the UK, everyone told me that I have a good English level, but I do not consider myself as good as what they describe, as sometimes I do not understand what the British are talking about. Maybe it is because of their accent, or sometimes they speak too fast and use difficult vocabularies. Although I studied English for a long time, I still find it difficult to talk to British students. I think it is not the language barrier that is the major problem but my personality and cultural background. I am not a person who is used to socializing, and I am not confident enough to speak to people who I am not familiar with. In my country, students should always be polite to teachers and do what they are told. They do not have choices, which is completely different to the UK education system. Therefore, when I first came to study in UK, I always relied on the tutors to tell me what to do instead of thinking for myself. The same situation happened when I was working with British students in a group. They always had lots of ideas and opinions, while I usually sat there and listened to them. Even though I had quite a good English language background, I had so many problems. This led me to think about the other international students who do not even read and speak English fluently. I would like to overcome all these kinds of difficulties, as well as find a way to help other international students that are experiencing the same problem. Hence, I chose to get involved in the research project concerning intercultural and international competencies.

When we had our first meeting for our research project, I actually felt very nervous because I was not familiar with other team members. Moreover, working in a team with tutors sounded serious. However, after we talked to each other through the introduction and team building exercises, I felt more comfortable. It felt good to have someone in the team start talking and get everyone involved, which helped break down the nervousness. It was interesting to fill in the self-perception questionnaire and understand what kind of person I am, as well as to find out what role I was playing within the team. When we were developing the questions for the focus group, we all suggested our own ideas and thought of what difficulties students might encounter, as well as their experience of internationalization within the course. I really enjoyed that session because I liked to know other team members' point of view. At the end, we came up with many interesting points and ideas.

After we developed the questions for the focus groups, we started to approach students and organized interviews. It was arranged for me to do interviews with groups of international students. I did not really encounter difficulties in finding students for the interviews. It was easy to talk to them, as we were all international students. Although we all came here as international students, sometimes what we have experienced and the difficulties we had come across were quite different. We had different ideas and points of view for some of the questions. Nevertheless, it was good to know others' opinions.

Throughout the research project, I have been trained to be more confident in speaking to people. At the same time, I have now begun to develop my own opinions and thinking towards different objects and I think that is really important. I used to think internationally towards my work but sometimes neglected my own cultural background, as I thought that I should use the opportunity of studying abroad to learn from other cultures. However, after the focus group interviews, I think that I should think internationally but also nationally, from my own cultural background, since there is also something in my culture that I should appreciate.

Getting involved in this research project has been a great experience. I have learnt a lot from other team members, as well as other students who participated in the focus groups. It has been really interesting to see how differently home students and international students think and the way they work. However, internationalization is still a large subject that needs further study and understanding. This project is not just a study that helps to develop intercultural competencies within the course; it helps us to perceive people's minds and increases communication that leads us to a better world to live in. The knowledge that I gained throughout the project is really useful and influential. I really enjoyed it and it is interesting to know how people think and their opinions about a subject; I would like to study more about this. I believe what I gained from the research project will help my studies and life experience in the future.

Oliver Worsley

My name is Oliver Worsley and I am one of five student researchers who represent the diversity of students studying on the fashion, textiles and knitwear undergraduate courses at Nottingham Trent University. Within this research group I am the only home student and also the only student to speak one language. Having admitted that, I will add that internationalization has always been an interest and is a strong focus of my practice as a design student and young professional. My first experience in international student engagement came from a role as a teaching assistant in the 2010 European Capital of Culture, Essen in Germany. Five different countries came together in Essen to celebrate cultural diversity and during this period I was fortunate enough to spend a length of time teaching in an international classroom. My interest in student engagement, and in turn internationalization of the curriculum/industry, was as a result of this project. Since that experience, I have understood the value of international competencies and continue to make efforts to maintain it, within this research project and externally. As part of assessment in level one, we had to present a concept we devised as a multicultural group to Oxfam and our year group. We concluded that our presentation should be spoken in one language, due to industry time constraints but presented on the PowerPoint slides with two: English and Mandarin Chinese. As all the group members had contributed equally to the work, it was logical that both languages were represented. It also further improved the strength of our presentation communication due to it being more culturally inclusive and visually diverse. My involvement in this research project followed organically from tutor recognition of this presentation.

I have found this project to be such a steep learning curve that it has felt like a microcosm of the continual learning environment experienced on my course at university. The first meeting of our research team filled me with a great deal of anxiety. It soon became clear to me that the challenges I faced would not only be socially within the group dynamics, but also with tackling advanced academic literature, learning and exploring appropriate research methods, as well as being able to competently record said research. After an initial discussion about project aims, it was inspiring to see that everyone involved was determined to make this project about action and improvement, challenging my fear that we might not be striving to affect change.

In hindsight, my fear was completely unfounded, having not considered that the other student researchers would want to change elements to their international student experience that could be improved. As this project began to develop, I felt compelled to inform my course-mates of inaccurate conclusions about international students, even going as far as to eliminate the use of sweeping terms such as 'international students', used to describe any student studying away from their home country. Within our research group we concluded that in order to move our course forward we would have to 're-label' the course as international to eliminate any pre-conceived ideas of ownership of the course.

The focus groups proved to be insightful and, at times, alarming. They have provided a catalyst in emotionally affecting our desire to improve the quality of international study at Nottingham Trent. Lengthy discussion was had at the time over which of us should carry out the focus groups. As we did not want to segregate groups, we were uncomfortable with assigning only researchers that had languages in common with students. However, for the purposes of quality research data, we concluded that an international group of students would be more comfortable talking to an international student about concerns, prejudices or issues than a student from the UK, such as myself. More pivotally, as a research team we are ambassadors for multicultural working and social relationships.

My perception of student engagement changed when I recently spent ten days in a Hong Kong Chinese classroom, equivalent to my level of study in the UK. For the students I met in Hong Kong, in contrast with the rotary style of education in China, it was their first time learning the practice of group tutorials. Group tutorials on a creative course require engagement from all of the students participating, in order to provide constructive criticism and review of their peers' work. More often than not, a tutor will be present to assist and provide structure to the process. When successful, group tutorials are a really dynamic way to generate an inclusive learning environment and in turn strengthen the students' work. In Hong Kong, as I joined the beginning of the course, the tutor took the opportunity to explain the value of group tutorials to the students and explain the potential value to everyone. To my surprise, the students grasped the concept of group tutorials quickly and went on to use them effectively. It was then that I realized that, for me, student engagement has to be carefully managed from the inception of the student to the learning environment. We go through education working in groups and it is gradually assumed that the skills required already exist. At some point in our education we become young professionals, which we are reminded of, so why does no one reiterate how to be professional? How to work in teams effectively? What real engagement with the course is? When acting as an ambassador, explaining our research to my peers, once we had illustrated the value and benefits, their stance and approach to the course, their own learning and their peers, regardless of culture and yet to be extensively validated, changed dramatically.

So part of our proposal for moving forwards with engagement of students from diverse cultural backgrounds is to create change from the beginning. When course-opening talks are held about credits, assessment, learning objectives and content, we hope to introduce the value of engagement to the new students. Firstly, that our course is an international one and that every student is important, in order to develop a sense of self-worth and value. Secondly, to explore how to get the most out of a course and finally what it is to be young, professional and engaged. If we don't see the value of completely engaging, I don't think we will ever be fully engaged.

Conclusion

All five students were keen to become involved in the project for similar reasons: their previous experiences of working in diverse communities and their desire to improve their own experiences and the experiences of other students. Language was perceived to be a barrier at the beginning of the project, but this was soon overcome. This was because of briefings where all individuals involved came to the project with a mutual respect and shared their cultural experiences, drawing on them for the design of the research and focus group questions. There was a lot of discussion around who was to lead the focus groups and this was successfully negotiated. The focus groups were all conducted very successfully, providing a lot of valuable insights into the interaction of students from diverse backgrounds, which can be used in the next stages of the project: designing materials and influencing the curriculum development to take account of internationalization and the development of intercultural competencies. Recently, the students have been interviewing academic staff and this has also been successful, demonstrating how confident these students have become by being involved in the project.

Chapter 10

Cross-cultural experiences

Exploring engagement as an international postgraduate

Shanna Saubert

There are two questions that inevitably come to mind for most people on first meeting an international student. The first question focuses on *identity*, namely 'who are you?' Answers are typically demographic in nature including name, nationality, age, etc. This then leads to the second, and perhaps more interesting, question of 'what are you doing here?' The emphasis changes depending on the person speaking but the essence of the question can be derived into the realms of student *motivation* and *engagement*. As an international postgraduate student currently pursuing a PhD in the UK myself, this chapter provides both an overview of some of the issues international students face as well as providing reflections on the importance of student engagement based on personal experiences. I have taken this approach as my current research is focused on the relationships between different types of engagement and experiences of international students in the UK. This chapter is therefore intended to consider the position of an individual student within a more generalized, wider perspective.

Previous research shows there are many diverse reasons students choose to study abroad, as well as multiple benefits for doing so. When students participate in international education experiences, they are given personal insight into how interconnected the world truly is as well as other benefits on a more individual and/or community level. Reasons for going abroad may include wanting to improve foreign language skills (Allen and Herron, 2003; Cohen et al., 2005; Engle and Engle, 2004), gain first-hand experience of living and studying in another culture (Di Pietro and Page, 2008; Freestone and Geldens, 2008; Van Hoof, 2005), and even potentially improve future career opportunities (Hamza, 2010; McLeod and Wainwright, 2009). Students often become more self-aware as well as develop intercultural skills during their time abroad while they enjoy what many believe to be once-in-a-lifetime experiences (Lewin, 2009).

In my case, there were many reasons for wanting to study in the UK for a PhD. The first hurdle to jump was actually deciding whether I even wanted to go for a PhD upon finishing a two-year research intensive Master's programme in the USA. I had been quite interested in my research topic for a couple of years already and saw discernible gaps in available research that I could attempt to fill. Once I had decided I did indeed want to pursue a doctorate, I then had to decide on where to apply. I had studied abroad before as an undergraduate, spending an entire year in Salzburg, Austria, before returning to the USA to finish my degree. I had enjoyed my time abroad and found I quite liked the ethos for learning in European Higher Education systems, which is based significantly upon student autonomy. I have always appreciated independent and self-directed learning much more than 'regurgitative' or rote learning based on memorizing facts and reciting them for exams. I ultimately chose to apply to universities in the UK because I knew of their reputations from the recommendations of friends and colleagues and liked the locations. While the university system appealed to me, I also made decisions based on the environment surrounding the university. Multiple questions went through my head, including 'what is the city like?' 'Where will I live?' And, inevitably, 'what can I do while I am there?'

Kuh and colleagues (2008a: 542) define engagement as 'both the time and energy students invest in educationally purposeful activities and the effort institutions devote to using effective educational practices.' This definition clearly follows the Higher Education Academy's proposed conceptual framework of student engagement in Higher Education. At the individual level, students become personally invested in their own individual and collective processes for learning and development. Some are even involved in assisting with curriculum design and providing additional feedback for improvements. At departmental and institutional levels, students may become involved as student representatives on institutional committees and through the Students' Union and may become part of disciplinary and interdisciplinary networks. Student representation, however, is not the only way students may feel engaged as they learn and develop as individuals within the university community.

I have been one of the so-called 'hyper-engaged' students since before I even got into Higher Education. It is honestly second nature for some students, myself included, as not being 'busy' or involved would be an anathema. The stereotypes of lazy students not waking up until noon or postgraduate students never leaving their seat in front of a computer are just that: stereotypes. There is not a single mould in which all students may be placed, whether domestic or international, undergraduate or postgraduate. Over the course of my academic career, I have been a student in three different universities as well as studied abroad at a fourth as part of my undergraduate degree. I have held various student representative roles, lived in student halls, worked part-time jobs, been on international student welcome teams, joined multiple national and international organizations, attended and organized various conferences, organized different student trips and events, and volunteered in various capacities. I have been a runner since I was a teenager and have joined different community running clubs over the years to break the monotony of training for marathons. I have also learned how much I appreciate both old and new activities like snowboarding, Irish dancing, and orienteering with friends I have met both in class and in different university clubs and societies.

I will admit that it all seems quite daunting when written down. However, having a schedule and learning time management is a necessary skill in life. Being involved in such a wide range of activities, I have also learned and developed other useful and transferable skills. For instance, I initially gained experience about budgeting and event management by planning various events for different clubs and societies. Developing coping skills to deal with the process of adjusting to new environments is an integral part of going away to university. 'Soft' skills such as those regarding effective communication and collaboration have also developed over the years as I have been a part of various teams, both academic and work-related. These opportunities have ultimately made my student experience much richer through the things I have been able to do and the people I have met. I became involved in the various activities initially because I wanted to meet people and have fun but then realized I could also help others through my experiences. In fact, if I had not currently been enrolled as a postgraduate student in the UK, I would not have been able to be a GamesMaker at the 2012 Olympics in London due to strict visa regulations. I have been very lucky by being in the right place at the right time it seems, but being a student is much more than just reading books, attending classes, and taking exams. As people, we learn and develop continuously based on the summation of all our experiences, whether this occurs in or outside of the classroom. Finding a balance between the personal and the professional aspects of life is oftentimes a juggling act but it is a crucial lesson to learn. In fact, being an international student can put even more emphasis on the importance of being engaged and having access to additional alternative systems of support in order to have a positive experience.

In their review of international education research, Engle and Engle (2003) recognized the influence of many variables in how students initially choose and subsequently reflect on their international experience. They noted important factors which may affect student experiences both in and outside of the classroom, including programme focus, choice of destination, cost to participate, programme duration, and participant preparation. Additional research has shown that social interactions and personal characteristics such as age, gender, nationality, education, previous experience, and familiarity with the local language, culture, and customs can also affect the perceptions international students have of their experiences (Arambewela and Hall, 2009; Reisinger and Turner, 2003; Yang, Noels, and Saumure, 2006). When compared with the experiences of domestic students, the experiences of international students are further complicated in that they are experiencing Higher Education outside of their home culture. Adjustment to a new environment takes time and often occurs in waves with undulating highs and lows, personally experiencing alternative feelings of culture shock and belonging. International students must continually cope with adjusting to a sociocultural system in which they encounter different attitudes, behaviours, fashion style, foods, sights, and perhaps even variations in language. I personally experienced various problems when studying abroad in Austria. They seem so miniscule now but were actually very challenging at the time. For instance, in my first week after arriving in Europe, I somehow managed to survive essentially only on fruit and a couple of bread rolls procured from the daily street market. I was not trying to be thrifty and save money, nor was I purposely avoiding new foods and learning how to cook for myself. Rather, I could not adequately make any distinction between grocery and department stores. I would wander around the city daily in awe of the sights and sounds, but return in the evening to the flat to an empty refrigerator. Luckily, my bewildered European flatmates kindly intervened and took me shopping once they realized what was going on. Looking at various types of engagement for international students is necessary as international students 'travel to study not just for an academic qualification but also for the language and culture experience' (HEA, 2012). When studying in a country with a foreign language, even simple daily activities such as shopping for food or going for coffee become a chance to learn, utilize, and improve practical foreign language skills.

Language can be a bit tricky sometimes. Despite being surrounded by beautiful but imposing castles and baroque churches one may find on postcards of most European cities, I felt a bit lost whilst studying abroad in that I had been learning German for two years but had absolutely no clue what was being said when I heard the local dialect being spoken. Admittedly, many Americans do not really understand dialect. English is hardly an easier language though. There are words and phrases in modern English that originated in Germany, France, Italy, Mexico, Greece, China, and everywhere else that immigrants have come from over the years. For most people who have not spent time studying linguistics and foreign languages, the English language has just been blended for centuries, spreading first across North America and then back across the ocean in movies and other forms of pop culture. Even native English speakers can have problems adjusting to culturally relevant idiosyncrasies, whether they are attitudes, behaviours, or language. For instance, I am regularly reminded that words are different in British and American English. I have learned to rely on the kindness of various people including friends and co-workers to figure out what is going on in various situations. I sometimes feel like I am Mr. Weasley asking Harry Potter, 'what exactly is the purpose of a rubber duck?' At the very least, I apologize for the confusion and everyone has a good laugh about it.

Most international students want to gain direct experience through interactions with peers from the host culture. Engaging international students with various opportunities for cross-cultural interactions at the university is therefore quite important. Most international students come with the expectation and intention to meet and make friends with domestic students rather than surrounding themselves with other international students. A sector-wide survey conducted by The Council for International Education (UKCOSA, 2004) found that international students who had been involved in activities on campus (e.g. sport, volunteering, arts, or clubs and societies) were found to be more likely to have British friends than those who had not participated. They also found differences based on programme level, as postgraduate students were less likely than undergraduate students to use Students' Union facilities or be involved in organized social activities. Cultural differences were also noted as international students coming from North America, the European Union, and South-East Asia were more likely to be involved in on-campus activities than those from the Middle East, Latin America, and East Asia. In fact, cultural idiosyncrasies can often play an important role in the international student experience. While engagement represents involvement in activities and making personal connections with others and the surrounding environment, the opposite can result in increased feelings of intense isolation and alienation far from home. There are stereotypes of certain groups of students clustered together in various cultural cliques and only socializing with each other, essentially isolating themselves from other students. While this idea of cultural 'silos' is sometimes true, it is not universal. There also may be other reasons for the emergence of the cliques. For instance, what is perceived as the traditional drinking culture of British students has been noted as a potential deterrent or barrier for some international students to integration with domestic peers (Byram and Feng, 2006; UKCOSA, 2004; Williams and Johnson, 2011). Those who do not drink alcohol do not always quite understand the social act of sitting in a pub with friends as opposed to going out to bars or clubs. However, there are multiple opportunities for students to interact professionally and socially with peers outside of these situations based on other common interests and even sometimes through the support of various university systems. At many universities, there are services and activities offered through the international office, the Students' Union, individual departments, various religious groups, and/or student run clubs and societies which are aimed at bringing diverse student groups together.

When I studied abroad as an undergraduate, I knew that I was only going to be there for a year so it was somewhat hard to establish friendships with Austrian students. It was also difficult as most Austrian students lived at home and I lived in university-sponsored halls, mainly with other international students. This experience is not unusual or unique as such, as other studies have reported the challenge of connecting domestic and international students. Unfortunately, the host university did not have a Students' Union or any type of structure for clubs and societies for students to be able to interact socially outside of lectures and seminars. My experience was further exacerbated in that rather than classes meeting two or three times a week, most of my seminars and lectures were upper-level courses and only met once a week for a couple hours. I found myself with loads of free time intended for independent study that I was not used to. I then found that I liked the independent learning and could spread my academic work throughout the week better. With the remainder of my free time, I was in a bit of a quandary. In the USA, university students tend to spend most of the week doing required coursework (studying for tests and writing essays which result in continuous assessment) and then have fairly free weekends. Whilst abroad, I was astounded that students wanted to consistently go out during the week and then would almost shut themselves away with open laptops and books to study on the weekends.

Most of my friends from this time abroad were other international students I met in various classes and within my residence who had similar experiences. For some of us, speaking in German was the only way we could converse which made practice essential. We would go out for meals and go to different cultural exhibits and museums that seemed interesting. We would also frequently travel together visiting various places and wandering around the countryside. Over the course of nine months, I made my way across a good part of Western Europe on various trips and tried to make the most of my limited time and funds. I had also stayed in touch with international students who had studied at my home university so I tried to visit them while I had the chance. I was not engaged as an international student the same way I had been at my home university as I did not have many connections to the university beyond my required coursework. However, I did not feel isolated as an international student but rather more connected to different parts of the world through the people I met and the places I visited.

Coming to the UK for a full three-year degree has given me another different perspective. In my first year I found myself somehow split between two communities: international students and the greater student body of the university. It was an undeniable change from living and studying in the USA but I had also already spent a year abroad. Some of the changes I had already anticipated such as needing time to adjust and idiosyncrasies between British and American English like using 's' rather than 'z' in certain words, for instance 'globalization'. I also found many familiar similarities, as my current university has a centralized campus with a great Students' Union and a very helpful international office. I did make the conscious effort to get engaged as a student but it took time. I knew that it was going to be difficult but I also did not want to have loads of spare time in which I would just constantly want to be on Skype missing friends and family in the USA and despising the time difference. Going to orientation programmes at the start of term, taking classes, joining clubs and societies, and living in halls were all choices that I made so that I could stay busy and meet different people. Like most international students I also wanted to travel and did so, when I could. However, knowing that I am in the country for an extended time has resulted in me putting off some activities and trips as less urgent than others. Like my British friends, I often put off some things I would rather be doing for various reasons and also in order to focus on the demands of doing a PhD. Like many other PhD students, I also often find it difficult to take a (sometimes much needed) break because there are not deadlines or set term times for postgraduates. I want to go on adventures and travel around to visit various places but I often rationalize that I can do these things later when I have the time and can relax. Now, preparing for my final year, I realize that this is why domestic students are always amazed that international students go traveling so much. It is not that there is a different timespan between the groups but rather a different attitude towards it. Domestic students and those international students who are at university for a full degree of three years or more perceive an infinite amount of time in the future to travel and do various things, while international students attending for only a semester or year want to fit in as much as possible because they do not know when, or even if, they will ever return.

Focusing on engagement in order to improve the experiences of international students seems to have recently become much more important as national and international policy debates attest. In 1999, Tony Blair launched the Prime Minister's Initiative (PMI) in the UK to increase the number of international students studying in British Further and Higher Education (UK Council for International Student Affairs, 2012). A second five-year stage, called the Prime Minister's Initiative for International Education (PMI2), was launched in April 2006 (Institute of International Education, 2012). This endeavour has included efforts to both increase the number of British students going to other countries as well as evaluating the range of services and support available to international students in the UK. In fact, most research regarding international education falls into one of two fields, either looking at domestic students who go abroad or focusing on international students who have come to study at a specific location or in a specific country. While PMI and PMI2 have been focused on evaluating and improving the student experience of international students, there have also been some negative developments more recently. When I arrived to start my degree in September 2011, there had been some student riots over the summer protesting a significant rise in their fees.

Adjustments to visa and immigration policies have also made it more difficult for some international students to travel for educational purposes. With the recent economic crisis, many branches of government offices have been consolidated and the workforce has been cut. This has left one centralized location with the responsibility to deal with work that had been spread across various regional offices in the past. Changes in regulations and bureaucratic processes can make applying for student visas extremely confusing and difficult. The UK Border Agency's (UKBA's) actions against London Metropolitan University's official sponsorship status in the autumn of 2012 has definitely brought the case of international students in the UK to the foreground of many current conversations in Higher Education communities. One of the main concerns has been whether international students are coming to study or to bypass immigration regulations. While international students pay higher fees than their domestic counterparts and contribute to the local economy through spending habits, there are some who worry about the strain on public resources such as healthcare and job prospects for the domestic population. Other conflicts, such as those in Syria and Greece, have made studying in the UK seem like a safe alternative to returning home for many students who are viewed as refugees. Engaging international students within the university community is thereby considered imperative as both a political and economic strategy. In fact, at the 2013 National Union of Students (NUS) sections conferences, various policies were proposed in order to address engagement and other issues specifically in relation to international students, postgraduate students, and mature and part-time students on a national scale.

Gaining personal experience by travelling and learning about foreign languages and cultures has been a part of Higher Education since the Grand Tours taken by aristocratic young men during the 17th–19th centuries in order to complete their classical education (Byram and Feng, 2006; Lewin, 2009). However, while only privileged individuals were able to benefit from these types of experiences in the past, there are now many different initiatives by which students are encouraged to undertake international education experiences. According to recent figures, there were approximately 3.5 million students worldwide who studied in locations outside their country of legal residence in the autumn of 2011 (Docherty, 2011). This is a significant number of individuals, and individual countries have further increased efforts to attract international students as well as send their own students abroad. A diverse range of students across the globe today are thus being permitted much greater access to international education experiences than preceding generations. Studying abroad is not perceived to be quite as 'elitist' as it once was. There are well established multinational programmes such as the European Community Action Scheme for the Mobility of University Students (ERASMUS) in addition to individual university exchange schemes and other independent options. I had done my year abroad with an independent group so was not traveling surrounded by a group of other American students. Instead, I took classes in different departments across the university and had to figure out a lot of things on my own. Some available options for international education are for a few weeks, some for a few months to a semester, and some for an entire year. While a shorter term would have undoubtedly been easier, I chose to be abroad for a full academic year as I wanted to be able to immerse myself in my experience without finally feeling comfortable only to jump on a plane to return home. I also wanted to be more comfortable with my language skills and knew that I needed practice in order to do so. I ultimately became more independent and internationally focused over the course of those nine months and learned a lot about myself which has left an undeniable mark on me as an individual. I was already studying for a degree focused on international affairs but my study abroad period had given me personal experience.

In conclusion, the student experience is undoubtedly complex and multifaceted. I realize my experiences, like those of many students, are unique and cannot be overly generalized. However, numerous themes found common in the experiences of international students are based on previous engagement and student experience research. In addition to the traditional academic requirements of getting a degree, there are also now additional pressures to gain both practical and soft skills during one's university career which are considered useful in future employment. Involvement in extra-curricular activities can further provide various opportunities to learn and develop such skills and interests as well as forge both personal and professional relationships which may become permanent fixtures in life. International students' experiences are even more convoluted as there are additional sociocultural variables which may affect how students are willing to be engaged. While there are directed programme provisions such as welcome week orientation sessions, individual students ultimately have the choice of what to do, where to go, who to interact with, and how they will be engaged with their own experience. The institution may provide targeted opportunities for learning and development but the student has to put forth the effort and make the final decision. I know that without getting engaged and attempting to make connections with my fellow students and the institution during my first year my experience as an international postgraduate student would be much different. Perhaps I do have a slightly biased, rose-coloured glasses perspective but I also know I now have friends all across the world in various academic and professional spheres and would not trade my experiences for anything.

Chapter 11

The NTSU Outstanding Teaching Awards

Student perspectives on engagement

Ed Foster and Jo Southwell-Sander

Introduction

In 2012, Nottingham Trent Students' Union (NTSU) launched its first student-led teaching award (Davies, Hope & Robertson, 2010). Nottingham Trent University (NTU) students were invited to identify outstanding tutors and describe what made them so. One hundred and twenty-five students from across the University responded. They often wrote highly detailed descriptions about factors that made specific tutors exceptional and, in June 2012, nine tutors and one support team were awarded NTSU Outstanding Teaching Awards. This chapter is based on an analysis of the students' descriptions of what made their tutors outstanding and identifies four distinct trends from amongst the respondents. We close by discussing implications for creating more engaging learning environments for students.

Student engagement

There are many factors that can influence student engagement with their studies (see Chapter 1), but in this chapter we are interested in the role of the tutor. Student engagement literature identifies the role of the tutor as crucial to engagement. Willis (1993) describes how students' intentions to be engaged were modified by the learning and teaching context, most often the lecturer. Students might take a particular module for instrumental reasons (such as convenient timetabling) but still find the learning and teaching context stimulating and therefore became thoroughly engaged. The opposite is also true. Students can commence a module with strong intentions, but the context causes them to become disengaged. Willis identifies five context factors: course content, class size/impersonality, the nature of assessment, provision for self-direction/depth and, most importantly, staff attitude and presentation. Similarly, a first-year student interviewed by Bryson and Hand (2007: 357) put it most succinctly: 'it's definitely the lecturer that can make it interesting or can almost destroy a subject'.

Perhaps the most motivated of students can sustain engagement despite a poor learning and teaching context. Nonetheless, there is clearly a role for the tutor in helping students to engage with learning and teaching. Leach and Zepke (2012: 246) state that 'we cannot underestimate the influence of teachers on student engagement. Teaching that ensures [. . .] successful teacher and student interactions [. . .] is most likely to engage students'. Broughan and Grantham (2012: 49) define one of the metaphors for teachers as 'an experienced navigator to explorers'. In this light, the tutor acts as an expert to help the students find their own pathways through the maze of learning and teaching. Broughan and Grantham emphasize the importance of focusing on the process, not merely the eventual destination. They stress the importance for tutors to respond to both the environment and how the students are operating within that environment.

A (very brief) recent history of rating tutors

Student opinions have long been sought as part of quality assurance processes. Students' unions have traditionally ensured that students' views are represented across the institution through direct representation in decision making at senior levels within the institution, or by training student representatives to speak up for their peers on course committees. The UK Quality Assurance Agency (QAA) now uses the term student engagement to describe 'the participation of students in quality enhancement and quality assurance processes, resulting in the improvement of their educational experience' (QAA, 2012: 4). The nature of such feedback has also become more public. Whereas at one point student views about the course and the quality of learning and teaching would have been expressed almost exclusively within course committee meetings, now student views are collated and are made publicly available through the National Student Survey (NSS).[1] These views have become available for prospective students to use to make consumer judgments about which courses to choose in the Key Information Sets (KIS).[2]

Changes in technology also now make it easier for students to pass judgments about individual tutors or institutions. At the time of writing, www.ratemypro fessors.com had over 15 million comments written about 1.7 million members of teaching staff. Concerns have been raised about whether individual academics might face cyberbullying from disgruntled students (Silver, 2006). The National Union of Students (NUS) has also flirted with controversy with its Feedback Amnesty campaigns. In these campaigns, students are asked to provide examples of good and bad feedback and the National Union has used this information to develop policy on best practice. Poor practice was 'outed', although, importantly, not linked back to the individual tutor or institution.

Changes in technology, and politicians' notions of the student as consumer, have therefore created an environment in which student opinions about their learning and teaching can become highly confrontational and potentially damaging to relationships between students and their tutors. It is in this light that the NUS's work on Student-Led Teaching Awards provides a valuable counterpoise. In 2009, NUS Scotland and the Higher Education Academy Scotland launched a campaign to promote Student-Led Teaching Awards (Davies et al., 2010). These are awards voted for by students to acknowledge and celebrate innovation and excellence in teaching. This campaign was then extended across the whole of the UK and more students' unions set up their own teaching awards.

The 2012 NTSU Outstanding Teaching Awards

NTSU is an independent democratic organization that represents the diverse body of students studying at NTU. Like other students' unions in the UK, it is led by a team of elected full-time sabbatical officers who serve a one-year term of office. The officers have portfolios relating to the different aspects of student life, including education, welfare, volunteering, sports and student societies. NTSU is affiliated with the NUS, but is operationally independent.

NTSU is partly funded by the University, but is again operationally independent from it. It acts as both a strategic partner to the University and as a campaigning organization, sometimes in opposition to it. The Union works closely with academic staff at the University to enable improvements to the student experience, particularly ensuring that student representatives are trained in ways to effectively represent their peers in institutional and course committees. NTSU also campaigns on national issues that may affect students' lives, such as tuition fees. At a local level, it has campaigned successfully to improve the students' learning experience by reducing late night lectures, increasing the availability of electronic resources and improving Wi-Fi access. The Union also provides various services for students, including advice centres and volunteering opportunities, and is a core element to the campus social and cultural life.

In 2012, NTSU implemented a student-led teaching award: the Outstanding Teaching Awards. It adapted the NUS's original concept by setting local criteria and award titles to best fit the institution. The University was positive about the idea and students were invited to vote for the best tutor and best support team in the summer term of 2012.

Students were asked to nominate tutors or support staff using an online form and write a short testimonial explaining why they felt the nominee should win the award. Students were encouraged to consider five criteria, such as 'encourages discussion, debate, co-operation and peer assessment' (NTSU, 2012), but students were not required to rate or rank each nominee against them.

There were 97 nominations submitted for the outstanding teacher award and 28 for the outstanding support team. Three nominees were shortlisted for each of the nine academic schools at NTU and invited to an awards evening attended by University senior managers and the NUS President. A student from each school presented the eventual winners with their awards. It was at the awards evening that the authors were struck by the richness of the detail included in the student nominations. The student nominees had written with conviction about the inspiring nature of their teachers and the exceptional levels of support they offered. This motivated us to explore the student comments further.

Data and results

For this section, we will concentrate on the 97 student testimonials provided about NTU teaching staff. Each student testimonial was analyzed for patterns. After several passes through the data, we identified four broad patterns. The results represent whether or not each individual student mentioned a particular feature, not every time they provided an example. We believe that this approach gives us an interesting insight into what students believe makes for outstanding teaching, although there are limitations. Firstly, the call for nominations asked specifically about the tutor, not the learning process. In our other chapter (Chapter 15), students tended not to talk about individual tutors, but rather the totality of the learning experience as being important to making their learning interesting. In this instance, students were asked to focus on the individuals at the front of the classroom. Secondly, each respondent felt strongly enough about their tutor to write a short testimonial and submit it at a busy time of the year. Therefore, these responses represent the views of students who are likely to already be engaged in the learning process. Nonetheless, the opinions cited below represent a fascinating snapshot of what students perceive to be inspiring teaching. We therefore ought to take every opportunity to share views like this as widely as possible.

The four main themes identified are shown in Figure 11.1.

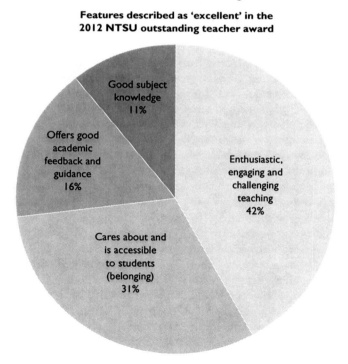

Features described as 'excellent' in the 2012 NTSU outstanding teacher award

Good subject knowledge 11%

Offers good academic feedback and guidance 16%

Enthusiastic, engaging and challenging teaching 42%

Cares about and is accessible to students (belonging) 31%

Figure 11.1 Major themes and characteristics of excellent teaching as defined by the NTSU Outstanding Teaching Awards nomination forms

Enthusiastic, engaging and challenging teaching

This was the most commonly reported factor. Students generally commented favourably about the tutors' enthusiasm for their subject and teaching, but more than that, described how this enthusiasm was translated into providing interesting learning experiences. Students described interesting classes, tutors' excellent communication skills and lessons that were both challenging and engaging. Eighty students (83 per cent of respondents) described these features.

Cares about and is accessible to students (belonging)

The second most-frequently mentioned aspect related to the quality of the personal relationships between the students and the tutor. The students described how the nominees made them feel that they belonged, would know them personally, would be helpful and, importantly, were accessible if a student had a query or concern. Fifty-nine (61 per cent) students mentioned belonging as an important part of excellent teaching.

Offers good academic feedback and guidance

The third feature described by the students related to feedback and guidance. Students reported favourably where tutors provided them with signposts and pointers about how well they were doing and where they needed to go in order to progress, particularly about forthcoming assessments. Thirty-one students (32 per cent) mentioned this aspect.

Good subject knowledge

Finally, students described the importance of each tutor's excellent subject knowledge. It is interesting to note that this is the least frequently mentioned feature. Clearly, good subject knowledge is needed to underpin most of the features identified by students above. Nonetheless, it appears that to this group of students, what is most important is how the knowledge is applied. Good subject knowledge featured in responses by 22 (23 per cent) of students.

We will now examine each of these four areas in more detail, using comments made by students on their nomination forms to illustrate our points.

Enthusiastic, engaging and challenging (pedagogy)

The most commonly cited responses relate to the ability of the tutor to engage and inspire their students, primarily through their interactions in the classroom (80 of the 97 respondents). Students reported that outstanding tutors:

- were enthusiastic, engaging and exciting teachers;
- offered stimulating, stretching and challenging learning;

- made learning interesting;
- possessed excellent communication skills and a good sense of humour.

The first thing is to note how much the students responded to the personal enthusiasm of the tutors. Students reported favourably about how the teachers possessed a love for their subject and how that enthusiasm in turn inspired the students:

> I always look forward to her lectures. She is engaging and talks to us like peers and not in the usual teacher to student way. She makes the subject exciting and the information seems to sink in better.

> Always has a lot of enthusiasm despite teaching a class that are normally hungover.

> She has an excellent teaching style, very engaging. She manages to make the subject interesting and use modem examples which are also humorous to keep the class motivated. I leave the lecture really feeling like I have learnt something compared to others where I walk out confused or bored.

However, students responded positively to more than just their tutor's enthusiasm. They responded positively to teaching that was intellectually stretching, was delivered in an interesting fashion and facilitated by good communicators.

Students were positive where they encountered challenging teaching, an important indicator of student engagement for both Chickering and Gamson (1987) and Kuh et al. (2008a). There appears to be a certain amount of pride in understanding challenging materials, but also acknowledgement of the role of the tutor in helping them to do so. Students spoke glowingly about how the tutor had helped them to grasp difficult concepts:

> The nominee's explanation of theories and mechanisms has allowed me to gain an improved understanding of [the subject], an area at the beginning of university which was a weakness, is now one my biggest strengths.

> His seminars are so well prepared they really do exercise your mind and really compliment the lectures. I am sure that the nominee could give me [a] lecture on absolutely anything and I would enjoy it and learn a great amount.

> Stimulating, enthusiastic, and consistently challenges students – she does this through setting work which is interesting and very relevant to our course.

For the most part, the nominating students described intellectual challenges, the classes that pushed them to develop in new and previously unknown areas. However, in one instance, a student nominee described how the teaching engaged them in deeper, more emotionally meaningful ways.

Her seminars are motivating, thoughtful and impact on everyone in a positive way. Her seminars have resulted in many tears because she always brings her own experiences into things making everything so much more meaningful. Genuinely loves teaching. Encourages us to debate and even if we go off topic yet it is still relevant to the course in some way she allows this and encourages this.

We received the most comments about those factors associated with good pedagogy, referring to the actual techniques used to make learning interesting for students.

She doesn't understand how amazing she is at teaching. She makes all lectures stimulating and is enthusiastic about the subject with personal on-hand experience that helps in understanding the theory into practice. She also challenges students to think about the subject and the challenges [for the] modern world. [The nominee] also involves the whole class in discussion and cooperation into a wide range of activities as well as field trips to put theory into practice [. . .]

Students cited a range of factors that made learning interesting. These included activities such as:

- group discussions;
- case studies;
- questioning strategies whilst students were conducting lab work;
- several students mentioned the use of alternative media such as films, music or lectures delivered remotely.

None of these factors are particularly innovative or original. In fact, they are likely to be included in any new academic's professional development programme. What appears absolutely pivotal is how the tutor delivers them. One student described how their nominated tutor included their own practical experience of working in industry to make the learning experience authentic. A second noted that the tutor worked to make the learning as interesting as possible with 'props etc. however [she was] also honest about the boring parts she knows we have to get through'.

As might be expected, the student respondents placed high value on the tutors' ability to communicate effectively. As they sought to describe excellence, students would often contrast the excellent tutors by comparing them to others who simply read from their notes:

He keeps his slides to a bare minimum, in order to have a free flowing intellectual discussion, rather than just citing off from the slides (which are probably siphoned from a textbook) like the average teacher [. . .]

Although, it is interesting to note that that different respondents had differing expectations of what constituted 'outstanding' communication:

> Her PowerPoints and handouts are always filled with information and with[out] them I would not be able to pass this course.

Students appeared to respond well to tutors who had a good sense of humour. Whilst we don't necessarily advocate specific humour classes as part of any educational development programmes for new tutors, we do feel it is important to stress the importance of humour in the classroom. Humour can demonstrate that the tutor is confident enough with their material to be playful with it. More than that, humour can be inclusive. Telling a joke about course content can work as a source of entertainment, but it can also demonstrate to students that the tutor feels those students are part of the academic community. There would be little point making jokes where the audience has no hope of understanding the punch line.

> She makes the lectures engaging. She interacts with us, she injects humour into them.

> Above all though, her style of lecturing is perfect. The nominee has the ability to make even the most complex issues seem simple while still finding time to make us laugh.

Of course students want to be entertained in the lecture theatre, but more than that, they were positive when the teacher acted as an expert interpreter to help guide them through the subject content. For example:

> She has kept me fully engaged all throughout the lectures with her teaching style of 'straight to the point.' I always go away knowing that I have learnt something new.

It appears that students valued more than just the dynamic, entertaining superstar tutor; they also valued the fact that tutors would take a personal interest in them and make time to ensure that the students had understood a concept:

> [They] would happily explain something to you repeatedly, even if it was for the 100th time.

Belonging

The primary finding from the 'What Works? Student Retention & Success' programme of work (Thomas, 2012c) is that belonging is crucial to student retention. Thomas argues that belonging is developed through a sense of identity with the course, confidence born out of progress in assessments and, crucially, the relationships formed with peers and tutors. Kember et al. (2001: 340) noted that 'those with a sense of belonging found study a more fulfilling and enjoyable process than those without much sense of affiliation'.

One of the anxieties about the massification (Teichler, 1998) of Higher Education (HE) is that students will feel that they are anonymous parts of a bigger machine, rather than members of vibrant and active learning communities. Fifty-nine of the students (61 per cent) reported that one aspect that made these teachers excellent was the variety of ways they had created personal relationships with their students. Tutors helped students to feel that they belonged within the course community and were valued as individuals. This was done initially through effective communication. Through day-to-day communication, outstanding tutors were perceived to be non-hierarchical and genuinely interested in their students:

> [The nominee] talks to us like peers and not in the usual teacher to student way.

> He also knows all of his students personally, not just by name. He has also gotten in contact with students personally, asking them if they find the course okay and if we have any issues.

However, relationship building went beyond the manner in which students were communicated to, it was also influenced by tutors' preparedness to support their students.

> [The tutor was] forever going above and beyond the call of duty to help me out.

It appears particularly important that the staff were accessible to students, both physically and, very importantly, via email or other electronic communications.

> He is always there for you when you need help.

> Really easy to contact and will offer a meeting the same day if needed.

> [The nominee] goes above and beyond the expected efforts of a University tutor. Many talk of having an open door policy but she really does.

As students often work late hours, they were particularly grateful when tutors responded to emails outside normal office hours. For example:

> He is always friendly and very approachable, even outside of usual lecture times. He goes above and beyond his responsibilities even to the point where he has responded to emails regarding important coursework at midnight the night before a deadline.

> Even after lectures finished for the year she is quick to respond to emails.

Students were also appreciative when tutors offered support that went beyond their role as tutor. For example, one nominee was grateful when the tutor put time and effort into supporting a course-related society:

> Supporting the ConSoc, going above the call of duty as he has put himself out a number of times even when he should have been doing other things!

Another referenced the role the tutor played supporting them to engage in their role in the quality assurance process:

> She is lovely, friendly and has been a great tutor and [committee name] chair. As school and course rep she has made me feel so welcome and valued.

Guidance

Thiry-one students mentioned the importance of the guidance and feedback offered by their tutors. Taken together, these functions appeared to fulfil the 'experienced navigator' role described by Broughan and Grantham (2012). Students appeared grateful that somebody was helping them to understand what they needed to do in order to perform well in their studies and was helping them understand how well they were progressing. For example:

> In class, she looks for pupil involvement without pressurising anyone and helping to understand structure to work to gain a clearer understanding.

He has a genuine interest in helping us to make the most of our degree, and wants us to achieve the highest degree possible, putting on extra seminars before exam period, so taking up his spare time to help us.

> I emailed her once asking if she'd mark some mock-exam answers I'd done. And she said that she would.

Student nominations were submitted from all years. Those in later years were particularly grateful for support with making the transition into more complex studying, or even into employment:

> The nominee also gives excellent feedback on assessed work for the module by the due date with the addition of an informative assessment to help with third-year marking and assessment criteria early within the year to help us understand the change from 2nd to 3rd year work.

> Given a lot of guidance towards my dissertation and helped me with a job and career guidance.

Students wrote about feedback too. They described how they found it useful for understanding how they could improve their work:

> [. . .] she never gives negative feedback without showing her students how they can do better.

She also gave particularity long feedback on assignments that were handed in allowing us to improve.

Excellent subject knowledge

In our survey, 11 per cent of students reported that what made the tutors excellent was their subject knowledge. When mentioned, students described being in awe of their tutors' knowledge and seeming omniscience. For example:

One thing that works strongly in the nominee's favour is that it would appear he knows everything.

Another student noted that the tutor brought her own research into the lecture theatre and classroom:

Having a lecturer that participates in research around her subject areas provides expert knowledge that she brings into the lecture. Knowing that she has such a broad knowledge base allows lectures to be concise and efficient.

However, of the four groups of factors identified, excellent subject knowledge was mentioned by the fewest students. It appears therefore that, for most, it is not what knowledge the tutors possess, but how they teach it. Our respondents are perhaps reassured that their tutors are experts but value effective communication, interesting pedagogy, personal relations and effective guidance far more.

Conclusion

At the time of writing, 909 nominations for the second NTSU Outstanding Teaching Awards had been received. It appears that this year students are even more actively engaged with the process. Moreover, the awards are seen as prestigious by staff, and those being nominated clearly feel recognized for the exceptional work they do. At a time where student feedback initiatives such as KIS can potentially damage student/staff relationships, it is encouraging to see how a student-led teaching award can help engender a more positive culture of partnership. There has been an indirect benefit for the Students' Union too. The Outstanding Teaching Awards have raised the profile of NTSU amongst academics. This has had two benefits: firstly, it has improved working relationships with academics and secondly, it has also increased awareness of NTSU services.

Students appear clear about what outstanding teaching looks like. The nominations describe how tutors engage their students through their enthusiasm, good pedagogy, personal interest and guidance built on solid subject foundations. This ought to provide us with a recipe for success. Coaching models used in professional development are clear: model and then teach behaviours and strategies that lead to success. Whilst we may baulk at notions of consumerism in HE, the customers have spoken very clearly about what they think makes a successful learning experience. One way forward is to use these excellent teachers as role models for peer development. Universities could benefit from developing academic coaching programmes around the approaches used by these academics.

However, this approach is not problem-free. For example, is it a reasonable expectation that tutors should be available at midnight on the night before a deadline? One of our student respondents felt that it was. Furthermore, what a student may feel is excellence in the short term, may not be helpful in the long term. For example, one student reported of their tutor that:

> She is organized, provides us with regular hand-outs which aid our own private study and runs us through the exact criteria that she knows examiners will look for.

Whilst this is an understandable and clearly supportive strategy in the short term and likely to make any tutor extremely popular, such approaches are problematic. At the end of their time at university, students are expected to operate with a high degree of autonomy and independence. Somewhere along the way, students need the opportunity to struggle with finding their own way to develop the maturity to cope.

The 97 students who nominated outstanding teachers in 2012 were pretty consistent in their views about what excellent learning and teaching looks like. Outstanding teachers are enthusiastic tutors who communicate well and who set challenging learning. They care about their students and help to develop or provide a sense of belonging. Outstanding teachers are guides through the HE environment who are also experts in their subject. The message from the students is clear: if we want to engage them, then subject expertise is far less important than enthusiasm, passion and authentic engagement.

Notes

1 http://www.thestudentsurvey.com
2 http://unistats.direct.gov.uk/

Chapter 12

The impact of co-curricular activity on student engagement

Sarah Johnson, Rebecca Murphy and Sarah Parnham

In this chapter, we hope to highlight the impact of the Student Mentor Scheme at Nottingham Trent University (NTU). This scheme is based on a Peer Assisted Learning approach and is aimed at increasing student engagement and enhancing the student experience. We will consider the experiences of two of the mentors, with differing motivations for their involvement in the scheme, and consider the link between their endeavours to enhance the engagement of others and their ensuing engagement in their own academic studies.

The Higher Education Retention and Engagement (HERE) Project (Foster et al., 2011b), a joint project between Nottingham Trent, Bradford and Bournemouth Universities, found that student doubting and subsequent withdrawal from university are often associated with course-related factors and anxiety about coping with academic expectations. When explored further, it was found that there appeared to be a correlation between increased confidence and support from fellow students. The research thus recommended that student mentoring may be a useful way in which we can support student retention and engagement in the first year of Higher Education. This echoes Kuh's notion (see Kuh et al., 2008a: 542) that student engagement is represented by 'the time and energy students invest in educationally purposeful activities', but also 'the effort institutions devote to using effective educational practices'.

The Student Mentor Scheme was set up at NTU as a cross-year scheme in which the learning of first-year students was scaffolded by more experienced others within the same discipline. This was based on a model introduced through the former Write Now Centre for Excellence in Teaching and Learning (CETL), where trained undergraduate student mentors worked with students of the same discipline to offer opportunities for discussion, thus promoting familiarity with the conventions of writing in that particular discipline. The intervention was introduced in order to encourage a sense of community within the educational setting and thus promote a sense of belonging (Perry, 1999), echoing Tinto (1987), who suggested that academic and social integration into the establishment can be directly linked to an enhanced experience and increased engagement, recognising the 'value of collaborative and cooperative learning'. Later findings suggested that the student mentors themselves also had an increased sense of engagement as a result of being involved in the scheme.

Feedback from students accessing the Student Mentor Scheme (2009–2012) has been positive and many have reported feeling an increased sense of confidence, having gained a greater understanding of course material and improved attainment as a result of having attended sessions with a mentor. But what we seek to highlight here is the impact on the mentors themselves in terms of their own sense of engagement, enhanced experience and improved learning as a result of their involvement in the scheme.

Much research exists outlining the supposed benefits of being a student mentor in terms of enhanced communication skills (Fleming, 2009), increased confidence (Nicol, 2010) and greater engagement in their own studies (Bryson, 2010). This chapter gives voice to two students, each outlining their experiences of meaningful engagement in response to such collaboration. Their narratives outline how their involvement in the Student Mentor Scheme, in place to support transition, retention and engagement, has served to enhance their own engagement in their studies. Here, we discover what they got out of being mentors, and why this was so powerful in terms of their own engagement.

Initial interest

Rebecca

Entering Higher Education at 20, I felt a lot more confident to get involved in university life than at 18. I had a clearer idea of what I wanted to gain from my time at university, and therefore tried to take advantage of the opportunities made available to me. I participated in a range of extra-curricular activities during my first year, including volunteering, student representation and student mentoring.

Sarah

On the information days prior to coming to university, I was inspired by the endless amount of information I received, not only about the course I had applied for, but about all other aspects of student life such as accommodation, clubs and societies, and the Students' Union. Students on my chosen course were available on the day to talk to me about what studying at university was like for them and how they were finding the course. I found this helpful because I found that the best people to talk to about my chosen course were the students who were currently studying it.

When I first came to university, I wanted to develop a deeper understanding of my subject and to explore my career options; I also wanted to gain the confidence that I lacked greatly. I planned to do this by moving into student accommodation, joining a society, and making myself familiar with everyone on the course; I tried to improve my engagement by taking control.

The students I met during the post-application day were outgoing, friendly and confident. It was clear to me that the students' academic achievement came from being happy and confident in themselves and other aspects of their lives; they believed that they had the confidence to do well so they were doing well, therefore social achievement and academic achievement must have worked together to become successful.

Belonging and becoming engaged

Rebecca

I found that the Welcome Week events arranged by the university gave me a number of positive experiences that helped me to become engaged very quickly, and as a result I did not experience the initial isolation or anxiety that some students describe. It was at this early point in the year that I applied to be a course representative, and I ultimately represented all first-year students in my school. This role allowed me to quickly form working relationships with lecturers, Student Union representatives and a great number of other students. I gained an understanding of the decision-making process and access to all levels of the university hierarchy, which gave me a feeling of being part of the wider university where I may otherwise have identified only as a computer science student.

During induction for my course, some of the events were run by second- and third-year student ambassadors who were engaged and involved in running an academic society. This was a key factor in ensuring my own engagement, as I joined the society and was able to meet like-minded students who would become my support network over the course of the year. This was invaluable to me not only because I felt there was less pressure to form friendships with the students in my accommodation, but also in that they were able to offer me resources and advice when I found course content more challenging. I hoped to be able to give other students the same level of help that I received, and ultimately became vice president of the society this year.

Further to this, when I had the opportunity to apply to be a student mentor, I wanted to get involved for similar reasons. The scheme has provided me with the ability to give structured support to other students who may be struggling with the transition to a university environment from college or work. I believe it is important to ensure that students are aware of the support that is available to them from the first weeks of their course as I was, and through speaking to new students about the scheme during induction lectures, I feel that I was able to make a difference.

Sarah

During Welcome Week, I took part in a range of activities alongside my course induction. The university's fresher reps encouraged me to get involved in the activities on offer, but they were also there if I felt like I could not get involved at times and needed someone to talk to about my worries.

On starting at university, I was very excited. I had high expectations for myself because I had achieved enough Universities and Colleges Admissions Service (UCAS) points to get onto my chosen course; I knew that I was smart enough to be there. I had hopes that I would continue to achieve good grades as I had always worked hard. However, at the beginning of my studies, I achieved very low grades. I felt disheartened as I had put in so much effort, and was simply shocked at the fact that I had only just managed to pass my assignments when I had already achieved so well to get onto the course in the first place. The feedback I received was mainly negative and I was not confident enough to ask for help from my tutors or other students about my academic work. I thought that I was a failure because I believed that the teachers expected me to do really well and I let them down, as well as myself. I was embarrassed more than anything and felt isolated socially, as I began to withdraw from going out with my new friends.

Halfway through the first year, I had to take part in a group presentation assignment with other students on my course. Fortunately, the students I had chosen to work with were already high achievers, and it was not until I worked with them that I was able to understand what was needed in order to pass the assignment at a higher level. Once I had received this help, my grades increased from a 3rd to a 2:1 classification in this assignment and others that followed. In this instance, learning from others was crucial to my engagement because once I understood how to write academically in the correct way I was able to connect with my course emotionally. I was over the moon at such amazing feedback which improved my confidence and increased my desire to pass on that information to others who were also struggling.

After becoming more confident in my studies, I became more confident as an individual because I knew that I was not a failure. Instead, I had been given the tools I needed to achieve higher grades; therefore I was not embarrassed anymore, which made me happier in other areas of my life such as going on nights out with my friends. In my case, my academic achievement greatly affected my social achievement.

After my grades improved I applied to be a Student Academic Writing Mentor. I applied for this position because I wanted to help people improve their writing and give them the confidence that it had taken me so long to develop. Although I wanted to support other students, I have also gained a deeper understanding of academic writing and the study skills needed by going over old ground; I have been there before so I understand how challenging it is and have the confidence to support others. I have been able to engage students through giving induction talks at the university and explaining how I could help and support them. I have also been given the opportunity to explain the struggles I faced when I first started university and how crucial it could be to gain the knowledge from other students that have been in the same position. After completing the induction talks, a tutor commented that:

> I thought they did an excellent job at putting across the service that you offer and it was a really valuable thing to introduce the first years to. It is definitely something that I would like to do again next year.

As a student mentor, I pose questions to students and provide them with techniques to enhance their academic writing and confidence in their ability to write. It has been said that learning happens when the more knowledgeable other, a teacher or peer with a better understanding of what is to be learned, poses questions and provides activities in order to motivate and help the learner to reach the more knowledgeable other's level. As a result of learning these skills, the student's confidence in their ability to write is increased; therefore, they become even more engaged. A student that has come to a mentor for help with their academic writing is a good example of a student that wants to become more engaged with their learning because they have added personal meaning to what they are studying. If a student wants to improve their academic writing and study skills then they are already committed to doing well at university as they are looking for ways to make it happen. Therefore, they must have a personal reason for why they want to do well.

What I get from it

Rebecca

Equally important to me is the positive impact that my involvement in the Student Mentor Scheme has had on my own success. There has been a considerable increase in workload this year and at times coursework deadlines and exams have fallen very close together, creating periods of high academic pressure. Students who access the scheme are often struggling with this pressure and, through my efforts to give them tools and resources for managing their time, I have become better at using them myself.

Being able to help other students has given me more confidence in my own abilities, which has helped me to be more proactive in my approach to learning. Additionally, I have noticed significant improvements in my own knowledge and awareness of academic writing as a result of my work as a mentor and the training I received for it.

In conclusion, support from peers has been vital to my engagement at university, as help and advice from second- and third-year students in my society has helped me to quickly understand and feel comfortable in my environment. My experiences as a Student Mentor have played an important role in equipping me to deal with increased academic pressure during my second year. I have been grateful for the opportunity to develop my own skills while providing vital support to other students.

Sarah

The Student Mentor Scheme offers students a range of employability skills; for example, students can improve their organisation, time management, presentation and communication skills. All of these can be transferred to the work environment, so when the student finishes their degree it gives them more than just their subject knowledge to include in their CV. When the student realises the relevance of these skills, they will become more motivated in their learning. This is because they can use them, as well as their subject knowledge, to help them find graduate employment.

I have become more engaged and involved in my own academic studies through being a Student Mentor, because I now understand how to be engaged. I have been motivated by students' willingness to achieve so I have become more involved with my own work. I feel that I am not only setting an example to the students, but I am also doing it for myself because I believe that I am able to do well. I also have the knowledge and experience to know that support from others can be the key to student engagement and academic achievement.

Links: endeavours to engage others and their own ensuing engagement

Van Gennep (cited in Tinto, 1987) describes the processes of learning to belong to a new community as 'the rites of passage'. Van Gennep is describing a social anthropological model whereby social stability is maintained in response to change. Initially, Rebecca and Sarah describe very different experiences of entering Higher Education. Foster et al. (2011b) similarly found that the periods of separation and transition may be made more stable by the introduction of strategies to familiarise students with the new community and opportunities to make friends, thus establishing incorporation to the new environment. In terms of the Mentors' own engagement, student involvement in, and engagement with, academic life can have a significant impact on student learning and development (Astin, 1993), and both Rebecca and Sarah cite how their involvement in extra-curricular activities increased their confidence in their studies and enhanced their sense of belonging, thus leading to greater levels of success.

Krause and Coates (2008) suggest that the levels at which students interact outside the classroom in activities such as clubs, societies and other extra-curricular activities could also be a measure of student engagement. Rebecca describes how such interventions within the curriculum have increased her sense of belonging to the university, as well as engaging her as a student within her School. She cites interaction with academic staff and the decision-making processes within the wider university as being integral to her increased sense of belonging. She states that involvement in the academic society meant that she avoided experiencing feelings of anxiety or isolation on first entering the university.

For Sarah, it appears that she had lower levels of understanding about what was expected of her at university; she experienced decreased confidence, struggled with her studies and was less confident about asking for help. Tinto (1987) recognises the 'value of collaborative and co-operative learning', and according to Colvin and Ashman (2010) 'teaching also occurs between and among students as they work together and, at times, mentor each other in and outside the classroom'. It appears that Sarah has benefitted from working with others who had a better understanding of how to achieve the higher grades, providing a springboard to greater levels of success.

Sarah applied to be a Student Mentor in order to access support from peers and identify learning strategies for supporting others in terms of their academic writing within the discipline. Research carried out at NTU indicates that student mentoring is a useful way in which we can support student retention and engagement in the first year of Higher Education. Feedback from online surveys has cited 'increased confidence' as being one of the many benefits of participating in the scheme, both as mentor and mentee: 'The mentoring helped to build my confidence in academic writing and structure from the beginning of the year' (Student Participant 2009–2010). A student mentor (2009–2010) cited seeing the improved confidence of mentees as being one of the most rewarding features of mentoring.

Student mentors at NTU are recruited for their own subject knowledge, competence in terms of writing and a desire to help others. However, sailing through their first year is not a prerequisite of becoming a mentor, as is clearly demonstrated by Sarah. Once recruited, the mentors undergo two initial days of rigorous training, followed by a top-up day closer to Induction in September. Initial training covers the basic tenets of mentoring:

- what is a mentor;
- skills and qualities required;
- effective communication;
- questioning techniques.

Student mentors are also grounded in the NTU graduate attributes to promote the notion of independent learning, notably: aptitude for independent, critical thought and rational inquiry; and intellectual curiosity, enthusiasm for learning and an aptitude for self-directed learning.

The reasoning behind this is to encourage the mentors to resist requests to proofread students' work, answer their questions or do the work for them. This maxim has become our mantra:

> Give a man a fish and you feed him for a day. Show him how to fish and you feed him for a lifetime.

The training is highly interactive and designed to progressively model behaviours expected of the mentors in their sessions, to encourage engagement. The following question from an online survey, sent following the training, elicited responses which all highlighted the engaging and highly social nature of the model demonstrated.

What Did You Like Best About the Training?

The role-play – it helped me to gain a deeper understanding of student mentor sessions.

Engaging in group activities, getting to know the other mentors.

That you got to know all the other mentors. The role play scenarios.

These responses appear to echo the benefits of the social nature of learning as proposed by Vygotsky (1978), and thus through promoting and modeling a pedagogy of engagement we also engage those we have employed to facilitate it.

Much evidence exists to suggest that students supporting students can be beneficial in engendering a culture of engagement. It would appear from our mentors' reflections that whilst institutional interventions put in place to improve and enhance the learning experience can deliver beneficial outcomes to students accessing such schemes, so those employed in these roles also benefit, in terms of their own enhanced engagement, development of sense of belonging and increased confidence. Rebecca and Sarah have outlined how their involvement in the Student Mentor Scheme, combined with other such interventions, has helped to erode a sense of isolation and anxiety and embed good practice into their own study habits. Moreover, their involvement in the scheme has helped to build confidence, increased their understanding of what is required at university and enhanced their ability to reflect on their own performance.

Part III

Engaging students

Chapter 13

'What matters in the end is to act well'

Student engagement and ethics

Carol Taylor and Carol Robinson

Introduction

This chapter focuses on ethics and student engagement practices in Higher Education. Many understandings of student engagement recognize that ethics are deeply embedded within student engagement practice and theory (Bryson, Chapter 1 of this volume; Nixon, 2012); yet ethical issues are rarely discussed explicitly, specifically or in any detail. In this chapter we aim to address this neglected area. The chapter considers various ways of conceptualizing ethics, proposing 'practical wisdom' as an ethical means to 'act well' in student engagement practices, before exploring some ethical practices, problems and dilemmas in detail through three empirical case studies of student engagement in Higher Education. The first case study focuses on a study of students and healthy eating; the second concerns ethical issues within a project on student transitions; while the third case explores the ethical challenges involved in student-to-student peer reviewing processes on an undergraduate module. The first and second cases deal with ethics in research projects, while the third considers ethics within teaching and learning.

The cases were chosen for three main reasons. Firstly, to illustrate how we have taken ethics into account at various stages of planning and designing student engagement within research and teaching. Secondly, to illuminate the ways in which ethics need to be taken into consideration at different 'levels', that is, at the institutional level, at the level of lecturer–student relations, and at the student-to-student peer level, although in practice these levels are not separate but intermingle in specific instances of action. Third, to explore some finer details of ethics in practice which demonstrate how knotty ethical issues arise unexpectedly and require a response 'in the moment'. Taken together, the cases illuminate aspects of the enactment of ethics and the need for an understanding of broader ethical principles in student engagement practices. Given that one of us (Carol Taylor) was, at least initially, responsible for originating both research projects and was the students' course lecturer, we spend some time considering the ethical issues which arise from the entangled nature of the staff/student power dynamics, authority and ownership in the three cases, which, as others have shown, is a recurrent concern of participatory research of various kinds (Bland, 2006; Bovill et al., 2011; Cornwall and Jewkes, 1995; Godwin and Neville, 2008). It is for reasons such as these that we hope the chapter will be of value to those new to student engagement who are thinking about how to take ethics into account in their own practice, as well as serving as a prompt for more experienced student engagement practitioners in their on-going reflections on the nuanced and contingent nature of ethical dilemmas which arise in situ with students.

Our understanding of student engagement in this chapter is consonant with Bryson's definition (Chapter 1 of this volume) which states that student engagement

> [. . .] is about what a student brings to Higher Education in terms of goals, aspirations, value and beliefs and how these are shaped and mediated by their experience whilst a student. SE [student engagement] is constructed and reconstructed through the lenses of the perceptions and identities held by students and the meaning and sense a student makes of their experiences and interactions.

Such a definition is important, in our view, because it recognizes student engagement as a holistic, dynamic and socially constructed process and acknowledges that every student is an individual and therefore different. In a similar vein, Taylor's (2012) view of student engagement as a heterogeneous field of practice which means different things to different people in different contexts has encouraged us to foreground the emergent and contextual nature of ethics. There is no doubt that this engages us as staff in working in more ethically nuanced and reflexive ways than we would if we were simply following a set of ethical 'rules', although it does seem at times (for example, where ethics committees are concerned) that aspects of university procedure work against adopting a flexible, contextual ethical approach. Thus, in what follows we have kept Bryson's (p. 17 this volume) comment in mind: 'Whatever method we use to study SE, we need to problematize the issues' – and this is what our discussion below aims to do.

The chapter begins with a discussion of different types and understandings of ethics. The three cases are then described. This is followed by a discussion in which the two authors explore ethical issues from the three cases in some detail. The chapter ends by promoting the advantages to be gained from adopting a bricolage approach to ethics in student engagement practices.

Ethics: types, principles and frameworks

Given the absence of explicit discussion of ethics in student engagement discourses, we begin with a 'back to basics' approach to ethics: we provide some useful definitions, consider two important philosophical understandings of ethics and, from this, propose a hybrid – or bricolage – approach to ethics. We then introduce Aristotle's (1953) notion of *phronesis* (which translates as 'practical wisdom') which, we argue, serves as a helpful guide to 'acting well', that is, in a principled and ethical way, in student engagement practices.

The common-sense view is that ethics concerns the rules or moral principles which govern behaviour. Such moral rules may be legal (socially proscribed behaviour punishable by law) or normative (socially acceptable codes of behaviour) but are often open to different interpretation and application by different people, which is why so many ethical disputes arise in society. The term *axiology* is used to describe the internal value systems which influence ethical decisions and actions. Philosophical discussions often make a distinction between morality, which concerns personal character and the moral principles of an individual, group or tradition, and ethics, which refers to the study of morality and, as such, focuses on the social systems within which those moral principles are put into action. In studying ethics, philosophers have distinguished between three different 'types' of ethics: normative ethics, social or religious ethics and positive morality. Normative ethics refers to standards of right and wrong, good and bad which *ought* to be accepted; social or religious ethics, relates to, for example, Sikh ethics or Confucian ethics; and positive morality derives from adherence to a doctrine or profession, for example doctors are regulated by the Hippocratic oath. In addition to such distinctions, some theorists separate a social science analysis of ethics which they call 'descriptive ethics' from a philosophical analysis of ethical concepts and beliefs referred to as 'metaethics' (Mautner, 2000: 180–181). We take a 'descriptive ethics' stance in this chapter, as our principle aim is to describe and analyze ethics in action within student engagement practice.

In the European philosophical tradition, there have been two contrasting ways of thinking about ethics: deontological ethics and consequentialist ethics. Deontological ethics derive from the Enlightenment philosophy of Immanuel Kant who thought that 'reason' was the highest human faculty. According to Kant (1997; 1998), we are free, autonomous and rational human beings and our reason enables us to recognize that our duties derive from observing consensual social laws in accordance with other rational individuals. Kant's deontological ethical scheme proposed the existence of moral laws which are universal, general and unconditional. Because the moral law applies to all rational and autonomous human beings it follows that the moral law is equitable, i.e. universally applicable, and the exercise of reason enables us to accept it as such. At a practical level, deontological ethics propose that universal ethical laws exist 'beyond' each individual; that they be applied irrespective of individual circumstances; and that reason obliges us to act in accordance with these universal moral laws. Applying deontological ethics to student engagement would, in simple terms, require us to regulate *all* relations with students on *all* occasions in accordance with a dispassionate, rational set of principles and laws decided *in advance*. Such a stance clearly has the distinct ethical advantage that all will be 'equal before the law'. However, it raises some profound questions for the practice of student engagement. For example: how does it translate into the need to engage students from different cultures or ethnic groups, or those suffering from inequalities due to gender discrimination, social class positioning or disability? Do we need a different sort of ethics for these groups? Should we not take into account the specific context in which the issue arises? And what about our relations with individuals – can they be regulated so rationally? What about emotion, altruism, personal likes and dislikes, prejudices even i.e. all those things that make us ordinary, fallible (and sometimes unreasoning and unreasonable!) human beings?

For those within the consequentialist tradition, the gap between the Kantian ethical ideal and the human actual is impossible to bridge and so they propose an alternative way of thinking about and 'doing' ethics. Consequentialist ethics can be traced back to Jeremy Bentham and, in simple terms, works on the idea that thinking about the consequences of our actions – their effect on others, or the outcomes or results our actions may lead to – will be the best guide in enabling us to act well and conduct ourselves rightly. For Bentham (2005) consequentialist ethics underpinned what he called 'utilitarianism', which is based on the view that social well-being is produced by maximizing happiness and minimizing pain for the greatest number of people, and that taking the consequences of our actions into account provides an effective practical and moral means of achieving this. In terms of student engagement, consequentialist ethics sounds promising: it enables us to pay attention to situations and contexts; to think about the needs of individuals and social groups; and it looks like it may lead to increased social justice if it is concerned for the happiness of the greatest number. But what if we can't foresee, or know, the consequences of our actions? Or if we misjudge them? What about unintended consequences which may, in the end, do more harm than good? What place do moral principles or religious ethics have in consequentialism? And who defines what is happiness for the greatest number? There may also be instances where we knowingly implement measures intended to improve experiences for the greatest number, while simultaneously being aware that such action may not be in the best interest of some, albeit a minority of students. These are thorny ethical issues.

To make matters even more complex Wiles (2012) argues that there are not two, but four, approaches to ethics. She supplements deontological and consequentialist ethics with a further two approaches: 'ethics of care' and 'virtue ethics'. Wiles advocates that 'ethics of care' focuses on participants and their communities and asks what constitutes compassionate and caring action for specific groups. Virtue ethics, however, focuses on the integrity and moral character of the researcher. In the discussion which follows, we draw on these four approaches to discuss details of student engagement practice in our three cases. We use this discussion to demonstrate that, like most other research and educational practices, student engagement practices require a judicious mix of all four ethical approaches. Drawing on Sikes (2010: 14) we argue that ethics-in-action in student engagement requires a bricolage approach, that is, an approach which combines elements of deontological ethics, consequentialist ethics, an ethic of care and virtue ethics. It is only by taking a bricolage approach that the ethical complexity of situations, contexts and relations can be adequately addressed.

It is worth pointing out that our three case studies are based within a research framework of 'positive morality'. This 'positive morality' is derived from our adherence as professional university researchers to the British Educational

Research Association's (BERA's) *Ethical Guidelines for Educational Research* (BERA, 2011). Like many ethical codes, the BERA guidelines cover responsibilities to participants, to the research community and to the general public. These responsibilities include: informed consent, access, disclosure and protection of information, the right to withdraw, the protection of children, vulnerable young people and vulnerable adults, the use of incentives, awareness of benefits or detriments arising from participation, rigorous data collection, and honesty in reporting and publishing findings. The BERA guidelines are also framed by an explicit set of principles which require that 'all educational research [. . .] be conducted within an ethic of respect for: the person, knowledge, democratic values, and academic freedom' (BERA, 2011: 4).

Having introduced four ethical approaches and the frameworks of positive morality to indicate why ethics is fundamental to student engagement practice we now consider Aristotle's concept of *phronesis* as a useful guide to ethical action within student engagement.

Phronesis, or Aristotle gives us a helping hand!

Aristotle's concept of *phronesis* is based on principles of good judgement and prudence and can help us decide what particular ethical response is called for in our everyday actions. Aristotle (1953: 150) sees *phronesis* as a link between the general and the particular, and explains that *phronesis* involves the 'prudence [. . .] to be able to deliberate rightly' not only about what is 'good and advantageous to himself [. . .] but what is conducive to the good life generally'. Putting Aristotle's concept of *phronesis* into practice in student engagement activities requires us to use our 'practical wisdom' to formulate concrete goals for virtuous action, in the knowledge that these goals and actions will differ with different individuals and circumstances and will lead to the general good. This leads us to the crucial point made by Israel and Hay (2006: 2) that 'ethical behaviour helps protect individuals, communities and environments, and offers the potential to increase the sum of good in the world'. If we see student engagement as infused with ethics both as immediate action and as an enhancement of the good life, then Aristotle's *phronesis* offers us a way of making ethics practical and it gives an ethical basis for *doing* student engagement in a principled and ethical way. As Eagleton (2008: 108) asserts, Aristotle thinks that 'to act really well we must have certain appropriate judgements, feelings and attitudes; but what matters in the end is to act well'. We now turn to our three case studies.

Three case studies

Case study I: Feed Your Brain: first-year undergraduates and healthy eating

The purpose of the Feed Your Brain project (Figure 13.1) was to map students' eating patterns during their first term at university. I (Carol Taylor) worked with

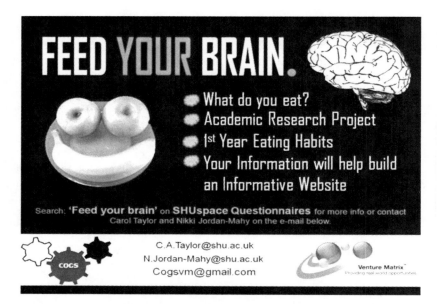

Figure 13.1 Publicity poster for the Feed Your Brain project

two other academics (Nikki and Peter) and a group of second-year undergraduate students from a university commercial enterprise called Venture Matrix which 'supplied' students on a client-contract basis to work with staff on research projects. Feed Your Brain was a student engagement project in two senses. First, it engaged the Venture Matrix students in a piece of real-world research. The students worked with Nikki and me to design a questionnaire which the students then piloted, redrafted and implemented via the university virtual learning environment. They also collected the data, analyzed it, and presented the results in a written report. Second, 147 first-year students from across the university completed the questionnaire. Their responses provided data on the relationship between students' engagement with learning, their eating patterns, moving from home to university or private accommodation, developing new friends, and participating in new leisure activities and study patterns.

Case study 2: the Student Transitions and Experiences Project

The Student Transitions and Experiences Project (STEP) was a six-stage project funded over two academic years which involved students on a BA (Hons) Education Studies undergraduate degree. The aims of the project were threefold: to research the first-year student experience in order to aid transition into university life and learning; to enhance student engagement through visual and

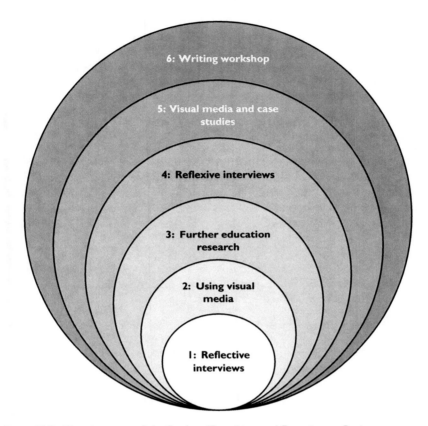

6: Writing workshop

5: Visual media and case studies

4: Reflexive interviews

3: Further education research

2: Using visual media

1: Reflective interviews

Figure 13.2 The six stages of the Student Transition and Experiences Project

creative research methods; and to support independent thinking, learner auton-omy and student skills development. The project used a collaborative, participa-tory research design which meant in practice that its development through the six stages arose through dialogue between staff and student participants. The six project stages are briefly outlined in Figure 13.2.

The project included interviews, the production of visual texts and creative writing which enabled students to capture their experiences of transition in ways which were meaningful to them as individuals.

Case study 3: a level 6 BA (Hons) Education Studies and Sociology module

This case study concerns an innovative approach to teaching and learning in a final-year module on a BA (Hons) Education Studies and Sociology undergradu-ate degree. Students used a narrative approach to write original creative texts, combined these with sociological analyses and produced an article for a web journal. Students participated in generating criteria for peer reviewing articles, participated in an anonymous class peer review process, evaluated peer feedback and redrafted their article in response to feedback. All student articles were published in a web journal. Overall, the module enabled students to engage in an authentic cycle of academic knowledge production.

Exploring ethics through the three cases: problems and possibilities

We now focus on some of the ethical issues which arose in these three cases and we use the cases to explore what we understand as 'acting well' in enacting ethics in student engagement practices. This section is a written account based on verbal discussions between the authors in which CR (Carol Robinson) asked CT (Carol Taylor) a series of questions which turned the spotlight on different, sometimes interrelated, aspects of ethical practice.

> CR: The most fundamental question with student engagement, whether it is through a research project or teaching and learning activities, is why was it carried out in the first place?

> CT: The three cases have different motivations for promoting student engagement. Feed Your Brain originated in a staff seminar to promote interdisciplinary research. The three members of staff discovered a shared interest in student cultures and healthy/unhealthy eating and followed this up by developing a research bid together, which obtained a small amount of seedcorn funding from the university. Each staff member had different motivations for modelling a research project around student engagement: Peter wanted to commission a viable project contract to engage his Venture Matrix students in a client-commissioned research bid; Nikki wanted to engage her BA and MA students in interdisciplinary research; and I wanted to engage students as researchers in order to incorporate their knowledge of student cultures in the design of the questionnaire. In contrast, the Student Transitions and Experiences Project (STEP) and the Education Studies and Sociology module were both 'disciplinary'-based initiatives, located respectively within a particular department, course team and subject (Education Studies). Both of these cases were more directly focused on enhancing students' engagement with their courses of study and more broadly with the university, whether that was by reflecting on experiences of transition and individual engagement (in the STEP project), or by facilitating increased student engagement via learning and assessment outcomes (as in the module).

> CR: How did the different origins and motivations for each case influence your consideration of their ethics?

> CT: The main thing in thinking about ethics in Feed Your Brain was that this project was based on a 'commissioning client' model of student engagement

where students were 'hired' to implement the wishes of the 'client' (Peter, Nikki and myself). This contrasts with the other two cases which originate in a dialogic tradition of student engagement and are much more closely aligned with the ideas expressed by Bryson, quoted above, which emphasize students' identities, meanings and perceptions. The 'commissioning client' model was more of a business-oriented 'professionalization' of institutional modes of student engagement in that lecturers are 'clients' who hire students to fulfil a particular brief within the terms of a contract which specifies the roles and functions of each party. From the start, this situates the lecturer–student relationship within a hierarchy of power. What I mean by this is that power clearly lies with the lecturer, who has an overtly directive (and perhaps even 'authoritarian') role in relation to the student, while the student's role is based on responsibilities to meet the client's needs and obligations to deliver the requisite outputs. Power is distributed unequally and hierarchically. Kreisberg (1992) refers to this as 'power over'. This feels very different to the way of working in the other two cases which begin with a presumption of dialogue and aim to minimize power relations between students and lecturers, a model which Kreisberg (1992) characterizes as 'power with'. There was, of course, some overlap: the Feed Your Brain questionnaire design came out of student–staff dialogue and negotiation but within the frame of 'meeting the client's needs'.

In terms of ethics, both of these ways of 'doing' student engagement highlight the importance of virtue ethics which, as we saw earlier, is about the researcher's integrity and moral character. In the cases here, the possession, use, and potential abuse, of power is an on-going and continuous test of the 'virtue' of the lecturer. In the case of Feed Your Brain, our virtue as lecturers was put at stake through the ways we sought to put in place mutually respectful relations with students so that any 'power over' was enacted with care and respect, and not with domination. In contrast, in the STEP and module cases it was crucial that the lecturers' virtue ensured that acts of 'power with' were perceived as honest, authentic and truly dialogic, not 'fake' or tokenistic. This was an on-going concern and meant that the sharing of explanations, open dialogue and honest listening was enacted at every step of the way. Thus, one's 'integrity as a researcher (as opposed to completing an ethical approval form) demands that we live out a series of moral virtues, not just espouse them' (Macfarlane, 2012: 14).

> CR: I like that phrase 'living out'. It points to the embodied individuality of ethical relations. One final question on the cases: did their different sources of funding influence the role of their 'stakeholders'?

> CT: In all three cases, the university was the 'primary' stakeholder, but had minimal influence in how the projects were run and what came out of them. Both Feed Your Brain and the STEP project were subject to approval from the university ethics committee, I was required to write a project report for each, and I was accountable for budgetary management. The institutional

managers for Feed Your Brain required students to attend a dissemination event along with all other projects they had funded. It is perhaps worth saying that I had extraordinary latitude with the STEP project. Once approved by the university ethics committee, the project belonged entirely to the participants and myself. This high level of trust – financial, organizational and methodological – was beneficial in a number of ways. In practice it meant we had complete freedom in implementing the collaborative ethics of the project and that, in turn, gave us a real sense of 'ownership'. It also meant that we were not expected to produce specific outputs and this acted as a spur for us to work collaboratively on a conference presentation, staff development events and a journal article. This degree of freedom is quite rare. The module was part of undergraduate teaching and learning but its reflexive and dialogic ethos meant we were all, if unequal, stakeholders. On reflection I think that, in the case of the two projects, the fact that the university as stakeholder took a 'hands-off' approach, once through the ethics committee, made me even more attentive to ethics on a day-to-day basis.

CR: Can you talk me through the process of obtaining institutional ethical approval? What issues arose regarding ethical approval?

CT: The university, similar to other universities, requires all research to be submitted to the ethics committee. Each submission takes the form of an ethics proforma detailing the project outline, a Participant Information Sheet, copies of research instruments, and proposed consent letters. The STEP Project was submitted to the university ethics committee and was rubber-stamped. Not so with Feed Your Brain! Off the record conversations indicated this was one of the 'trickier projects for the ethics committee' and it went back to the committee three times with further details, amendments and clarifications before receiving final approval. On its first submission, I received the following responses:

- On the questionnaire you need to stress that participation in any follow-up focus group is purely voluntary.
- The numbers of focus groups are not specified or numbers of student participants. Will students be trained to run these and instructed on ethical procedures?
- There appears to be only one participant information sheet, but participants in the focus groups need one so that they have contact details for the researcher, should they want to withdraw or gain more information etc.
- Participants logically cannot withdraw at any time. A cut off point for withdrawal of focus group or interview data needs to be given. This is usually two weeks after the data collection event.
- There is nothing about how the data will be stored and eventually disposed of.

I addressed these comments and resubmitted a revised ethics proforma. The committee then requested a revised copy of the Feed Your Brain questionnaire asking that I change the wording on one section of the questionnaire. I changed it and this third time ethical approval was granted. While these delays were frustrating, this case is an excellent example of the need to attend to the minutiae of ethical details. I think the ethics committee was concerned that this was a research project designed by students (albeit in collaboration with staff), implemented by students, which sought to obtain data from students. As such, it throws up ethical issues about students' involvement with peers which go well beyond the usual concerns relating to informed consent, confidentiality and anonymity. From this perspective, the detail, care and scrutiny the FYB [Feed Your Brain] proposal was subjected to in the end gave me greater confidence and security that I had 'acted well' in establishing an ethical basis for the project. To pick up on the terms used earlier, I felt reassured that the project's deontological ethical basis and its fundamental principles were sound.

CR: Were there were any issues around sample of students? Were students given incentives to encourage them to participate?

CT: The undergraduate module did not require a 'sample' as such. The module was part of students' third-year degree studies, it did not add to their workload, it was simply part of the teaching and learning design. Having said that, there was a high level of student choice around the content and style of their written finished article: students used narrative to explore personal experience; they worked together to negotiate the format and kind of peer review feedback they wanted; and they had choice in terms of their weekly verbal participation in sessions. In contrast, in each of the funded projects, students were self-selecting, and not a representative sample.

The whole BA (Hons) Education Studies first-year group were invited to participate in the STEP project. In stage one, 12 participated out of a class of 24, fewer participated at each subsequent stage, and by stage six, five students participated in the writing workshop. The issue of incentives for participation is clearly relevant to this case. Book tokens for £20 were given to those who participated in stage three in recognition of the amount of independent time involved, and there was a small hourly payment for the five students who participated in stages five and six. Given that the students pressed for the continuation of the project beyond stage three without any awareness of, or desire for, a possible payment, made the payment, like the book token, less of an incentive as such and more of a recognition of the commitment, time, energy and effort they put into the collaborative development of the project. For me, an 'incentive' is something of an inducement, whereas the STEP students did not need any persuasion to be involved; they were keen and willing to engage above and beyond my expectations, and in their own time. In recognizing this, I think the book token and small hourly payment is in line with BERA (2011: 7) guidelines which state that 'researchers' use of incentives to encourage participation must be commensurate with good sense and must avoid choices which in themselves have undesirable effects (e.g. the health aspects of offering cigarettes to young offenders or sweets to school-children)'.

CR: I want to pursue this a little further: first, can you comment on the question of who participates and what do you do about those who choose not to participate? And second, on payments to students – what do you pay them for? What does that oblige them to do?

CT: In response to the first question, I was aware that approximately half of the year group had chosen to participate in stage one of the STEP project and a small number continued through all stages. I was very careful to ensure that this did not privilege the participants above the non-participants. I did this in practice by ensuring that the project was not discussed in class sessions and by emphasizing that it was entirely separate from all teaching, learning and assessment on the degree. I also explained to the non-participants that the less tangible benefits which might be seen to accrue from participation in the project – such as the communication or presentation skills which come from attendance at a conference, and the confidence which may go with this – could be obtained through other avenues such as the careers service, and forms of participation in university life. Nevertheless, there was a felt sense at least from one participant that 'working with a doctor' (her words) on a research project gave her access to skills and beneficial dialogue closed off to her non-participating classmates. I did not anticipate such a comment and decided, in that moment, to call on *phronesis* to invite this participant not to see me as a 'benefit' but instead to think of herself in relation to others, so I asked her: what have you got from the project which will help you work in new or different ways with others? My hope was that, in shifting the conversation away from a presumed elitist alliance with me towards her ethical relations with others, I would be able to convey at least some of Kemmis's (2012: 10) point that 'the wise and prudent person [. . .] recognizes that to have an experience is to be formed by it'.

With regard to the other questions – what do we pay them for? What does that oblige them to do? – students in the STEP project were paid for designing and conducting research with sixth-form students (stage three), for producing a second video (stage five) and participating in the writing workshop (stage six). While the BERA (2011) ethical guidelines are right to draw attention to the bias incentives may produce, in the STEP project the open design meant that any texts, visual or written, students produced would be acceptable within the emerging remit of the project. Nevertheless, the payments as incentives did generate some unforeseen ethical problems. One student, Alicia (a pseudonym), came to the two allocated days for stage five of the project but did not make any effort to produce a video or to participate by helping anyone else make their video. Because she attended, however, she got paid. She also attended the first morning of the writing workshop, did not contribute, and got paid for that but failed to attend the rest of the workshop. Other participants expressed annoyance at Alicia's presence ('she's only turning up for the money') and subsequent absences ('we knew she wasn't committed to this'). The group discussed this with each other and then with me. I initiated a group discussion about how different people have different reasons and motivations regarding participation. While this discussion created a space for expression of emotions and led to expressions of greater tolerance of different levels of commitment, the group agreed that Alicia ought not to be allowed to continue in the project if she turned up again.

The ethics of the group's decision to exclude Alicia troubled me until I recalled Sen's (2001) idea of 'substantive freedom'. Sen argues that people have the capability – the freedom – to choose the life they value. In relation to the STEP case, the community constituted by the project expressed their freedom to put the collective life of the project above any individual. In doing so, they balanced intrinsic/internal commitments (to the collective project community) against external commitments (money and/or individuals). This instance remains ethically uncomfortable. However, the idea of substantive freedom is useful in accounting for inclusion and exclusion at this point in the project as it enables us to think about how ethics in their concrete, specific manifestations relates to communities and external inducements (payment for attendance). More broadly, it is based in a consequentialist view of ethics which explains that this particular event – the 'exclusion' of Alicia – is an outcome of a) Alicia's own freely chosen actions and b) the group's ethical commitment to the group's 'substantive freedom'. It seems to me that the group's decision was an enactment of *phronesis* and the idea that practical wisdom arises in specific contexts.

So, does payment carry obligation with it? With regard to the STEP project, for Alicia, and for the group, the answer is clearly no: Alicia got paid and did not feel obliged to attend; the group also got paid and did not feel that the payment required them to include Alicia because her motivations undermined their sense of group commitment, which was more important to them than money. Thus, individuals are not obliged to act in a particular way as a result of receiving a financial incentive.

CR: You mentioned earlier that you saw power as an ethical issue. Can you talk us through an example of this?

CT: The undergraduate module included a student-to-student peer reviewing process, the purpose of which was to engage students in a 'real life' experience of peer reviewing an academic article. Students peer reviewed each other's draft articles anonymously, received feedback, revised their drafts and submitted the finished article for publication in a web journal. There were two particular ways in which this process gave scope for the operation of forms of 'power over', to go back to Kreisberg's useful concept.

First, I had power over the students through my role as module leader: I drew up the anonymous list and allocated peer reviewers by making judgements about different students' 'level' and 'ability' to give constructive and developmental feedback to their peers. This process undoubtedly entailed making judgements about individual students and their capabilities based on normative and subjective inferences about past performance and what I could deduce from discussion about their orientation and commitment to the peer review process. On reflection, I was caught between using an anonymous peer reviewing process to promote an innovative form of student engagement in teaching and learning practice, and at the same time I was conditioned by the authority conferred by my role as lecturer to 'manage' the process. While my ethical motivation was guided by the question 'who will do the best job at giving peer feedback to this particular student?' my management of the process undoubtedly had differential results for different students and conferred differential benefits. Is there an ethical way round this, given that as lecturers we assess students in all sorts of formal and informal ways and that necessarily accords us power over them? I reflected a great deal on Noel's (1999: 274) contention that the origin for *phronesis* as a form of practical reasoning or wisdom is the question 'what should I do in this situation?' This influenced my decision in the second run of this module with a new group of students to abandon my role as 'chooser' of reviewers and, instead, choose names out of a hat. I feel this chance version is, on reflection, a more ethical process.

Second, there was the ethical issue that students ostensibly had the potential for 'power over' each other through the peer review process. In order to discuss this openly and seek to reduce this possibility (at least as far as I was able to), I engaged the whole class in collaboratively negotiating and agreeing the peer review criteria. The class agreed to be bound by the peer review criteria, which specified how much feedback to give, and the type, manner, style and mode of feedback. From this point, the criteria became an 'ethical contract'. Like the BERA (2011) guidelines, it outlined our own version of positive morality guided by deontological principles which all class members freely agreed to abide by. This meant that, without exception, students gave anonymous feedback to each other which was honest, kind and critically supportive. It was, I thought, perhaps too kind, not critical enough! When I commented on this during one-to-one tutorials, students said 'you showed us the horrible feedback you'd been given on your article and we didn't want to say anything that hurt another person's feelings. We thought about what sort of feedback we'd want to get.' What was most significant about this to me was that students had spontaneously and generously originated and put into practice an ethic of care: they showed care for each other's feelings, care for individual well-being, and care for group identity and cohesion. Without knowing of Buber's existence, in balancing developmental critical feedback with emotional support of the other they worked out that 'I–Thou' is a sound basis for good ethical relations (Buber, 2004). This example shows students actively choosing to get rid of their 'power over' one another and, instead, choosing to enact a positive ethic of care. It provides an excellent ethical illustration of Kemmis's (2012: 3) assertion that '*phronesis* is not something that can be taught; it can only be learned and only by experience'.

Conclusion: ethical principles and ethical practices for student engagement

This chapter has opened a theoretical space for what we hope will be the beginning of a lively debate about ethics in student engagement practice. The three cases provide useful insights into *why* ethics are a crucial aspect of student engagement, *how* ethics can be 'put to work' in student engagement practice, and *what* some of the ethical principles are which underpin those student engagement practices which we (as researchers, practitioners and co-authors) have been involved in. The cases illustrate what can be gained in taking a bricolage approach to ethics: on the one hand, it means that our practice is underpinned by certain moral principles; on the other, it means that we have the flexibility to 'tune into' details and devise an ethical response to an individual or group, in the moment, within a particular context.

The chapter has outlined four approaches to ethics (deontological, consequentialist, virtue ethics and ethics of care) and has discussed how these ethical approaches can be enacted and mixed within the particularities of student engagement practice. We hope we have clearly made the point that ethics is never about 'one size fits all'. It is about using our practical wisdom – what Aristotle calls *phronesis* – to act as wisely and as well as we can as embodied, unique individuals within the particular, social encounters we have, while acknowledging that some tensions may remain and some issues cannot easily be resolved. Nevertheless, given that ethics is about 'acting well', and if we can 'act well' in our student engagement practice, then we have the potential to, as Israel and Hay (2006: 2) say 'increase the sum of good in the world'.

Chapter 14

Academic engagement
Engaging who and to what end?

Sam Elkington

Introduction

Emerging student-centred approaches in Higher Education (HE) emphasize students as 'partners', as 'producers', as well as independent enquirers, creative thinkers, team workers, self-managers and reflective learners. In order to achieve these goals, students are expected to be presented with learning experiences that allow them to work with increasing independence, applying their competence and creativity to different types of learning activity. Such developments have been driven by a rhetoric of 'openness' and change, sectorally, regarding the idea of pedagogy and what it means for student engagement, repositioning students and staff to situate both within the dynamic context of the learning encounter, and what is referred to hereafter as 'academic engagement'.

Academic engagement is defined as 'engaging in the activities of a course with thoroughness and seriousness' (Hockings et al., 2007: 721). Here approach and engagement are inextricably interlinked through what Barnett (2007: 70) calls the 'will' of the student, which he claims sets 'the foundations for her knowing and her practical engagements'. Engagement in this sense has a pivotal role in the student's approach to their studies, ranging from a deep orientation towards learning activities in which the student invests something of themselves as a person, to a surface orientation, which lacks such a will. Listening to the voices of students, from this perspective, has less to do with conducting in-depth and wide-ranging interviews or focus groups, and more to do with staff and students working closely, and collaboratively, together on establishing the nature, content, direction and pace of learning.

This chapter documents recent institutional curriculum redevelopment at the University of Bedfordshire that has challenged orthodox thinking about effective teaching and learning. The redevelopment work shifted emphasis away from the traditional focus on structure and content of learning activities and programmes onto the student experience of learning. This has not only challenged educators to think differently about what is meant by engagement in teaching and learning but, perhaps more significantly, to seek out new ways of capturing and evaluating such student-centred approaches to curriculum design and delivery. This chapter draws upon one such attempt, in the form of a project entitled

'Thinking Differently About Engagement: Cases in Sport'. The project started life as a funded teaching and learning study (running from September 2010 to July 2011) and has since informed a further iteration as part of a continued commitment to student involvement in curricula design within my own department (Physical Education (PE) and Sport) between September 2011 and July 2012. I will use the following pages to demonstrate that student learning and development is directly proportional to student involvement, and that the effectiveness of educational practice is related to its capacity to increase the quality of that involvement. Finally, examples of how colleagues and students have tried to put these ideas into practice are presented.

Thinking differently about engagement

In early 2010, the University of Bedfordshire converted from 13-week semesters to 24-week units. All departments were encouraged to use this opportunity to re-conceptualize their curricula. The funded teaching and learning project was timely in this regard as it enabled a more considered and supported effort from my own department. There is little space here to detail the project in a traditional sense. As an overview, the project initially sought to capture the 'personal journeys' of students *and* staff within selected Sport-related undergraduate units. Utilizing a combination of personal reflective blogs and follow-up individual and group discussions over the duration of the 2010–2011 academic year, the approach was aimed at building a dialogue between students and staff so as to gather rich 'situated' data relating to the nature and quality of student and staff engagement amidst new curriculum redevelopment. The sample consisted of two members of staff each individually responsible for managing and delivering one undergraduate unit distributed across years two and three of the PE and Sport programme. Initially, each unit was represented by between 14 (year-two) and 16 (year-three) students, with a total of 23 students completing the full term of the project.

Participating tutors and students completed periodic personal reflective blogs, recording their thoughts and feelings in relation to their respective units. A total of five blog entries were recorded over the course of 24 teaching weeks, resulting in a total of six entries per student and tutor over the course of the project. Follow-up individual and group discussions around the time of reflective blogs enabled me, as principle investigator, to ask for clarification/elaboration on commentaries made, as well as filter and feed back student commentaries anonymously to tutors. Blogs were kept private to enable open and honest reflection, with only the author (tutor or student) and myself able to see entries. In this way, student commentary was used to inform critical friend discussions with tutors that allowed for (re-)evaluation of unit delivery and material, as well as identification of key themes or landmark events in relation to student engagement that might be continued or honed in future practice. Critical friend discussions aimed to be neutral with respect to personal educational philosophies, leaving the choice of position and approach for subsequent practice to tutors. It did, however, centre on a conversational framework that took students' learning needs and styles as the starting point.

The substantial data collected through the initial iteration of the project provided a rich, more nuanced, portrayal of student learning and revealed a number of factors found to determine the nature and quality of academic engagement experienced by both staff and students, namely: the benefits of gaining a better understanding of student engagement; the important role of student–staff interaction and dialogue in facilitating effective teaching and learning; as well as staff gaining a better insight into the nature and quality of their own engagement. These factors will now be discussed in more detail.

Academic engagement 'in-action'

Positioning students as peers who have valuable perspectives in learning is key to supporting equitable partnerships between educators and students with the goal of improving practice. Crucially, enhancing student participation in pedagogical development did not replace teachers' expertise and their role in facilitating learning as much as augment it. In the words of one tutor, this 'provided an invaluable window into how students perceived and were moved, or not, by my teaching inaccessible until now'. Similarly, students reported that working with academic staff to develop teaching approaches and content helped them gain a different angle on, and deeper understanding of, their learning through becoming more aware of, active in, and responsible for their learning both inside and outside the classroom. When tutors engage in dialogue with students about learning, expectations and pedagogical rationales are clarified. If done properly, and genuinely, such pedagogical transparency can lead to greater student responsibility and aligning of expectations in a learning encounter. Furthermore, where student commentary had resulted in noticeable changes in the teaching approaches of tutors, students reported enhanced feelings of respect for and ownership over their learning. A year-two student commented:

> It's a great feeling to know that your lecturer is listening to you and taking your ideas on board [. . .] there has been more emphasis on us coming prepared with ideas about how to explore and make sense of topics covered.

Students recognized the central role of tutors in personalizing their learning experiences, reporting that they best learned when staff encouraged interaction both one to one and collaboratively as a group, where there were opportunities to discuss views and opinions, as well as explore new interest areas. One year-three student acknowledged that 'there has been a definite shift in the way our tutor is involving us in sessions with more emphasis on us to be prepared to work out things both individually and together'. Similarly, tutors revealed that one of the major benefits of having student commentary on their units was that it enabled them to gain a more accurate insight into when students were most engaged (when they best learn) and what this might look like in practice. Crucially, a number of staff referred to the 'changing nature of student engagement' in HE revealing that what was seen 'in-class' (by staff) and what was felt (by students) is 'not always the same thing'. Recognizing the fallacy of the assumption that just because students are present and involved in a learning task does not mean that they are engaged to a degree that learning will ensue, tutors observed that there were perhaps different levels of engagement and that often student commentary would reveal that students had been 'going through the motions' or had not 'bought into a particular learning task'.

Student commentary implied that effective teaching and learning had as much to do with staff and students working more closely together as it did staff setting out a clear structure for learning. Indeed, it appeared that students valued the opportunity to contribute and collaborate on the nature and content of learning activities. One student noted: 'I learn best when I'm involved actively in the session and challenged by what is being discussed. Being lectured at for two hours just turns me off.'

Both tutors noted experiencing a reinvigoration in their practice, reporting feelings of energy and engaging more deeply in their work through opening up opportunities to students to engage actively. One tutor commented that this had provided 'fresh insight and detail into my own teaching that has really got me thinking about how I involve my students in each session'. The reduced immediacy between student and tutor forced both parties to reconcile a changing sense of their relationship with one another through an increasing sense of 'togetherness' that seemed to instil in students the confidence to participate and learn in an active and collaborative way. This confidence gave rise to new forms of engagement and was built on the foundation of trust relations between student, tutor and the learning environment being created. One student commented: 'seeing a difference come about because of your input, i.e. more emphasis on debating in class, has given me confidence and motivation to do my best'.

Unfortunately, such work in many instances is often too intermittent to be particularly valuable. It is important, therefore, to create a learning environment that consistently holds a recognizable shape and structure to allow students (and staff) to build a sense of familiarity, security and trust. Where staff had maintained a consistent and recognizable form to their practice over the course of a unit, it created a boundaried freedom of sorts, wherein student contributions encouraged a clear sense of ownership that took time to realize, as one tutor describes:

> There's definitely a greater sense of students leading the way [. . .] this is something that only became apparent towards the end of the unit, it's taken time I guess for everyone, including myself, to see it and appreciate it.

Such expressions of shared commitment, collaborative effort and trust, illustrate the power of repositioning students as co-creators of learning. A trusted learning environment is more likely to encourage freedom in intellectual risk-taking, creative thinking and complete task involvement. This sense of trust was experienced most often as a letting go (by both staff and students) of the need to control the learning encounter; instead, students become completely engaged with what they are doing in that situation. Letting go in learning means accepting a degree of uncertainty of an outcome which was not always immediately positive for students, as a year-two student explains:

> It was a shock at first, I have to admit, being asked for my input on the unit and how it was delivered didn't sit well with me, I think because I had been used to a certain way of working [. . .] but over time I've been able to see the value personally.

This form of uncertainty certainly resembles the sense of uncertainty captured in reports from both students and staff in relation to their shifting experiences of the learning units in the project. This form of uncertainty was characteristically internal, primarily to do with how individuals come to understand themselves, with their sense of identity (or lack of it). A number of tutors admitted to feeling uncomfortable with the necessary change in power relations that a more democratic pedagogic process requires, with such a shift posing a direct threat to existing privilege and power (of the academic), whilst also working to interpret the new possibilities for student ownership that this shift might engender.

Staff and students acknowledged the potential and very real discomfort experienced when adapting new practices, particularly in the early stages of the project, characterized by an efficacy deficit in taking any kind of risk in relation to their practices. This is perhaps to be expected given that, in the uncertainty of the contemporary HE environment, institutions have moved to reduce risk and, hence, trust, in the way curricula are taught. It is important to stress at this juncture that staff and student commentary implied that trust is mediated by individuals, not systems, and that the social context in which trust is exercised influences the degree to which it is practiced. A year-three student noted:

> The most positive sessions have been when each person has bought in to the material and committed to the session. You know straight away when there are people in the room who just aren't feeling it and it brings the energy down.

There was inevitably a high level of variance in this practice across units, owing to the range of subjectivities which participants in the learning environment bring with them to its culture as a result of their own histories and predispositions. Crucially, however, these differences appeared to provide the spaces for much of the most engaging practice reported by participants, with both tutors and students recognizing the benefits of shared learning experiences. Staff identified benefits not only to themselves and their students but also to the programmes and institutions more broadly. Students, however, reported benefits that related only to themselves and their own learning, suggesting a degree of distrust, perhaps appropriately so, of the wider relevance of such experiences.

Establishing new terms of engagement

While the initial iteration of the project had been effective, in part, in challenging the orthodox thinking about effective teaching and learning in general, an evaluation of the practice implications of the intervention with participating tutors invariably located practices of trust and positive engagement with students' 'best learning', with learning contexts themselves, and the social interactions had therein. This led to calls for a second iteration of the project and greater emphasis on creating an 'experimental culture' of learning, rather than a culture in which curriculum and pedagogy is fully locked-in in advance. In addition to building on the rich data and emergent practice outlined above, two new elements were added as foci for this second iteration of the project.

First, the focus of attention shifted to learning settings rather than isolated pragmatic issues of course delivery (i.e. lecturers, assessments) as had been the case the previous year. Feedback from tutors and students suggested that effective learning stands in relation to, and takes its direction from, socially defined learning environments that can and should be designed in ways that promote and hold concentration, interest and personal growth, presently as well as over time. While there were high levels of student engagement reported across each of the units followed in the initial iteration of the project, these reports remained largely isolated instances of individual student engagement. A second element to be introduced was a focus on unit composition in terms of its aims and objectives, as well as its constitutive activities. Indeed, the first iteration of the project had demonstrated that the places to search for meaningful engagement appeared not to be in the conventional descriptors for individual performance such as learning outcomes, assessment criteria, though these remain important, but instead in the 'process' of student learning itself. It was felt that over-emphasis on aims and objectives often neglected the fact that existing units and how they are taught may be a less than ideal fit with students' learning needs, and could be improved by opening up the range of activities they involve and how these are established through regular dialogue with students so as to encourage a 'process-focus' in student learning.

For the purposes of continuity, the second phase of the project involved the same two tutors delivering the same year-two and year-three undergraduate units. Of the 23 students who completed the first phase of the project, 13 final-year students had graduated, while three second-year students had chosen elective units delivered by another department and so would not be available at level three. Seven year-two students continued onto the designated final-year unit, while a cohort of 17 students chose to undertake the year-two unit. In the end, a total of 18 students completed the full term of the second phase.

Phase two moved beyond merely capturing the 'personal journeys' of students and staff to draw upon those instances during which high levels of engagement had been reported by students in the previous phase, to articulate the kind of conditions that tutors felt could be used as a framework for setting the scene for a more experimental culture of learning and more positive student engagement. To avoid pre-conceived ideas of teaching and learning the constitution of learning settings were left to tutors to work out with their students through dialogue facilitated using the same reflective blogging tool and conversational framework (student commentary anonymously informing critical friend discussions with tutors) initiated in the original iteration of the project. However, this time I would be coordinating this dialogue between tutors and students in relation to three key features that emerged through phase one evaluation that tutors felt could be used as a framework for creating a more experimental culture of learning, namely:

1   pedagogic structure (what to teach, how and by who);
2   feedback and reflective mechanisms;
3   learning environment and atmosphere.

The following discussion draws upon comments of participating students and tutors derived from individual reflective blogs aimed at capturing their continued experience and progress throughout the second phase of the project. These comments highlight different aspects of the nature and quality of student engagement during this time and say something of the range of different approaches to fostering deep engagement that emerged.

Pedagogic structure

The intellectual stimulation necessary for deep engagement is never purely intellectual and, with courses which have a more practical orientation, such as Sport, there is a need to see that energy is generated to enable the intellectual changes to translate into individual, as well as collective, action. This stresses the importance of the emotional and personal side of learning and is dependent upon giving students a strong sense of identity and confidence, generating an important sense of responsibility, commitment and trust that extends beyond the confines of the discrete educational event. For this to happen there must be a supportive system of interaction between the person and the learning environment and its associated activities that engenders and sustains attention, keeping the person motivated and involved. This was most effectively realized when an 'experience first, explain later' approach was adopted, wherein the tutor looks for ways to engage learners in some meaningful experience as early as possible and then uses this experience as an anchor for later, more disruptive work. Here, notes one tutor, 'the requirement of new ideas and information needs to be met by different means than merely through formal and didactic input common to traditional courses'. On the year-two unit, this had evolved to take the form of film reviews, wherein initial student orientations in relation to new topics and material were made through reviewing a series of classic sport-related motion pictures or documentaries. This had initially been rolled out as a one-off seminar activity the previous year, but in the words of the tutor the film reviews:

> Really captured and enhanced the students' sociological imagination to the degree that many had, quite independently, themselves initiated a series of film reviews around other topics. I wanted to build on this good practice and make a bigger deal of it.

This led to more structured interactive workshops being used to discuss and explore students' initial reading of each film. The concept of 'reading' a film involved an active process of students making sense of what is experienced and trying to understand the interrelationships between film text and social theory. In light of the diverse sports-related experiences possessed by students taking the unit, the meanings embedded in the films examined assisted them to make greater sense of their own familiarity with the inner workings of the world of sport and generated a positive approach and attitude towards addressing relevant aspects of theory for practice, rather than the intellectual detachment of the two, as one student explains:

> The film reviews always marked the start of a new topic or series of ideas and helped me connect my thinking and made my learning more real because I could see the different theories at work. Discussing our different interpretations in class then meant I had to be open to other ways of looking and understanding a film and its narrative. This was far more powerful than doing a lecture and seminar. I felt we built a collective appreciation not just of each film we reviewed but also of other peoples' backgrounds and relationships to sport.

Here emphasis is on creating an environment in which students are open to, and become increasingly adept at, learning from each other. This has encouraged a sense of student autonomy in learning and the understanding, skills and disposition necessary to become critically reflective of their own assumptions and to engage effectively in discourse to validate beliefs through the experiences of others who share similar values. Student autonomy in learning is not an add-on. It is the essence of effective engagement.

Feedback and reflective mechanisms

Building in regular reflection on the quality of their engagement through dialogue functioned to offer students clear feedback on how effectively they achieved a balance between the challenges of a particular activity and their capacity to act accordingly. Focusing reflection on the specific quality of individual learning experiences (what interested them about topics and how this could be aligned with their 'best learning') through tutor–student dialogue allowed direct access to the experienced detail of learning. At this point, learning can become intrinsically valuable and was typically characterized by a deep sense of enjoyment, as one year-two student reports:

> We have been constantly challenged with making the material relevant to us and how we learn best [. . .] it's a different mindset, a positive one that really gets you thinking about what's interesting about topics and how you can relate to it. When that connection is made, there has been a real sense of delight and enjoyment for me!

Quality of learning experience can be further enhanced with external supports such as the presence of other learners collaborating and tutors who mindfully model thinking/learning around deliberative tasks. Too much support, either in the form of being told too much information or required to work within tight and controlling structures, may result in feelings of distance and little owner-ship. Too little support is likely to cause anxiety and anxious students will be less willing to take risks. Support from tutors (and peers) needs to be matched by challenging tasks, the opportunity to take risks with new ways of working and the opportunity to re-think assumptions. Achieving a better balance of support and independence is often mediated through specific tasks but can be aided and enhanced by experiencing a wider range of specific roles. For example, a student tells, at length, of their experience of student-led seminars on their final-year unit:

> Planning and delivering a 40-minute seminar for other students in the group was a completely different and very challenging experience but has been one of the things I have learnt most from. Taking a topic and looking at it from a tutor's perspective changed how I saw things. It wasn't enough for this topic to make sense to me; how could I make this make sense to others? And what was the best way of doing this? After agreeing a course of action with our tutor, my group decided to turn the task back around on students to get feedback on their viewpoints. This was invaluable because it gave us something to go on for the debate task we had planned. By the end of the seminar series we had expe-rienced a range of different and interesting sessions and styles of delivery. The fact that we weren't assessed for it didn't even come into it because we were all committed to doing the best we could by the group as well as ourselves.

Asking students to pursue what is intrinsically valuable in each activity requires them to take responsibility for finding an appropriate balance between their own skills and what and how challenges are set. One final-year student wrote about how his awareness of this intrinsic value helped continually reaffirm his commit-ment to full participation in his work:

> I've found concentrating on what interests me and discovering what else I can do in each activity enjoyable. It could be boring to do the same thing over and over, but this way it is never the same. It's a challenge and the chal-lenge for me is enjoyment.

Presenting material through formal inputs, such as lectures, can be difficult to engage with. Transforming sessions into student-managed learning environments has allowed students to find out what is relevant and helpful to their own learning by collaboratively exploring material. This open form of engagement requires each learner to develop their own understanding of a topic, building on what they know already, and sometimes requiring the dismantling or re-conceptualization of existing understandings.

Paying attention to the quality of their engagement with tasks offers students the tools to question and reformulate their approaches to learning in light of their own learning experiences. Helped by someone with a better knowledge of the actual pedagogic challenges attached to tasks, students can start to break down the idea of learning into the pragmatics of confronting certain tasks or activities. In the words of one year-three student, emphasis was on 'finding ways of being present in my own learning that allowed me to see and do more'. Building in regular opportunities to reflect on and make sense of experiences, both inwardly and collaboratively, with significant others was deemed crucial for effective learning, allowing students to refine self-knowledge moving them beyond the detached reflective practice so often adopted on courses.

Learning environment and atmosphere

The sense of intellectual continuity of learning is often difficult to generate in traditional courses, particularly those trying to acquaint students with a wide range of issues. As one tutor noted: 'often we do not make clear to students the areas of the curriculum that they need to concentrate on and which will enable them to access higher level learning later'. Topics that are personally meaningful enable learners to access a different level of thinking about a subject and their ability to grasp these concepts enables them to understand them more deeply. It is important, therefore, to devise learning environments that consistently hold a recognizable shape and structure to allow students to build a sense of familiarity, security and trust in relation to the approach being adopted. Assuming that students can experience timely feedback on their progress during tasks, they can work at bringing appropriate skills to bear on challenging, self-directed, tasks that, for one student, 'gave me a confidence and purpose in my learning. I am definitely more sure of myself and happy to try things out.' The idea of confidence demonstrated here is not confidence per se. Rather, it is students having a heightened sense of themselves and of the world around them; a confidence and investment in their own selves that enables them to match increasingly sophisticated skills to more complex challenges and move deeper into their learning. It is a confidence to have a go, a willingness to go on by themselves through self-motivated individual and collective action. Here, students move forwards in their learning not only because they have the skills and knowledge, but because they sense a self that is adequate and sensitive to such uncertainty. It is a way of looking on what they perceive to be insightful learning experiences, helping them to develop a sense of plausibility in their practice. This is at once a process of engagement in the act of learning and characteristic of the person engaged. A tutor captured this well, observing:

> It is one thing to 'know-of' something in order to satisfy some assessment task and quite another to function in those situations in which knowledge has value and another still to choose to seek out and engage in such situations.

In practice this requires more than 'active' involvement from students. Rather, it calls for a certain orientation to learning, most eloquently captured by one final-year student:

> We have been given freedom and encouragement to think and work in ways that match how we best learnt. But this has meant that we take responsibility for not just our own learning but others' too. You have to be mindful and see the bigger picture.

Such 'mindful' activity has opened spaces for development in which students are able to explore, test, expand, enhance and reflect on their capacities to learn, and to act. In the words of one year-three student: 'I guess you could say we have been encouraged "to be the change".' Here is an orientation to learning that is founded on shared beliefs, values and trust, in relation to learning, that displays a distinctive ethical and moral character. With this in mind, educators have an obligation to assess the consequences of their pedagogic decisions; are they developmental and emancipatory, are they open, or do they reproduce and legitimate traditional approaches? Framed in this way, the tutor must teach the student as much as they teach the subject. One tutor notably reflected:

> It's not knowing when or even how to teach, but when not to teach, when to let go. There's a point when it doesn't belong to me [. . .] it is the students' own, I don't want to institutionalize anything in that sense by assessing this process. To do so would destroy its value.

What has been depicted here is a shared concern for and commitment to intrinsically valuable academic engagement most effectively realized through discursive practices that construct new ways of working, creating new spaces in which to act, requiring both individual and collective participation by students and tutors alike. This has necessitated a reconsideration of the term 'academic engagement' and subsequent recognition that 'engagement in learning' is not a simple state, but a complex of subjective experiences most powerfully realized through immersive engagement brought about through achieving a deep sense of enjoyment in learning tasks.

Focus on enjoyment

We need to be asking ourselves how we, with our students, are going to find such intrinsic rewards within learning activities. The alternative perspective – namely, how to most efficiently hurry through the educational process so that the student can attain the extrinsic rewards, be they a qualification or simply the chance to get on with their 'real' lives – betrays our experiences as educators, belittles the potential of our students, and calls into question the whole idea of a 'Higher' Education and thinking. Enjoyment has been shown to be something that is achieved through effort – is something individuals work for. Crucially, it is a sustainable and repeatable state, though it is sustained only if we commit ourselves to the process of sustaining it. This demands of the student that they place themselves into a conscious relationship with the work they are engaged in and that tutors provide opportunity for them to do so. They must be mindful of their work, observe the task before them, make a conscious decision on how to pursue and engage with that task, and be prepared to take responsibility for the outcomes of their work. But like engagement, we cannot manufacture authentic student enjoyment in learning. Rather, it is a state that sometimes visits us when the conditions are right. Placing the pursuit of enjoyment at the heart of the learning process offers an alternative perspective through which to focus attention onto high levels of involvement in learning and identify, structure and personalize the significance of a learning encounter. This can be used to shape and develop teaching and learning so as to set the scene for the kind of deeply involving self-discovery that would allow students to more regularly experience enjoyment and positive feelings about themselves and their learning. This, in turn, is determined by tutors providing students with the opportunities and expectations to become involved. Certain conditions were found to be prerequisites for encouraging the kind of deep involvement necessary for enjoyment to occur. These conditions are outlined below.

Balance challenges and skills

Deep enjoyment and immersive engagement usually occurs when students confront challenging tasks they have a realistic chance of completing.

Student: How do your skills 'fit' with the task before you?

Tutor: How can you offer a range of potential challenges to your students, both horizontally, from easy to difficult, and in a vertical sense, allowing students to be involved on a variety of levels requiring various skills in order to enjoy it?

Establish clear goals

A connection with the task is usually possible because the task undertaken has clear goals.

Student: What motivates you and what do you want to achieve from the task?

Tutor: How can a student balance their personal goals with the educational goals you have set them?

Clear and timely feedback is needed

There is clear and frequent feedback available on progress in relation to the task undertaken.

> Student: What mechanisms can be used to gather information on your progress?

> Tutor: How do we value different forms of feedback? What is the relationship between feedback and repetition of a task; are students challenged to feed-forward in their work?

Concentration is key

A positive relationship with a task is mostly likely to occur when there is ample opportunity to concentrate on the task at hand.

> Student: How can distractions be eliminated from the learning environment?

> Tutor: What are the structures/mechanisms you are going to put in place at the start of a session/activity to enable students to cross the threshold from distractions of the outside world to complete concentration of the learning encounter?

Let go of the ledge

Allow for and exercise a degree of student control and choice in the configuration of learning activities.

> Student: How can you use your skills and experience to shape the activity in new and meaningful ways?

> Tutor: How do you help students decide where it is appropriate for them to focus their attention?

Look to stretch yourself

Provide opportunities for students to 'stretch' themselves by seeking new challenges in both new and familiar tasks.

> Student: How can you raise the challenges of the activity and what skills will you need?

> Tutor: How do you facilitate self-reflection by students on how learning has changed them? How do you encourage them to value those changes?

Asking a learner when they 'best learn' immediately confronts them with some of their foundational attitudes and preferences in relation to learning, gently questioning their usefulness. Similarly, asking them to then provide personal justification for engaging in certain forms of learning, by pursuing enjoyment, shifts the focus from achieving tutor-set objectives to the achieving of their own objectives. Here, tutors set the parameters of the task in collaboration with students and, therefore, the details of the task, the pursuit of their 'best learning', is a private and self-generated terrain accessed only through on-going dialogue between both parties. This does not imply that the student should avoid difficult or unpleasant tasks. On the contrary, it has been shown to encourage them to construct a positive will to understand and learn from tasks they might otherwise have avoided. Such a will to learn sees the learner seek out engagement in increasingly complex tasks for its own sake.

Clearly this places certain obligations on both learner and tutor in that learning tasks need to be structured in ways that enable a learner to succeed and revisit tasks with increasing subtlety and detail over time. Admittedly, converting from 13-week semesters to 24-week units has provided greater capacity for this to be worked out in the units discussed in this chapter. Here, a focus on practices that might yield enjoyment in learning has offered students an appreciative mechanism for choosing and establishing appropriate levels of challenge that allows them to engage with their learning without boredom or anxiety, or, as one final-year student put it, 'to learn without hiding and be open to difference and difficulty [. . .] because that's what's real'.

Final thoughts

This chapter has presented evidence demonstrating student engagement to be proportional to student involvement, and that the effectiveness of educational practice is related to its capacity to increase the quality of that involvement, more specifically, whether enjoyment is regularly achieved therein. Relatedly, the emergent framework presented in the latter portions of this chapter has been a useful starting point for structuring student engagement. It has been a point of entry for tutors and learners alike, offering both a grounds for dialogue and an 'appreciative' method (seeking students' 'best learning') for charting progress through increasingly sophisticated use of tasks and a reflective and practical language through which the learner can encounter and transform how they learn.

As an appreciative methodology, it takes the idea of the social construction of learning to its positive extreme, especially with its emphasis on dialogue, relational ways of seeing, and its potential as a generative tool. In its broadest sense, it involves systematic discovery of what gives 'life' to learning environments (what is effective and most constructively capable in developmental terms), asking questions that challenge and strengthen both individual and collective capacity to apprehend, anticipate and heighten positive change through learning. It is crucial, therefore, that academic engagement be identified and satisfied holistically, if we are not, by the back door, to reintroduce anxiety, boredom and disengagement in student learning. Why not offer those we teach an unshakable rationale for committing themselves to their own development, based on the simple fact that they enjoy it?

Chapter 15

Using student engagement research to improve the first-year experience at a UK university

Ed Foster, Michaela Borg, Sarah Lawther, Jane McNeil and Ellie Kennedy

In this chapter, we explore student engagement from the perspective of those first-year students more at risk of early withdrawal. These 'doubters' were researched as part of the HERE Project, one of seven studies that formed the major report 'What Works? Student Retention and Success' (Thomas, 2012a; 2012b). We build on our earlier work about those factors that led students to have doubts in the first place (Foster et al., 2012c), but also explore what helped students to engage and to be interested in their subject. We are particularly interested in how universities build up students' capacity to make the transition into Higher Education (HE) and so in the final section share three case studies of strategies adopted by Nottingham Trent University to support students through the pre-entry, initial induction and extended induction phases of the first year (Cook and Rushton, 2008). These strategies were developed in response to, and have influenced, our on-going research into student transition and engagement.

Student engagement

For this chapter, we are primarily interested in academic engagement; specifically how students engage with their studies and how institutions enable such engagement to take place (Kuh et al., 2010). Astin (1977; 1993), Tinto (1987) and Pascarella and Terenzini (2005) all found that the impact of a HE experience depended upon the degree of individual student's efforts and their engagement with the campus environment. At one end of this engagement continuum, we find highly engaged students undergoing transformative learning experiences (Solomonides et al., 2012b). At the other, we find students engaging in a highly instrumental manner (Bryson and Hand, 2007) or withdrawing from university altogether (Ozga and Sukhnandan, 1998; Foster et al., 2012c).

As educators, we are interested in what prevents all students from engaging fully with their studies. One key factor is the fact that studying only forms one aspect of students' lives. Bryson and Hardy (2012: 25) describe student engagement as 'a multi-faceted and dynamic concept that is closely linked to the student's sense of identity and purpose'. This sense of purpose can be unclear, confused and conflicted as university students struggle to manage competing pressures on their time. For example, does a student prioritize paid work with the short term benefits of cash in their pockets, or put more time into their studies with the longer term, but often vaguer, transformative benefits? Furthermore, many students are also engaged with social and family lives (Leach and Zepke, 2012).

Even without the personal distractions, academic engagement is challenging for students. One of the hardest issues is the transition from earlier stages of education into the first year at university. For whilst students clearly possess the skills and strategies to complete their earlier education, they often find that they need to adapt and develop these approaches in order to succeed in a HE setting. Banning (1989) noted that the opportunities for personal growth are greater when the gap between sending and receiving institutions is greatest, but the larger the gap, the more difficult it can be to make the transition. Foster et al. (2011a) noted that in the United Kingdom there are significant differences between the sending colleges and receiving university. Students entering university often possessed naive perspectives of what their coming education would be like and, to make matters worse, the differences between the two systems were often not well explored once they entered HE. Bryson and Hardy (2012) noted that students often found it easier to make the social transition than it was to make the academic one and some students continued to adopt inappropriate strategies for learning at university well into their final year.

The HERE Project (2008–2011)

Between 2008 and 2011, the Paul Hamlyn Foundation (PHF) and the UK Higher Education Funding Council (HEFCE) funded seven projects to explore factors that helped improve student retention. Collectively, this work was known as 'What Works? Student Retention & Success?' (Thomas, 2012a; 2012b). The 'What Works?' programme funded seven studies to explore those factors associated with effective student retention.

Most of the seven 'What Works?' studies set out to test whether or not specific interventions impacted upon student retention. These included targeted co-curricular activities, different types of personal and pastoral tutoring and the impact of student mentors (Thomas, 2012b). The Higher Education: Retention & Engagement (HERE) Project took a slightly different approach (Foster et al., 2011b). The three partner institutions, Nottingham Trent University (NTU), Bournemouth University (BU) and the University of Bradford (UoB), were interested in exploring two areas that appeared to influence student retention: these were the impact of 'doubting' and the impact of course teams. We deal with recommendations for course teams in Foster et al. (2012d) so will concentrate primarily on doubting in this chapter. As the partner institutions were already working in the areas of transition into HE (Cook and Rushton, 2008; Johnston, 2010) and the first-year experience (Upcraft et al., 2005), we focused on the experiences of first-year students.

The HERE Project used a mixed methods approach. Seven large-scale online surveys of first-year students were conducted between 2008 and 2011, with 2992 respondents; in 2013 a further survey was conducted at NTU only, with 441 respondents. We interviewed 67 students individually or in focus groups to provide richer details about their experiences. Finally, respondents' progression was analyzed to test the impact of doubting on subsequent retention.

We would argue that doubting is a legitimate and valuable behaviour for anyone entering a new environment such as the first year at university. We use the term 'doubters' to describe those students who have considered withdrawing from their course or university, although it is important to stress that we do not use the word negatively, or to criticize those students with doubts. We refer throughout this chapter to those who considered leaving their course as 'doubters' and those who had never done so as 'non-doubters'. Although some students will withdraw due to a sudden trigger event or crisis, Ozga and Sukhnandan (1998) argue that more students leave due to a gradual accumulation of problems and doubts. Two UK studies, Mackie (2001) and Roberts et al. (2003), added that if a student had considered withdrawing, they were subsequently more likely to actually leave. Moreover, both studies found differences between doubters who stayed and doubters who withdrew. Importantly, there were far more students who had considered withdrawing than had actually left. Doubting therefore increased the likelihood of withdrawal, but did not make it inevitable; most students who had considered leaving had found a reason or motivation to continue. We wanted to find out what that might be.

At NTU, we have seen the proportion of doubters decline each time that we have surveyed our first years. In 2009, 37 per cent of respondents had considered withdrawing at some point during their first year; in 2011, it had dropped to 32 per cent; and in 2013, to 25 per cent. We believe that this partly relates to improvements in our practices, particularly around supporting students' transition into the University, but it is also likely to reflect the changing financial arrangements over the same time period. In 2011–2012, UK universities could charge a maximum of £3375 tuition fees; in 2012–2013 the maximum rose to £9000. Students were aware of these changes at the time and we believe became increasingly concerned about the financial costs of withdrawing and starting again. At the time of writing, early indications suggest that, across the sector, the number of students who left early in 2012–2013 has also declined steeply. This may have implications for engagement. If students feel that they cannot afford to start again, there is a risk that they will feel trapped, engaging resentfully as hostages rather than willingly as partners.

In Foster et al. (2012c), we reported in detail our findings from the first research cycle. In March 2009, we used an online student transition survey to ask first-year students about their university experience and whether or not they had considered leaving. At NTU, 656 NTU first years responded and 370 granted us permission to track their progress. The following academic year, we checked which students were still at our institution and found that doubters were more likely to have left than non-doubters (98 per cent were still in HE, compared to 91 per cent of doubters[1]).

Importantly, doubting appeared to be part of a pattern. In the 2009 survey, fewer doubters felt that completing their course would help them achieve their future goals (77 per cent compared to 91 per cent of non-doubters). They also reported a more negative experience across 17 different student experience factors, for example 'my subject is interesting'. We conducted a factor analysis of the 17 experience factors and grouped them into three sets: 'academic experience', 'support, resources and future goals' and 'student lifestyle'. A logistic regression was used to test whether or not these factors had any statistically significant association with doubting. The 'academic experience' was shown to be statistically significant. 'Those students with the lowest scores in this factor were twelve times more likely to be a doubter when compared to those with the most positive scores' (Foster et al., 2012c: 103). Student doubters also appeared to have more difficulty engaging with their studies; just under half of all doubters (49 per cent) reported that they were enjoying their course, whereas 83 per cent of non-doubters felt the same. Only 48 per cent of doubters reported that they were working hard, whereas 59 per cent of non-doubters reported the same. Perhaps unsurprisingly, 42 per cent of doubters also reported that they found coping with their course difficult compared to only 29 per cent of non-doubters. The main reasons doubters cited for wanting to withdraw related to their course, particularly issues about confidence about coping with their studies. When asked about reasons for staying, students identified four main reasons. The most frequently mentioned was 'support from family and friends', particularly friends made at University, followed by 'adapting to the course/university', 'personal commitment and drive' and finally, 'future goals, particularly employment'.

In 2011, we repeated the online survey, with slightly changed questions to reflect findings uncovered in 2009. This time, 452 NTU students participated. We were particularly interested to uncover when students encountered doubts and what had helped them to engage with their studies.

In our study, the incidences of doubting were influenced by the time in the academic year. We asked doubters whether or not they had considered leaving at the following times: prior to arrival, during welcome/induction week, during the first term, after Christmas and at the time of the survey (February–May 2011). We also asked them to identify what issues had the strongest influence on them doubting at each time. Relatively few of our respondents had doubted prior to arrival or during Welcome Week. The times when most students considered leaving were immediately before and after Christmas, both times in UK universities when students are facing the first major coursework deadlines and are awaiting feedback from their tutors. The most important reasons for doubting also changed over time. Although relatively few students doubted prior to arrival, their doubts were dominated by anxieties about the student lifestyle. For 57 per cent of those doubting at this time, student lifestyle was the most important factor. However, concerns about lifestyle fell away and by the time of the survey, only 10 per cent felt that it was the most important issue. Prior to arrival, students also had concerns about finance and whether or not the course would help them with their future goals. Both factors declined over time. Other factors fluctuated; homesickness, for example, is not mentioned until the first term but it had dropped away entirely at the time of the survey. The only factor to rise over time related to anxieties about students' courses. No students perceived it as the most important factor prior to arrival but gradually it rose until, at the time of the survey, it was the most important reason to doubt. Forty-two per cent of all doubters cited it as the most important reason to consider leaving. It appears that during Purnell's initial encounter phase (Purnell and Foster, 2008), students are primarily anxious about fitting in and developing a sense of identity amongst their peers. Anxieties about the course appear to rise as assessment starts to loom large on the horizon.

In 2011, we repeated several questions from the 2009 survey in order to check that patterns of engagement were broadly consistent between the two groups. Once again, we found that doubters were struggling to engage when compared to their non-doubting peers. They were less likely to report that the course would help them with their future goals (75 per cent compared to 92 per cent) and were less likely to report that their lecturers were enthusiastic (55 per cent compared to 68 per cent). Eighty per cent of doubters reported that they had struggled with an aspect of their course, whereas only 52 per cent of non-doubters felt the same way. Doubters were less likely to report that they were studying on a friendly course (68 per cent compared to 77 per cent) and had made fewer friends since starting university. Taken together, these results reinforced the picture from 2009: student doubters appeared less engaged with their course, their peers and their tutors. They appeared have been less successful at making the transition into HE than their non-doubting peers.

Numerous writers make recommendations for improving student engagement. These include large-scale institutional models (Chickering and Gamson, 1987; Kuh et al., 2010) specific recommendations for engaging first-year students (Whitaker, 2008; Yorke and Longden, 2008; Foster et al., 2012c) and classroom-focused strategies (Bryson and Hand, 2007). We had already identified that doubters were less engaged than non-doubters and so used the 2011 survey to see if there were any factors that might be more useful for helping doubters to engage with their subject. After some debate, we chose the question 'What makes your subject interesting?' rather than one that specifically used the word 'engagement'. Whilst students would clearly use the word engagement as part of their everyday vocabulary, we felt that its use in an educational context might be slightly ambiguous without extensive clarification. It is possible to be 'interested' but not necessarily 'engaged', nonetheless we felt 'interest' would provide us with more useable responses.

As with the other factors, once again doubters were less likely to report that their course was interesting (60 per cent found it interesting, compared to 86 per cent of non-doubters). We received 340 open responses from the survey respondents. The responses were coded according to the number of reasons given, providing us with a total of 394 reasons given. We then grouped the responses into the categories, as shown in Table 15.1.

Table 15.1 Responses of doubters and non-doubters to the question 'what makes your subject interesting?'

What makes your subject interesting?	Total responses (n = 392)	Non-doubters (N = 293)	Doubters (n = 99)
Intrinsic subject interest	n = 184 (47%)	n = 147 (50%)	n = 37 (37%)
Nature of studying	n = 126 (32%)	n = 85 (29%)	n = 41 (42%)
Career goals	n = 54 (14%)	n = 41 (14%)	n = 13 (13%)
Staff	n = 21 (5%)	n = 15 (5%)	n = 6 (6%)
Other	n = 7 (2%)	n = 5 (2%)	n = 2 (2%)

If we look at the responses from doubters and non-doubters, there are almost identical patterns for 'career goals', 'staff' and 'other'. However, there appear to be important, and possibly useful, differences in the responses relating to 'intrinsic subject interest' and 'nature of studying'. Throughout this section, we have used student quotes to illustrate these themes and coded them with (D) to indicate a doubter and (ND) to indicate a non-doubter.

'Intrinsic student interest' describes those comments in which students reported a strong interest in one or more aspect of the subject matter. This often appeared due to a long-standing interest in the topic, for example, 'I have always enjoyed history' (ND). However, from many of the respondents, we saw a sense that was deeper than just prior interest. These students appear to also feel that the experience of uncovering more about their subject was developing them as an individual. For example, 'It is something I am passionate about. Something that challenges not only my thoughts but also my beliefs. With the knowledge I gain I feel I could make a difference in the world' (D).

'Nature of studying' refers to the forms that learning and teaching takes rather than the subject. Clearly, there will be some crossover between the two, but we were interested in students' reactions to *how* they were taught in contrast to *what* they were taught. The most frequently mentioned themes involved active learning. This related to both opportunities to be creative, but also where students were able to be practical and apply their knowledge, for example, '[I like the] theory side as it helps inform my practical work in the workshops' (D). Our respondents described a range of opportunities to be active, including field work, art and design workshops, architecture projects, practical work with animals and psychology experiments. Secondly, students appeared to like the variety and choice in their course: 'I like the diversity of areas to study within the subject. The course is a mixture of essays, exams and coursework, so there is a variety of ways to work' (ND). Thirdly, students described how the opportunities for independent learning and pursuing topics that interested them had helped make learning interesting, for example: 'I have the freedom to do whatever I want, even when given a brief [. . .]' (D). Finally, a few students described how relationships with their peers made learning interesting: 'I enjoy reading and discussing characters' identities in depth in small groups' (ND).

'Career goals' was the third factor. Students reported both that they were interested in how their studies reflected the world of work and how they believed that it was also preparing them for future employment. One student commented that the course was interesting because 'I want to be the best primary school teacher that I can be and this course teaches me the skills to achieve this goal' (ND). One student doubter went further and reported that 'It's not a subject I've studied before, it has confirmed for me that I want a career in this industry' (D).

Relatively few students mentioned staff directly, although they are implicitly linked to the 'nature of studying' factor. Where students mention staff directly, the most frequently mentioned aspect is responding to lecturers' passion and enthusiasm. For example one student reported: 'I have some good enthusiastic lecturers which helps make even the boring bits interesting' (ND). Secondly, students described situations where lecturers demonstrated genuine interest in the students: 'They are interested in what I think. They are never absent' (ND). Finally, students mentioned how lecturers have an in-depth understanding of their subject, '[lecturers] are really supportive and extremely knowledgeable' (D). As is the case in Chapter 11, tutor knowledge was less important than passion, enthusiasm and interest in the students.

Finally, 'other' factors were those that were more difficult to categorize, including the almost zen-like 'Stupid answer, but it just is' (ND) and heartening 'everything; a bit broad I know, but I don't think I would enjoy my course half as much if it wasn't here at NTU' (D).

The main differences between doubters and non-doubters related to the relative importance of two factors: 'intrinsic subject interest' and 'nature of studying'. As might be expected, those who have never considered withdrawing appeared to have a stronger intrinsic subject interest; 50 per cent cited it most frequently as the factor that made their subject interesting. It appears that these students have found a good match between their goals and aspirations for coming to university and the learning and teaching environment they have entered. However, for student doubters, the 'nature of studying' factor was most frequently cited, accounting for 42 per cent of all the responses. We would suggest, therefore, that the majority of students will be engaged by a combination of their own intrinsic interest in the subject and rewarding, skilful teaching. However, for doubting students, the intrinsic subject interest may be weak, or even non-existent, and so an engaging learning and teaching environment becomes even more important.

Embedding research into the first-year experience

One aspect of NTU's strategy to enhance students' learning opportunities has been recognition of the importance of successful student transition into the first year. From 2005 onwards, NTU has invested time and resources supporting this process. In this section, we present three institutional case studies developed to support student transition and create an environment in which students can engage within both academically and socially (Tinto, 1987). Our work reflects Kift et al.'s (2010) third generation approach to the first-year experience, in that these three initiatives support students' transition through both curricular and with co-curricular initiatives.

For this section, we have slightly adapted Cook and Rushton's (2008) transition model. The three case studies are presented in chronological order. 'Starting at NTU' is an online resource designed to help students engage during the pre-entry stage. The web pages contain both information to prepare students for their forthcoming life and activities to engage with, thereby effectively starting their course induction before they arrive on campus. The second initiative, 'Welcome Week', is a large-scale institutional programme of activities and improved inductions to help students begin to build peer support networks and friendship groups. This takes place during the period Cook and Rushton describe as initial induction. The third case study is also the newest of the three: the NTU course tutorials offer students a small group environment to both build peer support networks and develop a more holistic understanding of their whole course and takes place during Cook and Rushton's extended induction phase.

Case study 1: 'Starting at NTU' (a pre-arrival transition initiative)

'Starting at NTU'[2] is an online resource available to students in the six weeks prior to arriving at University. The site was developed from several different existing online services that enabled students to complete functions such as online enrolment, or find out about the forthcoming Welcome Week programme. However, our transitions research suggested strongly that students would benefit from a more joined-up set of pre-arrival services and resources. We were particularly keen to help students maximize opportunities for developing friendships as early as possible and to help them understand the differences between learning at college and university.

Our overall goals are shown here.

Academic engagement

- Offer students early, timely insights into what studying at university would be like through the use of videos and other resources.
- Help students to engage with the academic aspects of their course through the information provided and pre-entry induction tasks.
- Provide an opportunity for students to start modelling behaviours appropriate for university, particularly independent learning and short research tasks.

Social engagement

- Create opportunities for students to start to engage with their accommodation, course and interest communities through social networks.

- Raise student awareness about the university environment through video and written resources.
- Raise awareness of the social opportunities available to students during Welcome Week and create a sense of anticipation about the forthcoming activities.

One of the most important elements of the resource is the online course induction. Every course is required to upload resources and activities designed to be used before students arrive on campus. These include a welcome from the course team, the induction timetable and information about learning, teaching and support. Perhaps most importantly, every course also provides a short pre-arrival induction activity. These short activities are designed to help students start the process of becoming a learner at university. Academics at NTU have developed four types of activity: short research tasks, engaging with the literature through reading activities, engaging with peers through social media, or reflecting upon key questions about the academic discipline they are entering. These activities are expected to be embedded into the induction week programme.

Evaluation and improvements

We evaluate students' reactions to 'Starting at NTU' in our annual Welcome Week surveys and with focus groups. Overall, the site is well used by new students. In 2012, 85 per cent of students reported logging in at least once and 72 per cent of them reported that the site was useful for understanding what university life would be like. Student feedback about the pre-entry course induction materials has also been positive. Students in the focus groups reported that they valued the fact that they were starting their inductions early. However, we have encountered problems with communicating to students. Not all new students were aware that they had an online induction resource. Furthermore, some students reported that the pre-arrival tasks were not properly integrated into their course inductions and this led to a sense of some frustration on their part. 'Starting at NTU' remains a valuable resource and we will continue to develop it over time.

Case study 2: Welcome Week (an initial induction initiative)

NTU has provided an institutional Welcome Week since 2005 (Foster et al., 2011a). This is a programme of around 450 social, cultural, academic and sporting activities designed to help students cope with their initial encounter with the university and is delivered jointly with our students' union. It is a huge undertaking, but as we have seen from earlier in the chapter, early doubts appeared not to arise about the course, but about fitting in socially and developing a sense of belonging within the course community. Although primarily focused on social transition, we have also dedicated resources to better understanding students' early academic experiences and improving the induction experience.

Our overall goals are shown below.

Social engagement

- Create opportunities for students to develop friendship/peer support networks, particularly for groups of students not living in halls (often mature, local and international students).
- Create positive social experiences other than the alcohol-fuelled events traditionally associated with Freshers' Weeks.
- Promote the wide range of cultural activities available through engagement with student clubs and societies and beyond the university's campuses.

Academic engagement

- Improve the quality of course inductions by informing academics about students' anxieties and experiences of initial induction.
- Encourage the use of activities that build learning communities such as small group work, field trips and ice breakers.
- Continue the earlier work from 'Starting at NTU' by integrating the pre-entry task into the induction programme.

Evaluation and improvements

Welcome Week is now a mature programme of activities. The Welcome Week survey (conducted immediately after Welcome Week ends each year) shows a steady improvement in student satisfaction with their early university experience. In 2005, 80 per cent of all students reported that they were 'satisfied' or 'very satisfied' with their initial university experience. Those students in NTU halls were even more positive: 86 per cent of those students felt the same way. However, in 2005, there were some disparities between the feedback from these students and some of their peers. For example, only 63 per cent of mature students rated their initial experience positively. However, by 2012, 95 per cent of all respondents were 'satisfied' or 'very satisfied' with their initial experience and 90 per cent of mature students felt the same way. Doubting also appears to influence students' satisfaction with Welcome Week. In the 2011 HERE Project survey, 57 per cent of doubters reported that Welcome Week had been a good opportunity to make friends, whereas 65 per cent of non-doubters felt the same way.

Since 2005, we have found that course inductions have got slightly longer and the range of activities is more engaging (Foster et al., 2011a). NTU inductions typically contain less lecturing, more seminars and group tasks to aid both social and academic engagement. In the 2012 Welcome Week survey, despite the wide range of social opportunities available to them, students reported that the place they had made the most friends was through their course induction. When asked to rate their inductions, students rate the professionalism and approachability of their tutors most highly, but report that more could be done to make the inductions interesting.

Case study 3: course tutorials (an extended induction initiative)

In 2011–2012, NTU implemented a new programme of course tutorials. These were designed specifically to improve the student academic experience, enhancing new students' transition into HE and developing both academic and social engagement. In tutorials students are expected to explore meta-themes that bind the course together or to deepen understanding of the individual modules contained within the course. The development of the tutorials was directly influenced by our work on the HERE Project, combined with other research interests, particularly Lave and Wenger's (1991) communities of practice.

Our overall goals are shown below.

Academic engagement

- Use the tutorials to develop a sense of course cohesion. The tutorials are designed to look across modules and help students identify with the curriculum holistically rather than one module at a time.
- Encourage a sense of disciplinarity/professional identity, particularly in later years.

Social engagement

- Develop a core of strong peer relationships.
- Build a meaningful relationship with at least one member of staff to help develop a sense of belonging within the course community.

Academic/social engagement

- Engage students in active learning while encouraging course community building among peers through this structured provision.

Evaluation and improvements

As this is a new and large-scale initiative, we have focused on formative evaluation of the implementation, in order to identify and share successful practices across Schools and disciplines. We found that students value the contact with tutors in a small group setting, appreciating the opportunity to ask questions in a non-threatening environment. In a similar vein, tutors are positive about the close contact with a small group of students and feel that this provides them with an opportunity to understand student support needs better. They also gain an insight into students and their learning that can feed into their teaching. The evaluation also identified challenges to implementation, such as logistical issues around appropriate rooms and timetabling and other issues, such as student attendance and course team ownership of planning and resources.

In addition to our qualitative approach, we collected data through a student transition survey in which, amongst other things, students were asked to identify the benefits from engaging in tutorials. Just over half of the 441 respondents (53 per cent) reported that tutorials had helped to build relationships with academic staff, while half of the respondents said they had improved their understanding of assessment by engaging in tutorials. Slightly fewer (46 per cent) reported that tutorials had helped them feel part of a peer group and the same number said that they better recognized how the course fitted together. Once again, however, the survey illuminated the differences between doubters and non-doubters; non-doubters were more likely to find the tutorials valuable and doubters less so.

As the newest of the three case studies, requiring resources and buy-in from the largest number of people, we envisage that perfecting the tutorials will be a longer process.

Conclusions

Our research continues to show that doubting increases the likelihood of students actually leaving early. It appears clear that early doubting tends to be associated with a student's social life, but that as time progresses, more important anxieties about coping with studies come to the fore. However, even here doubters report that there are factors that help them to engage effectively with their studies. Chief amongst these is an interesting learning and teaching environment.

We have tested the number of student doubters three times since 2009. Over that time we have seen the incidence of doubting fall from one third to one quarter. Although there are other factors to consider, particularly finance, we believe that we have been able to take major steps improving students' early engagement with their new university environment. Clearly we still have room for improvement. However, in each iteration of these three initiatives we have used research findings to explore ways to improve the experience for students.

Notes

1 These rates of continuation are better than those for NTU in the 2009–2010 academic year. We suspect that by answering the survey, these students demonstrated that they were more engaged than many of their peers.
2 www.ntu.ac.uk/startingatntu

Engaging experienced students as academic mentors in support of the first-year experience

The Epistemic Apprenticeship Project

Kay Sambell and Linda Graham

Overview

This chapter describes a project in which second-year undergraduates took responsibility for helping to promote and support first-year students' academic transition. Our model of student engagement framed students as change agents (Kay et al., 2012) who worked as academic mentors within the first-year curriculum, encouraging newcomers to engage in dialogue about effective approaches to learning on the course, where Assessment for Learning (AfL) approaches were routinely used by their teaching staff to promote students' academic engagement. In particular, we draw attention to the insights of seven student mentors who, at the end of the project, decided to produce a booklet for future first years, based on their own experiences of making the transition to university education. The chapter aims to highlight the ways in which the students' voices in the booklet represent a strong sense of personal transformation, which they linked to changing learner identities, the importance of active involvement within programme learning communities, and a perceived sense of belonging (Astin, 1999; Mann, 2001). The importance these students place on the social and affective aspects of learning, rather than purely cognitive or subject-related elements, corresponds strongly with studies which demonstrate the salience, from the student viewpoint, of social integration, community dimensions and the perceptions and identities held by students as conditions for intellectual engagement (Bryson and Hand, 2008; Solomonides et al., 2012b).

Teachers' viewpoints: AfL as a means of improving the first-year experience

In this section, we explain our own perspective on the initiative, and our reasons, as teachers, for bidding for funding to support it. We established the Epistemic Apprenticeship project to further support students' academic transition in an area which had already been the focus for considerable teacher-led pedagogic development and enhancement activity. As part of a five-year university-wide programme of pedagogic innovation, research and development, we had been spearheading the implementation of a holistic model (Sambell et al., 2012) of AfL in a range of programme areas across the university in order to improve student learning. The Epistemic Apprenticeship project sought to take AfL a step further in our own disciplinary field of Childhood Studies.

AfL has, over the past 20 years or so, gained popularity and prominence in universities. It is often seen as a means by which university lecturers can promote first years' academic engagement (Nicol, 2009), largely by promoting deep approaches to study (Marton and Saljo, 1976; Ramsden, 1992). AfL varies in different contexts and encompasses a range of practices but is always based on the fundamental principle of using assessment to improve learning, as well as fulfilling its more traditional function of simply measuring learning. For us, AfL represents a holistic culture-shift, which extends beyond what is commonly regarded as 'assessment' and blends into what is often thought of as student-centred teaching and curriculum redesign based on the integration of learning, teaching and assessment. In practice, this means making a determined move away from a curriculum simply defined as structure and content, towards a view of the curriculum as student learning experiences or the educational conditions in which students are placed. When focused on the first year, the approaches we used shared important elements of Nelson et al.'s (2012) transition pedagogy for student engagement, albeit with a focus on creating pedagogic approaches to encourage the development of understanding, learner autonomy and sophisticated views of knowledge and learning. Indeed, AfL can be seen to represent what Nelson et al. (2012: 127) refer to as 'second-generation' first-year experience (FYE) approaches, with a primary focus on teacher-led interventions within the curriculum via pedagogy, curriculum design and learning and teaching practice in the physical classroom (Kift, 2009: 1).

In the programmes of study which this chapter focuses upon, our main emphasis had been on creating constructivist and dialogic learning and teaching environments which, from AfL perspectives, are seen as key to providing high-quality, timely and sustainable feedback which enables students to self-correct and supports them to develop independence and the capacity for self-regulation (Nicol, 2009; Boud and Molloy, 2013; Sambell et al., 2012). To achieve this, students need to be explicitly supported by their teachers to become assessment literate, which means becoming au fait with disciplinary or professional views of appropriate standards and criteria, and developing the skills to choose and apply appropriate approaches to improve their own work (Price et al., 2012). Active and participatory methods are intentionally created by teachers to give students a fair chance to present and test out their own mental models in formative situations, giving them opportunity to begin to recognize, via informal peer and teacher assessment and feedback, the extent to which they have mastered relevant skills, qualities or understandings, so that they are enabled to monitor and control their own learning (Boud and Associates, 2010). Meaningful interaction with subject matter importantly helps students identify the unspoken assumptions of the discipline, which are crucial to assessment literacy because they underpin the real (but often tacit and therefore invisible) requirements of the assessment tasks that students are asked to undertake (Bloxham and West, 2007). Examples might be, for instance, the design of classroom activities which enable students to apply criteria and standards to previous examples of student work by becoming involved in self and peer assessment activities (Rust et al., 2005), or which encourage students to conduct formative tasks and discuss work on-display by means, for example, of informal poster work (see Sambell et al., 2012). Thus by designing active and participatory learning environments, teachers prepare students for the ways in which they will be summatively assessed, giving them a fair chance to present what they know and can do informally, without being 'caught out' by not having appreciated what is required or not realizing that their approach to a task is misguided or is not meeting the standards required.

Teaching and learning methods based on participation also relate strongly to a student's developing sense of the deep-level principles and rules of engagement in the subject community, which, from lecturers' perspectives, manifest themselves, again tacitly, in the ways of thinking and practising (Meyer and Land, 2005) of the discipline. In order to learn and participate in the complex and situated epistemological practices which characterize Higher Education, learners need opportunities to make meaning and build their own mental constructs, rather than passively receive information and didactic instruction. A main way of developing this appreciation is via active and social learning experiences, where students learn, gradually and over time, to absorb the ways of thinking and practising of the subject domain by being collectively immersed in a constant flow of disciplinary discourse (Northedge, 2003) which they work on with peers and 'old timers', who model their approaches in a process of epistemic apprenticeship (Claxton, 2011). From this viewpoint, dynamic interaction and collaboration between staff and students helps students to perceive what sort of questions a disciplinary expert asks, allows them to think about what makes a good question, and to see how those questions might differ from the ways in which other disciplines might frame them.

Acknowledging potential gaps between staff and student perspectives

However, while such teacher-led AfL approaches relate strongly to two of the dimensions of engagement outlined in Trowler and Trowler's (2010) substantial review, through individual engagement and the development of disciplinary identity via participation, they arguably tend to mainly construct a view of an engaged student in the lecturer/researcher's own image, that is, as someone who shares the teacher's own intense interest in and passion for the subject (Brennan et al., 2010). Recent FYE research is beginning to illuminate how such pedagogic approaches designed to support academic engagement do not work with all students (see, for example, Hockings, 2010). Further, we are also becoming more aware of the inherent complexity and the challenges of developing shared understandings amongst students and staff (see, for example, Sambell, 2010; Price et al., 2012). For instance, recent work on students' views of exemplars (Sambell and Graham, 2013) illuminates the substantial gaps that exist between staff and students' capacity to notice the 'things that matter' (Sadler, 2013) in an academic assignment, even when staff believe they are spelling out their expectations extremely clearly.

Given these challenges, it seemed valuable to explore the potential for enlisting the help of students themselves to enhance the first-year experience. In the following section, we describe the next step in the evolution of AfL approaches in our academic area: the development of a project focused around student-led developments within the curriculum. Here, experienced, highly engaged students volunteered to act as change agents (Kay et al., 2012), who were then given responsibility for aspects of quality enhancement, making active contributions to the shaping of the first years' learning experience on their course.

Student involvement in enhancement activity

The work of the project was supported by funding from a Higher Education Academy Teaching Development Grant scheme, a UK funding stream with a particular focus on student engagement. The basic idea underpinning the Epistemic Apprenticeship project was that the second-year student mentors would be particularly well-placed to directly support newcomers' academic engagement within the context of the discipline, because they had recent first-hand experience of making the transition to academic study themselves, so seemed likely to be in a good position to understand the challenges and issues from learners' perspectives. They also seemed well-placed to help first years look ahead to future possible selves. The grant enabled a range of academic staff and students to work together on an introductory module. Twelve second-year undergraduate students were recruited to become academic mentors who participated directly as agents in the learning experiences of first-year students, working with them to help negotiate what some newcomers experience as quite radical differences between appropriate approaches to study in school/further education and effective approaches in university.

The project developed a bespoke training programme which prepared the mentors to undertake the role of supporting their first-year undergraduates. It is important to acknowledge that the second-year students who were recruited to become mentors in this instance had already successfully undertaken a year-long module, established as an important aspect of the AfL developments introduced by the staff team, as a core aspect of their own first-year academic induction. The module is 'Approaches to Learning'. As the module's title suggests, it draws heavily on the theoretical concepts and paradigm of the student approaches to learning literature, which have deeply influenced the scholarship of learning and teaching in the UK and beyond. Rather than acting as a straightforward Study Skills module, the participants are encouraged to become aware of what Hutchings (2005) calls 'the tricks and truths of the learning trade' or 'pedagogical intelligence', by starting to share the growing body of work on pedagogical knowledge in Higher Education with students, as well as with staff. For Hutchings, pedagogical intelligence involves developing an understanding of how learning happens, and an appreciation and embracing of the disposition to shape one's own learning; to be an active agent of learning; to seek out proactively and consciously engineer experiences in which one's learning is advanced. It is widely accepted, she argues, that learners who are self-conscious about the processes of learning and teaching tend to be more successful. It seems sensible to assume they will also be better placed to support and develop others' learning.

Because the mentors had already experienced some involvement in the scholarship of learning and teaching, their formal training programme included refresher activities which enabled them to revisit and reflect upon the core content, concepts, focus and aims of the formal academic induction programme that would be followed by their mentees. Other elements of the training sought to ensure that the mentors understood and adhered to the specific boundaries of their role. A few already had experience of being a mentor on the programme in another scheme, but most did not.

Throughout the whole process, the mentors were encouraged to promote active, independent learning in their first-year groups. During our joint planning meetings, they decided to achieve this by facilitating collaborative, informal cross-level discussions about being a learner in Higher Education, predominantly by sharing their own experiences of learning to learn in the first year. In this way, the model of engagement we eventually adopted most closely resembled the definition of 'students as partners' described by Kay et al. (2012: 367), with students helping staff to tackle the challenges of supporting first years by explicitly asking, from their current viewpoint, what they wished they had known about approaches to studying the subject when they were in the first year.

This meant that, throughout their involvement in the project, the mentors often found themselves reflecting together, and with us, on the ways in which in which their own perceptions of being a learner had changed and developed during their time on the course so far. They then led face-to-face meetings with groups of first years, where they worked on previously negotiated tasks related to the general focus of selected teaching sessions, opening up discussions about their personal experiences of transition with them at key points within a core introductory module. At the end of the module they organized a Student Collaborative Conference for all the first years, which focused on supporting newcomers to gain feedback from experienced students, as well as staff, and encouraging them to reflect collaboratively on effective approaches to the module assignment.

As well as working directly with first-year students in class time, the mentors also acted as advisors to the module teaching team, supporting them to redesign elements of the curriculum and the classroom activities which the first years would be encouraged to undertake. For instance, they redesigned a two-hour large-group teaching session about making the most of lectures, which the students then co-delivered with the staff teaching team, sharing the ways they saw the lecture material now, after nearly two years of study, and reflecting on how they used to approach complex lecture material when they were in the first year.

Some of the student mentors were keen to try to ensure that their involvement might continue to have an impact on newcomers in the longer term, after the 'live' element of the project was over. They had decided to invite Professor Phil Race as keynote speaker to the Collaborative Conference, and he produced a leaflet for the first years, based on the discussions held at the conference. This inspired some mentors, who decided they would like to work with us to produce an informal booklet, entitled *Developing Learnership in the First Year: Students' Perspectives*, which we agreed might be placed on the Approaches to Learning module reading list for next year's first years. Seven volunteered to contribute to a series of editorial meetings organized and facilitated by the project leaders, whose role in the meetings was to simply to elicit students' viewpoints on topics covered by the module (more in the manner of an open-ended interview) rather than impose particular concepts and structures on the publication. We also got the job of acting as note-keepers during the meetings, and arranged to have any recordings of students' voices transcribed between meetings.

During these highly informal editorial get-togethers the students collectively brainstormed ideas for the publication and gradually refined them into a set of headings and themes, which they felt indicated some of the major challenges and conceptual shifts that first years typically encounter as they make the transition into studying in Higher Education. They collectively planned each theme on a piece of poster paper and prepared an agreed group summary, which represented their shared overview of the particular theme. The remainder (and bulk) of the text, however, was formed by recording individual student voices. Here the group 'talked aloud' about their recollections, giving their views and experiences in relation to the topic. These were captured, transcribed, selected and agreed for inclusion in the booklet in subsequent meetings. Finally, students decided on the final formatting and presentation features of the booklet, which included a brief general overview of the project (written by the project leads) and Phil Race's leaflet, which they included as an epilogue.

However, the voices of the mentors themselves formed the mainstay of the publication and the chapter will now turn to illuminate the viewpoints they offered. These are interesting because of the insights they reveal into the factors they chose to identify as being fundamental to their development as learners and their academic engagement. They foreground the ontological aspects of learning, especially a sense of being, belonging and transformation, as well as the epistemological aspects of learning and the apparently cognitive level which teachers' discourse and the approaches to learning literature tends to forefront (Solomonides et al., 2012b).

The student booklet

The publication, *Developing Learnership in the First Year: Students' Perspectives*, started out as a 'mythbuster' with the aim of illuminating some common urban legends that are rife in the first year, which could subsequently be challenged and changed. As the guide took shape, however, the writing team began to feel that this approach risked casting the first-year student in deficit and also risked suggesting that certain remedies or solutions to a 'student problem' were appropriate. This actually went against the grain of the scheme and the feelings of the group, which revolved around the sharing of individual experiences and the variety of ways forward that individuals had taken themselves.

To this end, the publication was eventually restructured around a series of key themes, such as lectures, assessment, reading, feedback and so on, which the mentors felt were useful elements of the first-year experience for readers to (re)consider. What actually emerged was a set of aspects that, in these second years' experience, seemed to epitomize the kinds of conceptual adjustments in relation to these themes that they had experienced in their transition to becoming a learner on the course. These revolved around shifts they had made in thinking about the nature of knowledge, learning, teaching, feedback, reading, assessment and the role of the student.

They sought to raise these to visibility by presenting, under each theme, three key headings. The first concerned dominant conceptions first years hold in relation to the theme; the second was about mentors' views of the likely consequences in terms of approaches to learning that flow from them. Finally, the last heading ('How We Think Now') was designed to document the mentors' views and approaches after nearly two years' of Higher Education study, with a view to illuminating the ways of thinking and practising they felt they had developed in the light of their experiences. These were collectively agreed amongst the group, but illustrated by individual voices (which they presented in speech bubbles) to acknowledge the diversity and range of individuals' approaches and preferred ways of working. The students felt this was important, as their introduction to the guide articulated:

> We are a mixed group of second-year students: young, mature and some-where in the middle! The common thread between us is that throughout our university experience we have become passionate about learning. We understand, though, that the first year at university can be exciting and scary at the same time. So we wanted to talk about our learning experi-ences, and the ways in which we have begun to develop as learners, with first-year students.
>
> Our idea was that hearing from people who have gone through similar changes may help [. . .] It must be stated that [. . .] there cannot be a perfect way of learning [. . .] every student goes through university as an individual.
>
> It's important to emphasize that we're not saying we're right, or brilliant, or that it's easy, or that there's a set of strategies to follow – we're trying to show readers of our guide just how, as second years, our ideas about learning itself have changed since we were in the first year – and continue to change as we go through our degree. Good luck, have fun, and enjoy!

In what follows, we briefly present some of the most striking features to emerge from their booklet, which revolve around the dramatic shifts with regard to learn-ing they felt they had made during their own experiences of transition into Higher Education. Interestingly, these strongly echo some of the conceptual shifts in thinking about the nature of 'teaching', 'knowledge' and 'learning' that Kember (2001) pinpointed in an early study of student transition, but also illustrate shifts in their views of the nature of 'feedback', 'reading' and 'assessment' which the students felt were important to point out for their first-year audience.

Changing views of the self as a learner

In a recent study of final-year students' experience of university study, Kember et al. (2013: 32) asserted that:

> At university, the interviewees reported going through an interconnected set of transitions that included the following:
>
> 1   Developing self-discipline and self-management to cope with the relative freedom as a university student.
> 2   Developing the ability to learn independently, without the accustomed close supervision of schoolteachers, to adjust to the different types of teaching and learning at university.
> 3   Becoming confident enough to engage in discussion in class.
> 4   Developing more sophisticated epistemological beliefs so as to be able to make judgements on multiple perspectives.
> 5   Learning to write [. . .] in a style consistent with these more sophisticated beliefs.
> 6   Getting to grips with the nature of their discipline.

The first three of these acted as compounding influences for the other more demanding transitions.

It is interesting to note the extent to which our mentors emphasized the first three of these, encapsulated in the following extract of a section of their booklet on their chosen theme of 'You as a Learner'. In what follows, we reproduce it exactly as they wanted it to appear in the booklet:

You as a learner

How people often think about being a learner when they're in the first year

When you come to uni you might think that being a learner is about sitting in a tiered lecture theatre waiting to write down lots of knowledge. That it's the lecturer's job to tell you everything you need to know and to give you all the information you're going to need.

What happens if they think that way

If you think like that then you will only see your job as waiting. You're waiting to be spoon-fed.

How we think now

But university is a really different way of learning. There are different ways of doing things here. You need to realize that and see that you need to get switched on. You need to get really engaged.

'First years don't think like that though. They're not used to working like that – even at college we didn't. It's not how it's done. You're fed too much at sixth form. The jump to university is MASSIVE.'

'You have to move away from expecting to be spoon fed. You have to think about learning in a different way.'

'At uni it's about learning. College wasn't about learning. It was just about stuff to put in the assignments.'

'It's not like a tick box exercise any more. I feel like I'm actually learning something. It's not just getting by to get the grades.'

'It puts the ownership back in your court.'

'You have to start to think differently, here. You have to think about the way you're approaching ideas. It's a big shift you have to make. And you have to see it's not just a matter of being clever. But, like many people I came to university thinking "I won't be able to do this. Everyone will be so much cleverer than me!" But you need to get to a point where it's about digging deeper and getting into it. It's an approach you take, which allows you to think you can aim high.'

'I have to say, though, that's not easy. It can make you feel really uncomfortable. At the start if there was something I couldn't understand I used to feel really uncomfortable. But now, I think the whole point is, that if you feel uncomfortable that's how you learn! You could be thinking one thing, then someone puts a completely different perspective on it, and you think – whoa! I've never thought like that about that! So you try to make new sense of it. But actually, that's the *only* way you're actually going to make sense of it!'

'It's a real leap, to think of yourself as a learner like that!'

The students' collective sense of becoming an active participant in the knowledge community of a course was one of the features they felt characterized learnership (the role or state of being a learner) at university and they were at pains to explain how, from their viewpoint, this sense of belonging to the course differed radically from their prior educational experiences. As one put it:

> At university the respect levels are much more, like, level. You're part of a whole thing. Even though you're like, a student, obviously, you're part of the whole thing – the lines blur more – your opinions are respected. At first that was weird – it takes a lot of getting used to.

The ways in which this felt unsettling and became linked to a sense of identity is extremely conspicuous in the students' talk. It is also important to note how, from these students' viewpoints, the notion of reducing a sense of alienation is not synonymous with eliminating stress or effort, or even discomfort, but something they saw as being part and parcel of learnership.

The emphasis on working with peers

Another striking element of the booklet is the emphasis these students placed on the significance of social engagement within, and beyond, the classroom. This emerged across the whole book, but was encapsulated in a section they decided to include, entitled 'Working With Peers':

How people often think in the first year

When you first start uni you can feel that you're basically on your own when it comes to working on your studies. Sometimes you don't want to share your ideas in case someone takes them from you. You think that others might take the information that you've found, so it's best to keep it to yourself.

What happens if they think that way

If you think that way you can feel very isolated and you don't give yourself chance to see how other people think about things that you are working on.

How we think now

In our experience it's important to discuss your ideas with other people, and talk about whatever you're working on, because that helps you learn to see the different ways a thing can be seen. You need to see the different perspectives, and talking helps you do just that. It also helps you get yourself clearer in your own mind about the different viewpoints on a thing you might want to bring in. So we find we all go and talk about a lecture or whatever over a coffee, because chatting it through helps you so much!

'I like talking with the girls – it helps me get understanding more. It helps you see different ideas and different approaches. It's one of the most helpful things – being put into groups.'

'It makes you rethink your thoughts, and helps you adapt and change, or makes you think more and get deeper into it. It might not make you change – it might just help you realise that things can be seen differently – that there are other approaches. And that's important. To see more.'

'I often ask "do you think this?" which helps me to see where I'm completely off the rails. Talking about uni is really important. It kind of then escalates, and you see different points of view.'

'But first years don't think like that, though. They're not used to working like that. Working with peers – that's so different to college! At college, you do your work, and you're on your own, basically – you do your work – you do your assignment. But here, it's like, you work together.'

'Because if you're on your own it's hard to develop your understanding. But if you talk about it in groups it really helps. But in the first year it feels really alien to sit and have a coffee and chat about work. But now we're in the second year that seems like second nature. It just happens naturally. We start talking about the lectures. Asking what do you think about that?'

'I don't think I could have survived the first year without working with other students! They were a lifeline!'

The first year doesn't count!

Finally, another striking feature worthy of comment is the emphasis these students placed on debunking the idea that the first year is, as Bryson and Hand (2007: 355) found many students thinking about it, 'a big doss'. The student writers were keen to explain, instead, that the first year is 'not just about knowledge: it's about getting the hang of how to go about your work'. Much of this, as in Bryson and Hand's (2007) study, focused on the university as a whole as a different sphere for engagement, which they explained in their booklet to their first-year audience as follows:

> You need to learn to put yourself out there, finding out who can help you, where to go for support, all the people and materials that can help you – all the support that you need to find for yourself. If you think the lecturer will just tell you all you need to know: how to use the library, how to suss out all the little things you need to know, and that's it, think again! You need to use the first year to get your head around the whole community of people – all the networks – not just lecturers and other students, but also all the people in IT, the Library, visits, the Students' Union, Student Services, Careers, Finance. And you have to get to grips with new things like how to set out references, how to download journals, how to use the IT facilities. In fact, there's so much more to everything than you probably imagined and you have to learn to make it your job to find out what's on offer [. . .] It's much easier when everyone's new and you don't feel such a twit not knowing!

The final sentence tellingly acknowledges how alienating it is to feel, as Mann (2001) suggests, like a stranger in a strange land and how hard it is, for some students, to 'put yourself out there'.

One student drew attention to the importance of AfL teacher-led pedagogies, which seed peer relationships in class, in helping to develop this sense of belonging to the wider community of the university:

> It was really hard for me to get into the university thing – databases, emails, getting used to all that – it felt like I was really putting on peers. But without them I wouldn't have managed the first year. That's why group work and helping each other was so important.

Overall, the student guide placed huge emphasis on the linkage between social and academic affiliation and the ways in which, from these students' viewpoints, being a member of a learning community felt like a prerequisite which sustained and developed their learning. Their association with a learning community seemed supportive, both intellectually and emotionally, and helps to explain the prominence their booklet placed on working with peers and finding mutual support from their informal social networks (Morosanu et al., 2010). The sense of belonging to a trusted peer community was a key feature of their academic engagement. As one student put it:

> They [the first years] need to see that there's a divide opening up, it happens in the first year, about the ones who are taking it seriously and getting on with it, and the ones that are not. Because there's more of a community in the ones that are getting on with it.

Final reflections

This chapter has sought to illuminate how, while the staff on the teaching teams tended to take a view of an engaged student as someone who shared their own intense interest in and passion for the subject, these students tended to represent the transitions they had made into 'new' forms of learnership as more a multi-faceted, dynamic phenomenon which was closely linked to their developing sense of identity and purpose in being a student in Higher Education (Bryson and Hardy, 2012). In their booklet they strongly foregrounded issues of identity and participation, with a strong social element, based on developing good relationships with staff and students and a keen sense of belonging. In this sense, then, the students' contributions to the publication draw attention to the importance of theoretical perspectives which emanate from the student engagement literature. For instance, Solomonides et al. (2012b) argue that ontological issues, and the sense of transforming as a person, are key to academic engagement and play a pivotal role in the student's approach to study.

Student engagement can consequently act as a useful lens through which to view the nature of effective AfL practice, especially in relation to its espoused development of learning for the longer term (Boud and Associates, 2010). Students need to transform as people in order to become professionals and need sustainable assessment and feedback practices which enable them to learn prospectively, beyond the immediate context (Boud and Molloy, 2013). These practices frame students in particular ways, as active agents who seek information which can help them. To this end, Boud and Molloy argue (2013: 711), AfL must focus holistically on creating an effective learning system which needs to include 'the learners and what they bring, the curriculum and what that promotes and the learning milieu and what that affords'. Teachers definitely have an important part to play in this. But, given that many newcomers struggle to see themselves as active learners, and tend, instead, to subject themselves passively to the experience of learning, we believe there is also value in engaging students as partners and change agents in the first-year experience of academic transition. The students in our project, for instance, communicated ideas about learning to learn in ways which seemed more accessible to newcomers than any advice that we could have produced, however student-centred we might have tried to be, and the first years referred to their booklet enthusiastically. From our perspective, their contributions had a really important part to play in co-creating a model of AfL which is in line with recent theory about how best to support the development of students' assessment literacy. This strongly connects the scholarship of assessment to ideas and assumptions drawn from the student engagement literature via the conscious development of learning communities:

> The basic underlying enabler of assessment literacy (for both staff and students alike) is community.
>
> (Price et al., 2012: 150)

Chapter 17

Enriching the student experience

Engaging students and staff

Andrea Jackson and Katie Livesey

The School of Earth and Environment at the University of Leeds is home to over 600 undergraduate students enrolled on a variety of programmes, spanning earth and environmental science, sustainability and business. This chapter firstly presents the development of an online resource to support pre-entry and induction stage students in their transition from school to university. It then outlines a programme of research within the School that has explored the barriers, enablers and effective practice in engaging undergraduate students in order to enhance their sense of belonging to the School community and with their discipline. This research recognises that social interaction, as well as involvement in the academic and research community, all contribute to the student experience and that students learn by being involved and learn more the more they are involved in both the academic and social aspects of their university experience (Astin, 1985; Bransford et al., 1999; Chickering and Gamson, 1987; Krause, 2005). Actions as a result of this work have focused on facilitating educationally purposeful co-curricular opportunities that promote supporting peer relations and meaningful interactions between staff and students in order to enhance undergraduate student engagement (Kuh, 2001). These are intended to complement the engagement opportunities provided through the academic curriculum. This research has also raised awareness amongst academic staff of potential mismatches between their perceptions and the reality of the student experience. It has resulted in the development of a School Student Experience Framework, achieved through a student–staff partnership, and brought about strategic change and investment in the student experience within the School of Earth and Environment.

It is hoped that the engagement opportunities outlined in this chapter will provide inspiration for others to trial within their School or Department. However, it must be acknowledged that the student body is diverse and complex and that developing a student experience to foster engagement and belonging must therefore be implemented in different ways, through providing a range of opportunities and using innovative methods that are relevant to student interests and future goals. Our work has shown that really understanding and working in partnership with your student body, and the multiple communities within it, are fundamental to the success of any interventions that are put in place to facilitate student engagement.

Part one: early engagement with Higher Education

The engagement challenge

Students arrive at the School of Earth and Environment from a diversity of educational backgrounds, with differing life experiences and varying levels of pre-university preparation. These all influence their engagement with Higher Education and can result in a mismatch between students' expectations and perceptions of university with the reality of the experience (Edward, 2003; Lowe and Cook, 2003; McInnis and James, 1995; Ozga and Sukhnandan, 1998; Yorke and Longden, 2008). Focus group work with our first-year undergraduate students in 2008 showed that some were finding the transition from secondary education and early engagement with Higher Education challenging. For example, some students were having difficulty understanding what was meant by critical thinking and independent study; some felt intimidated arriving at induction meetings taking place in large lecture theatres, with over 200 students, without knowing anyone; some were unsure what equipment they needed to purchase before they arrived; some had difficulty with the university terminology. We therefore wanted to find a mechanism to help align their expectations of Higher Education with the reality of the academic experience to assist with this transition period.

The engagement intervention

In early 2009 the School developed 'Countdown to University Study', an online informative and supportive resource intended to align students' prior expectations and perceptions of university with the reality of the experience. The resource was developed through consultation with staff, current university and secondary school students and supports the School's induction programme. It was specifically intended to help build academic community awareness, inspire development of independent learning/critical thinking, and guide expectations and enhance understanding of the institution, the school and the discipline. It promotes the student experience at the beginning of the student life cycle, not only for early engagement and retention, but for later success in learning and professional practice (Kift, 2009).

Students are invited to use the resource through e-mail, a link from the School's Facebook page, and in a welcome letter sent from the School as soon as their place at Leeds is confirmed. Key features of Countdown to University Study (which can be seen at www.see.leeds.ac.uk/countdown/SEE) include:

- a collation of pre-induction materials;
- video welcomes from key members of staff;
- advice from current students;
- degree programme information and optional activities;
- written content to introduce teaching approaches and demonstrate the integration of research within teaching;
- photo storyboards to show fieldwork locations and activities;
- links to social media provision where they can meet others before they arrive.

Academically, the resource helps students understand the difference in learning style between school and university by inclusion of resources related to independent learning, critical thinking, and other study skills links. It also provides the opportunity for students to familiarise themselves with key staff from an early stage through finding out about the academic staff responsible for the management of their programme.

The social dimension to the resource is intended to help students to form friendships with other incoming undergraduate students before they arrive, as Thomas (2012a) has shown that friendship groups formed early in the student experience are enduring and that friendships are critical to many students' retention and success. The resource also provides them with the opportunity to obtain peer support through questions and conversations with current students via Facebook.

The resource relates to the professional services in ensuring that all appropriate links to central support services (student services, library, study skills services, disability services, Lifelong Learning Centre for mature students, International Office for such students, etc.) are collated for ease of access and introduced to students at an early stage. It also introduces students to the School's dedicated professional student support team, explaining individuals' roles and how students might interact with them.

The resource has been in place since 2009 and both quantitative (Google Analytics and use of Facebook) and qualitative (focus groups and interviews) evaluation has allowed assessment of the effectiveness of the approach in helping students with their transition from school to university. Quantitative evaluation shows that the resource has been used on average by over 60 per cent of incoming students in each year (annual undergraduate intake 200+) and has been viewed from 23 countries across the world. The pages that are viewed most frequently each year are those related to the Freshers' week programme; field trips; and programme specific pages.

Focus group work has explored whether the students have found the resource helpful for their transition to university, the most and least useful aspects, what other content they would welcome, and aspects of the design. The majority of positive comments have related to the clarity of outlining what students need to do and when; being able to recognise key staff when they arrive; and the usefulness of hearing advice from the perspective of a student. Comments include:

- 'The Freshers' Week pages helped me know what to expect.'
- 'It was good to be able to see what equipment I needed to buy.'
- 'It was good for Foundation Year students, I didn't feel excluded.'
- 'I was able to identify my programme manager when I arrived and recognised faces.'
- 'It was interesting to hear from the perspective of a student and helped with my expectations.'

These positive comments indicate that the resource is proving useful in supporting students accessing it in their transition. A postgraduate version of the resource

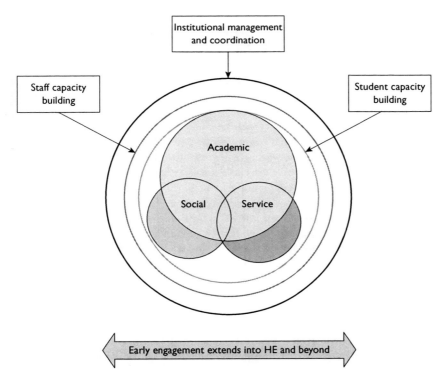

Figure 17.1 The *What Works?* Model: improving student engagement, belonging and retention for success

Source: Thomas, 2012a.

has subsequently been developed, with 'Step up to Masters' supporting all of the taught postgraduate programmes within the School.

Part two: enhancing undergraduate student engagement

The engagement challenge

The Higher Education Academy's 'What Works? Retention and Success Model' (Figure 17.1) (Thomas, 2012a) puts student engagement and belonging at the heart of improving student retention and success and embodies promoting early and continued engagement across the student life cycle; nurturing engagement through the academic, social and professional services; and developing the capacity of both students and staff to engage through a partnership approach. We have been working in the School of Earth and Environment to enhance the sense of belonging to the School community amongst our undergraduate students and to enhance their engagement with their discipline.

This was primarily driven by a merger between the School of Earth Sciences and the School of Environment in 2004 which brought about a larger and more diverse staff and student body, which in turn increased the engagement challenge. There are also additional challenges to undergraduate student engagement in the School, including our degree programmes not directly mapping onto the traditional A-level subjects that the majority of students have previously studied (only a small number of students will have taken geology or environmental science A-level). This makes it challenging for students in understanding and engaging with the academic research going on within the School.

Furthermore, students receive very little formal teaching within the School building itself, thus having little opportunity to meet with students enrolled on other degree programmes and for student–staff interaction. Students are not easily able to see the interconnectedness of their interdisciplinary degree programmes (i.e. linking social and physical sciences) to enable them to set their own learning in a broader context. We therefore carried out a series of focus groups with our undergraduate students to investigate their sense of belonging which revealed that students:

- mainly felt a sense of belonging to a degree programme, not to the wider School student community, but that they wanted the opportunity to interact with students from across the School;
- felt there was little need to go into the School building other than for administrative purposes, thereby minimising the potential to interact with staff and other students;
- felt that a sense of belonging was generated in the School through the friendliness and approachability of staff, especially support staff;
- talked about engagement through membership of School and University student societies, and by working as a student representative;
- wanted more opportunities for interaction with staff and other students.

A School audit of activities that students were undertaking to engage with the School and their discipline was carried out alongside this focus group work. The activities obtained from the audit were categorised according to the Higher Education Academy Dimensions of Student Engagement (HEA, 2013) which encompass the ways in which students become active partners in shaping their learning experience, the results of which can be seen in Figure 17.2.

From our initial findings, it became apparent, as expected, that there were multiple student communities in the School that were engaging in different ways. We therefore set about a programme of research to understand the barriers, enablers and effective practice in engaging our undergraduate students, with the intention of targeting educationally purposeful co-curricular opportunities, to supplement their academic provision, and to enhance their sense of belonging to the wider School community.

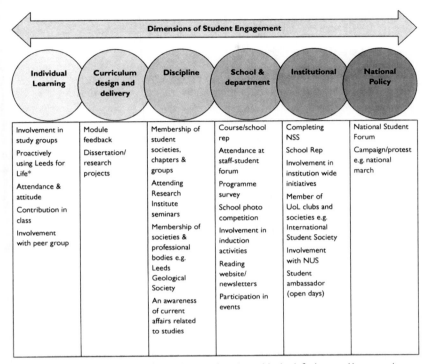

Individual Learning	Curriculum design and delivery	Discipline	School & department	Institutional	National Policy
Involvement in study groups	Module feedback	Membership of student societies, chapters & groups	Course/school rep	Completing NSS	National Student Forum
Proactively using Leeds for Life*	Dissertation/ research projects		Attendance at staff-student forum	School Rep	Campaign/protest e.g. national march
Attendance & attitude		Attending Research Institute seminars	Programme survey	Involvement in institution wide initiatives	
Contribution in class		Membership of societies & professional bodies e.g. Leeds Geological Society	School photo competition	Member of UoL clubs and societies e.g. International Student Society	
Involvement with peer group			Involvement in induction activities	Involvement with NUS	
		An awareness of current affairs related to studies	Reading website/ newsletters	Student ambassador (open days)	
			Participation in events		

*Leeds for Life is an online tool to support the personal tutoring model at Leeds. Students are ables to record co-curricular activities and build on a living CV to enhance employability.

Figure 17.2 An audit of engagement activities within the School of Earth and Environment categorised according to the Higher Education Academy Dimensions of Student Engagement

Source: HEA, 2013.

A combination of focus groups, interviews and, primarily, a survey adapted from the National Survey of Student Engagement (NSSE) were used to explore student engagement in the School. The NSSE explores the activities that contribute to a student's experience according to five indicators of Effective Educational Practice, known as Benchmarks:

- Level of Academic Challenge.
- Active and Collaborative Learning.
- Student–Faculty Interaction.
- Enriching Educational Experiences.
- Supportive Campus Environment.

Given the scope of this project in enhancing engagement through involving students in educationally purposeful activities beyond the classroom, our School

Student Experience Survey explored student engagement according to three of these Benchmarks:

Student and staff interactions

These interactions are shown through research to be among some of the strongest determinants of positive learning outcomes (see, for example: Astin, 1993; Kuh and Hu, 2001). Questions in our survey related to the level and nature of students' contact and interaction with teaching staff outside the classroom and on an individual level, such as through feedback on their academic performance; discussing ideas from their classes; working with staff on research or activities other than coursework.

Enriching educational experiences

A considerable amount of learning at university takes place outside the formal learning setting and students' participation in broadening educational activities play an important role in their personal and educational development (Griffin et al., 2003; Krause and Coates, 2008). Questions in our survey related to participation in experiences such as research seminars, volunteering, field trips, membership of societies and working as a student ambassador/course representative.

Supportive learning environment

Students' perceptions of the extent to which the School has supported their learning can provide an indication of their sense of inclusion with their learning community. Questions in our survey regarding students' feelings of support within the School community include those based around quality of relationships with other students (academic, support, demonstrators and technical), as well as how induction activities had helped them settle into University.

The School survey, including 55 quantitative questions and 2 open questions, was administered to all undergraduates through lectures within the school in 2011, 2012 and 2013, and a prize was offered to encourage students to complete the survey. Response rates of over 60 per cent were obtained for the Student Experience Survey in each of the three years and the results from this work have enabled many student engagement interventions, examples of which are given below. These interventions have been introduced over the last three years and evaluation through the student survey has enabled us to refine these over time. Interventions are co-ordinated by a School-based Student Experience Officer, a position that was developed as part of the School's student experience investment plans. It is now a permanent position within the School.

Summary of engagement interventions

Student experience ambassadors

These are students employed by the School and who work closely with the School's Student Experience Officer to help identify and facilitate engagement activities such as those described below. Working in partnership with the students in this way is invaluable to developing the portfolio of engagement interventions. During the course of this research, we have learned lessons about what we can expect from the ambassadors and the level of training and mentoring required throughout the course of the academic year.

Student-led newsletter

The Leeds Earth and Environment Pages (LEEP) is produced by the student ambassadors each semester, and involves interviewing staff about their research, student society news, field trip reports and forthcoming events. The intention has been to involve the students in creating a resource that informs them about the research that is being carried out within the school in a way that they understand, and bring together relevant information for them in one place, and the Student Experience Survey results show that this is proving useful to students in delivering these messages.

Event listings

A weekly LEEP event listing is sent by e-mail to all students including information about all research seminars within the school and other discipline-related events that students are encouraged to attend. This was originally sent to students from a generic student support e-mail address, but student feedback revealed that they were becoming overwhelmed with messages through this route and therefore not able to distinguish this from student support messages. We therefore created a LEEP-specific e-mail address and this has received positive student feedback, with survey results revealing that they find this a useful source of information.

Use of social media

We have been using social media, such as Facebook and Twitter, to inform students about activities and opportunities, but also to engage them in dialogue about expectations of their student experience. Facebook in particular has been a successful communication mechanism, with our School Facebook page membership continually growing.

Establishing a school student societies' forum

This forum was established to bring student groups within the School together, encourage collaboration and raise awareness of each society's schedule of activities.

We have found that working in partnership with the student societies, along with the student ambassadors, is one of the best ways of engaging our students. This partnership has also brought about benefits to some of the school societies who have seen an increase in their membership, through raising their profile within the School. We have also been able to provide them with feedback as to the kinds of activities that students would like them to organise.

Student Experience Fund

A Student Experience Fund enables students to apply for funding to support projects that encourage collaboration and community building within the school. This is now in its second year and has provided funding to support student-organised, educationally purposeful activities such as: caving trips; degree programme-specific site visits such as wildlife reserves and mines (of interest to students on earth and environmental science degree programmes); biodiversity work with bees including funding a beehive and beekeeper training, a project which has subsequently grown to provide secondary school outreach activities; organisation of a one day student conference; and to enable guest speakers to visit the School. Lessons learned from this experience include the appropriate level of guidance to students for completing application forms, and the importance of having an academic lead in guiding the educationally purposeful aspect to their proposals. We therefore run workshops to guide students through this process.

Conference Bursary Fund

This fund has enabled students to attend conferences such as the British Conference of Undergraduate Research (BCUR). Students who have attended the BCUR have found it an incredible experience that enabled them to put their research in a wider context as well as being an important networking experience. The response was so positive we have diverted more funds towards this activity.

School-based events

We have held events such as the 'SEE (School of Earth and Environment) Behind the Scenes' building open evening. World class research facilities and equipment referred to in lectures and taught sessions are seldom seen by students. This event therefore opens up these facilities through guided tours enabling students to hear from staff and research students about the activity that takes place within these and how this relates to their teaching.

A slam event piloted in 2012 was designed to showcase to staff and students the outstanding activities that students are involved in during the summer through short, three minute presentations. It is also intended to inspire students to seek out similar experiences for themselves, and presentations have included an overview of a student's study year abroad in New Zealand, working with children in Guatemala, a wildlife ranger in Canada and a student who supported disabled children on an overland expedition in South America. Both students and staff have requested that this event be run again next year.

We have introduced a BBQ during induction week to encourage new students to meet each other. This has now grown to include a School Student Societies Fair to provide students with the opportunity to get involved from the outset in one of the many student societies.

Our Finalists Farewell is an event for our final-year students and occurs in the last week of teaching, coinciding with the University's Celebrate Week. An informal awards ceremony followed by lunch enables us to mark the students reaching the end of their undergraduate journey within the School. The awards nominated by students and staff celebrate achievements in engagement in the School community and include awards for outstanding students, engagement with research and engagement in the School and University community. Students are also able to nominate their 'most inspirational lecture'. This has been a very powerful tool in engaging some of our busiest research staff with the aims of this project.

The list above provides a snapshot of the interventions that have been put in place as a result of this research programme. The student experience survey has also provided information according to year group which has enabled engagement interventions to assist with transition points throughout the student journey. The survey results have also helped us identify differing engagement characteristics of the broader undergraduate subject areas in the School, for example BSc Earth Science, BSc Environmental Science and BA Environmental Science. Understanding and appreciating the needs of these multiple communities has enabled us to offer a greater breadth of engagement opportunities, facilitating student engagement across a greater number of students.

Enhancing staff engagement

The engagement challenge

Our increasingly diverse, complex and ever more discerning student body means that we need to ensure staff are fully engaged and informed of the student experience in order to enhance practice and manage expectations. However, our staff understanding of student engagement often differs from the reality of students' experience due to staff's anecdotal evidence or beliefs based on cultural or professional background, personal experiences, etc. As such, we wanted to provide an evidence base for staff to help them identify the gaps in their understanding and expectations of the student experience. A staff survey was administered to the 95 academic staff within the School in 2012, with a response rate of 40 per cent. This mirrored the student experience survey and included 54 quantitative questions and two open questions to measure the academics' perceptions of:

- the proportion of their students who engage in different activities and the frequency with which they do so;
- the importance staff place on various areas of learning and development;
- how students feel about support within their academic community;
- the nature and frequency of staff–student interactions.

The following section brings together some of the key results from both the staff survey and the student experience survey and outlines how they have been used to stimulate evidence-focused conversations about student engagement activity amongst staff; to stimulate new thinking about good practice that should lead to the enhancement of student engagement; and to increase staff awareness and understanding of the initiatives and policies surrounding student engagement.

For example, from the student experience survey 85 per cent of students rated their overall student experience within the School as either good or excellent (on a scale of excellent, good, fair, poor), with 30 per cent rating their experience as excellent. In the staff survey, 86 per cent of staff thought students would rate their experience as 'good', but only one member of staff thought the students would rate their experience as excellent. This difference between student and staff responses provided the starting point for the presentation of results to teaching staff at a Teaching Enhancement away-day. The event proved a successful forum for engaging staff in discussions about enhancing the student experience and the following results are framed around the three benchmarks described above.

Engagement interventions

Student–staff interaction

Over 80 per cent of students in their survey responded that they had 'never' worked with teaching staff on activities other than coursework. However, from the staff survey 86 per cent of staff thought that students had participated in such activities either 'sometimes' or 'often'. Qualitative responses indicated that students wanted 'more opportunities for involvement with staff research projects' and that staff wanted to be able to offer such opportunities but that there was no effective mechanism within the School to be able to facilitate this. In response to this, a set of guidelines for internships were established, offering a centrally administered mechanism to enable staff to offer these opportunities that are then clearly communicated to students. There are now a greater number of such opportunities available to students, including four School-funded internships.

Enriching educational experience

Over 40 per cent of the students responded in their survey that they had 'never' attended talks/presentations/seminars within the School that were not timetabled. Qualitative responses indicated that students felt that the School provided seminars that were of interest to the subjects taught, but they felt that they were pitched at too high a level for them to understand, they were not always sure whether they were able to attend and often didn't know about them. In response to this, we have worked with the student societies to include seminars that are more accessible for students and they all now receive a weekly email listing all forthcoming events across the School. As a result, a greater number of students are attending seminars to hear about the research that takes place within the School.

Fifty-six per cent of students felt that it had been made explicit 'quite a bit' or 'a lot' where an academic member of staff's research had been used in their teaching. In contrast, although staff felt they had made their research explicit in their teaching, with 75 per cent of them believing they made it explicit 'quite a bit' or 'a lot', only 37 per cent of staff thought that the students would give the response 'quite a bit' and no staff thought that students would respond that their research had been made explicit 'a lot'. Staff therefore felt they were taking the time to make their research explicit in their teaching, but were then underestimating the extent to which students were seeing this. The students are therefore much more aware of the academic research taking place within the School than staff realise which has been particularly encouraging for them. This has made staff more willing to participate in events that enrich the educational experience through showcasing their research, and which in turn enhances student–staff interaction.

Supportive school environment

The majority of first years felt that the School had helped them settle into University life either 'quite a bit' or 'a lot', which was encouraging given the efforts the School has placed on helping students during this transition period. However, the survey revealed that students in later years, particularly those entering the second year, felt less supported, and this has helped identify and target interventions for these cohorts for the beginning of the next academic year.

Quantitative and qualitative analysis of the survey showed that the most influential benchmark in determining the overall rating of the student experience was the Supportive School Environment. As outlined above, this benchmark explores the quality of relationships with other students and staff and is related to creating a school environment that helps students thrive socially and succeed academically. The supportive school environment is, of course, linked to the other two benchmarks explored within the survey as enriching educational experiences will in part enhance student–staff interaction leading to more positive relationships.

Summary

This chapter has described how information from a School Student Experience Survey has enabled us to tailor and target formal and informal educationally orientated interventions across the student life cycle and across degree programmes to improve the quality and outcomes of the student experience. A staff survey has also helped academic staff have a greater understanding of the student experience. Importantly, the work has facilitated the development of a school student experience strategy, developed in partnership with students and staff, and which recognises that social interaction as well as academic involvement is an important contributor to the student experience. The qualitative and quantitative methodologies used in this research programme will also enable us to monitor and evaluate the impact of these engagement interventions as they further develop.

Over the last three years, we have learnt that effectively enhancing student engagement is a developmental process that takes time and in-depth understanding of the student body. For those embarking upon enhancing the student experience, you should not be disheartened if your ideas do not work the first time but try to work on the principles that initiatives need to proactively engage students through being informative, relevant to their interests and future aspirations, be well timed, encourage collaboration with fellow students and members of staff and be explicit about the potential benefits of engaging.

Chapter 18

Reflections, and considerations about the future of student engagement

Colin Bryson

There have been contributions in this volume from a wide range of students and staff studying and working in an equally wide range of contexts within universities in England, and are therefore broadly representative of the Higher Education (HE) sector. They have brought to light a cornucopia of high quality evidence about the nature of student engagement. All the authors have shown a mutual consensus that engagement is located in the being of the student, thus is unique to that individual. This supports and vindicates the position taken in the opening chapter: that student engagement is complex, dynamic, not amenable to measurement and impossible to fully capture or predict in any overarching single model. Nevertheless, some recurrent themes emerge.

An issue that permeates the three longitudinal research studies at the beginning of the book, and is given salience by the subsequent accounts from some of the students, is that persistence and success in HE can be really difficult. However, such a major factor in mitigating all the alienating forces is peer support and social networks. Without these supporting sources, many of these students would not have got through to a successful culmination of their university studies. Indeed, we might add to the normative outcomes of a degree, the award and the development of graduate attributes, the further point made by Julie Wintrup. Another important achievement by students is the development of the virtues of altruism, persistence (commitment and resilience) and collectivism the students showed so well, in the support given to and received from, their peers.

These support networks did not derive from, or were not well supported by, the actions taken by universities or their staff. The design and delivery of courses often got in way of creating and sustaining social networks. Many staff might argue that this is all extra-curricular, and therefore not their concern or responsibility. Notwithstanding this, it is very clear from this evidence about how much this social dimension really matters.

A wider feature of these major studies in the early chapters is the weakness of trust relationships between staff and students. This is not intended as a criticism of busy staff who indubitably had a host of competing priorities and many responsibilities which prevented them from giving much attention to individual students. Work intensification for staff has been a feature of HE for some considerable time

(Bryson, 2004) and staff too have been subject to alienating forces (Mann, 2001) that privilege the transactional outputs, over the relational. Nonetheless, the large, anonymous courses featured here created a rather soulless culture where students were reluctant to approach staff and, particularly in the first two years of degrees, had no member of the staff that they knew well enough to approach.

Another feature of these research studies is the point that for at least some of their degrees, the students seemed content to 'get by', in the sense of not 'moving on' in their intellectual development and developing into a critical and independent learner. Sadly for some students, they never got past that 'stuck' position throughout their degrees. Thus, the student experience for them was more about 'having', getting some sort of degree, than 'becoming' (Fromm, 1978). The need for an initial transition is very clear, and students cannot be expected to adapt immediately and be 'ready to engage' from the outset. However, that does not mean that the first year should not be challenging and designed to stretch students, allowing them to take risks and *learn*. The first year is a period of adjustment, and while some students will take a bit longer to adjust than others, all need to be scaffolded through this stage. However, surely students should be encouraged to be entering into the 'transitional' way of knowing before the end of the first year (Baxter Magolda, 1992). There should be space for more 'interesting things' beyond just settling in. Some courses had features such as early project work that enabled this, but some curriculum designs failed to encourage this at all, and this alienated students who were ready to do so and desired more.

This all sounds rather negative, and clearly some students in these research studies had very positive experiences. This sense of transformation and becoming emerges strongly in the chapters written by students. So many of these student authors demonstrate the strongest levels of engagement: they are truly 'super-engaged'. The precursor for this seems to be getting involved in a substantial role or project where their engagement flourishes, which becomes a catalyst for transformation. That might be taking on a role such as being a student representative or peer mentor, which often seemed to lead to taking on multiple responsibilities and activities. Or, it might be getting involved in a project such as the one taken on by Susan Lund at Sheffield Hallam University, or the intercultural competency project at Nottingham Trent. Alternatively, it may involve taking an unusual module, as Zoë Baker did. These activities may seem very different but all share the characteristics of allowing the student the chance to devise creative and risky ideas and put them into practice. These initiatives involved the student taking ownership of the task, with the tutor/project supervisor stepping back to do no more than facilitate and support (e.g. as a coach); in Zoë's words: 'a marked shift of control to students' (p. 103). The way that the students have much more control of the whole process is central to alleviating or even beginning to eliminate the alienating 'norms' built into the conventional curriculum where the students enact the process as set out for them by staff.

The students need to be ready to engage in such initiatives and it should be noted that an important part of that is having the confidence to do so. Sarah would not have become a mentor (Chapter 12) if she had not gained confidence in her own academic work through the serendipitous peer grouping, which had enabled her to learn from her peers and recognize how to improve her own work. That is another example about the need to be 'ready to engage', and to be self-assured enough to be self-critical and change (Nicol, 2010). It really does not matter that some students did not enter into such roles for the reason of wanting to transform themselves. A more prosaic incentive such as enhancing their curriculum vitae is fine, as it is once they do the role that they become engaged in a much more relational way and all the good possibilities start to open up.

There is an interesting question about whether such opportunities should be in the curriculum or not. Most of these projects were entirely extra-curricular. As these roles are substantial, that can create a bit of a tension in terms of competing with academic work and deadlines, and with other priorities in their lives. The students at Newcastle were able to use some of the roles they undertook as the basis for a graduate development module. This allowed them more space to devote time and energy to the roles, but also to have support to develop as reflective practitioners (Schon, 1983), to learn from others about how to enhance their own practice and that of their peers. For Zoë and her autoethnographic research project within a final-year module, the scholarly dimension was even more explicit and connected directly to her disciplinary study.

However, undertaking this type of 'engaging practice' in modules raises the thorny issue of assessment, which can inhibit risk taking and return control and power to the tutor. Note that these problems were addressed carefully in Zoë's case by the sort of approaches discussed in Chapters 13 and 17, by considering this ethically, and through the tenets of assessment *for* learning rather than *of* learning.

The element of reflection is another important part of these projects and initiatives in which the students participated. This was facilitated in a number of ways, such as being a key part of modules, but also through the role of the students in disseminating their 'work' to peers and wider audiences. This necessitates the students thinking through the underpinning ideas and a consideration of how others will receive and respond to the messages; this is reflection in and on practice.

Where these transformative experiences are not located in the curriculum, there was another connection to the 'academic' dimension, for example, in the intercultural competencies project (Chapter 9). This is a good exemplar of undergraduate research, and notable because these students undertook this in their first year. Although the content of the project may appear to be not very connected to the discipline of study, the students certainly considered it to be relevant to their future professional practice, thus authentic, and the processes they were putting into practice were likely to be of direct use subsequently in their degree.

Two of the chapters are written by international students and focus on that experience. These chapters bring out how international students face more powerful alienating forces that make it harder to integrate both socially and academically than home students. That is ironic given that a key driver for students to study abroad is precisely to create the opportunity to integrate into another culture.

It should be noted that although international students may not get so involved in their course or university as other students, this matters less because they are getting involved in the extra-curricular experience of being in another country. This may be rather invisible to university staff. From my own professional experience of having students who go abroad to study, they show major development in confidence, maturity and graduate attributes upon their return. Shanna Saubert (Chapter 10) makes that point too, demonstrating that although studying abroad brings all sorts of challenges with it, it can indeed be a transformative experience. The project at Nottingham Trent shows that language and cultural barriers can be overcome when a high trust staff and peer group is created, with the students' own participation in the project group being the perfect example of that.

Chapter 11 has a different significance as it based on a very different type of project. The student-led Teaching Awards permitted students to express what they appreciated in terms of what staff bring to teaching, and to their learning. The point that the key features of being enthusiastic and engaging in the classroom, and relating well and caring about the students, topped the poll is not surprising to scholars of engagement. These features link well to the importance of the affective domain in student engagement and the positive influences on student engagement identified in the first chapter. The authors make a wider point: that this approach to listening to the student voice positions the student as partner rather than customer, in contrast to mechanisms such as the surveys and ratings based on 'satisfaction'. Such an 'appreciative' approach also emphasizes the positive factors rather than seeking to identify the negative.

The final section about engaging student is also full of good evidence gathered from students within the context that enhancement policies and practices were being introduced. This emphasizes the point that such policies and practices should be based on such evidence and endorsed by the students in that context, to have the best chance of success. Chapter 13 reminds us to consider carefully the ethical dimension, an issue to be returned to later. This chapter is complementary to the two student chapters (6 and 7) which covered the perspective of the students participating in initiatives which are used as the main part of the case studies for ethical scrutiny.

The focus within Chapter 15 on 'doubters' is important, because it considers students who bring a disposition to HE from which it may be a bit harder to engage and get to a position of being engaged. Of course, these students are not 'in deficit', but the point that they are more likely to perceive nearly every aspect of their experience, social and academic, in a more negative light behoves the staff to address that issue. Note again the importance in fostering social networks and relationships. The authors have introduced a whole range of initiatives designed to do that and to foster a sense of belonging and community. Chapter 17 introduces and evaluates a holistic student engagement strategy in addressing the same goal within a school. As with Nottingham Trent, the authors at the University of Leeds demonstrate a particularly useful way to deploy surveys, as an evaluative approach and to gather the student voice, in checking systematically that innovations are delivering their intended outcomes. Another crucial dimension is also emphasized here though, and that is getting the staff on board and ensuring that staff are aware of student perceptions about their experience. This evidence showed that the staff underestimated how much their work was valued by the students, establishing a positive footing for enhancement work.

There is also a strong staff component in the initiatives to enhance academic engagement in the 'project' in Chapter 14, again based within a single school. At the heart of this curriculum reorganization was the creation of a much stronger dialogue between staff and students, with a view to co-owning the 'learning environment'. The focus was on processes which enabled students to 'best learn' in the 'learning encounter', something which is most likely to occur when the students enjoy what and how they are learning.

All the chapters in this section about ways of engaging students embrace so many of the principles set out in the first chapter, which were collated from all the research about the nature of student engagement. They focus on: being inclusive and accommodating the point that each student is different; that trust relationships between and within all parties is key; fostering belonging and community; fostering autonomy and creativity through enriching experiences inter alia. Notably, they all have a strong element of working with students as partners. A very notable example of this is in Chapter 16, where the experience and expertise of peer mentors is applied to the epistemic development of new students, to offer them 'learnership' and induct them into successful ways of gaining value from their course. Thus, instead of assuming that the perfect student is one 'in the image of the academic', the student is allowed to develop their own identity with the guidance of more experienced peers. This invokes a different role for staff, which involves letting go. This notion of partnership, a change in the position of student (and staff) is a recurrent theme throughout the whole book and leads to a strong pointer about the future direction of student engagement.

Partnership: the way forward for student engagement

Among the many strands that lie behind the notion of partnership is 'student voice'. This concept has emerged through two contrasting approaches. The first approach is both pedagogical and political and is derived from work over the last century about broader education (for a full review, see Bovill, 2013a). Thus Dewey (1916) argues for 'progressive' education to have a 'social democratic' basis. This critique of the rigidity and prescriptive nature of the curriculum continued through the work of humanist and constructivist theorists, such as Rogers and Freiberg (1969). Freire (1972) called for education to be opened up, to be 'public', and to focus on the needs of the learner and to enable social emancipation. This notion of radical pedagogy was followed in the next decade by advocacy for critical pedagogy, which challenges pre-established knowledge and argues for teacher and student to co-create, through collaboration and negotiation, new forms of knowledge (Giroux, 1983). Therefore, in such approaches there is a change in the position of the student and the teacher: a more democratic relationship where the student's view is drawn on and valued and the teacher's role changes to facilitator and becoming a co-learner. Ellsworth (1992) critiqued an important element of critical pedagogy. She argued that empowerment cannot be simply achieved by teachers sharing power with students, as power relations are not nearly as simplistic as this in the diversity of educational settings, and that teachers themselves do not hold all, or even many, of the reins of power. Taylor and Robinson (2009) showed that another important element, dialogue, was also problematic, as it assumes communication between teacher and student as transparent and not influenced by the values and identities that each party brings. However, these criticisms are not arguing against the principles of critical pedagogy but posing challenges as to how it may be achieved in practice.

The other approach to student voice has less of a pedagogic character, although it does have a political element. This is about taking students' views into account more broadly. This may have a collective nature through collective representation. There is a long tradition of student unions and representation by their officers at a senior level in universities. In addition, at course and department level, there have been staff–student committees or their equivalent for some time too. The degree of power and influence these student representatives have generally had in the past is limited, and is very under-researched. Lizzio and Wilson (2009) did find some evidence that, given the willingness of staff to engage in constructive dialogue and if the student representatives were supported to overcome barriers such as role ambiguity, these bodies could be effective in influencing the curriculum and the student experience.

Another, much more dilute, form of the student voice has risen in prominence recently. This is in the format of student feedback and evaluation. There is a plethora of survey instruments to gather evidence from students. In the UK, there is the National Student Survey (NSS) applied across the sector. Australia's latest version of such an instrument is the University Experience Survey, and Chapter 1 of this volume noted the widespread use of the NSSE in America and beyond. Other authors in this volume have already critiqued such instruments. There are two profound concerns. The first is that such surveys aggregate the student voice through the use of a narrow, prescriptive and closed format, as a proxy of quality. This evidence is then used for two purposes, neither of which has anything to do with pedagogy, partnership or collaboration.

The first purpose follows an overtly managerialist agenda. For example, institutional managers setting 'key performance targets' (such as a minimum of 90 per cent of students 'who are satisfied'), using data from the NSS to threaten departments with 'poor' scores with remedial measures, or even closure. Similarly, at the level of modules or units, it is now commonplace in the UK to require module evaluation questionnaires, with the data being used to threaten individual staff (though also influencing promotion decisions or leading to disciplinary procedures), an approach similar to the way that Student Evaluation of Teachers methods in the USA are used to determine tenure track staff appointments (Marsh, 1987). Such processes disempower both staff and students. Nearly all this type of evidence is gathered from the student after they have completed the course or module, which is of weak benefit to their personal, future experience.

The second purpose of the NSS, currently, is its use in league tables and in marketing courses with the simplistic promise to the prospective student that the higher the position or score, the better the 'quality' of the experience will be at that university or on a specific course. This positions the university sector as a competitive market, HE as a commodity, and the students as a consumer of that product. Naidoo and Jamieson (2005) and McCulloch (2009) present damning critiques of such a model, but current UK government policies and its endorsement by much of the popular media have promoted this position. Changes to admissions rules and the introduction of high fee levels have resulted in universities very much competing for high achieving applicants, as measured by their pre-qualifications.

McCulloch (2009) proposed a model of co-production between student and staff. In a direct challenge to 'student as consumer', Neary and Winn (2009) posited the model of 'student as producer'. This model addressed wider concerns too, arguing that universities are for public, not private, good and was rooted in a Marxist counter-position to capitalism. The model proposed that students should work with staff, through scholarly endeavour, to create work of 'social importance'. This model was developed at the University of Warwick (Taylor et al., 2012) but is now being fully implemented at the University of Lincoln (Neary, 2010).

A key component of this model is undergraduate research: students working with staff to produce knowledge and to integrate teaching and research. This links directly with the work of Healey and Jenkins (2009) who have been advocates of research-informed teaching more widely but particularly this type of approach. A manifestation of undergraduate research is the growing number of undergraduate journals (Metcalfe et al., 2011) and conferences, most notably the British Conference of Undergraduate Research. This is clearly a form of partnership, but does this fully embrace the wider student experience, drawing in the teaching and learning experience of both the individual and their peers?

There are three strands of work that do address the teaching and learning environment more explicitly. The first arose out the Centres of Excellence for Teaching and Leaning (CETL) initiative between 2005 and 2010. The unprecedented scale of investment in these CETLs (some £315m) permitted some very innovative approaches and the deployment of students in substantial internship roles within the projects over an extended period of time. Examples of these collaborative projects are detailed in Little (2011), with two particularly strong exemplars of partnership being in the Universities of Sheffield and of Manchester based on inquiry-based learning models. Some of these students subsequently formed the Student Learning and Teaching Network, which is currently still promoting partnership and engagement.

The second strand is concerned with initiatives that invite students to come forward with ideas to improve teaching and learning. They are then supported to gather appropriate evidence and then promote and implement enhancement – to act as 'change agents'. Leading examples of these include a body of work at Exeter (Kay et al., 2012) and the Academic Partners project at Birmingham City University (Nygaard et al., 2013). In a similar vein are the types of projects which involve students as consultants to academic staff, such as advising module leaders (Crawford, 2012).

The final area is student involvement in the design of the curriculum. Bovill (2013b) has reviewed recent developments in this domain in both the UK and elsewhere (also see Werder and Otis, 2010). She identified a range of approaches, with significant variation in the level of participation by the students involved, from initiatives where all the students in a module were actively involved in the design and undertaking of the module, to models more akin to a few students acting as consultants at a pre-design stage. This diversity raises an important consideration in approaches to partnership, about the balance between the collective and individual.

I began this discussion noting a contrast between pedagogical and collective/ representational imperatives in partnership. Much of the subsequent discussion has been on individuals participating as collaborators with staff and the developments taking place in that domain. There have also been recent initiatives in the area of collective partnership, for example, the approach at Bath University to include students in many committees and spheres of university life (Van der Velden, 2012). This more than meets the code of practice set out by the Quality Assurance Agency (2012) to encourage universities to include students in all their quality assurance and enhancement mechanisms. However, merely including students in committees could be just a box-ticking exercise. How would we know that this embodied a real ethos of partnership? To address that question a second one must be addressed too: how does the collective and individual join up?

Wenstone (2012: 8) rejects both the old model of student as apprentice and the newer model of student as consumer. She makes the case for partnership and contends that:

> At its roots, partnership is about investing students with the power to co-create, not just knowledge or learning, but the higher education institution itself [. . .] Community engagement, widening access, transnational education, research, sport, capital investment [. . .] are all part of the educational project and prospectively the business of the student body.

Perhaps unsurprisingly as a representative of the National Union of Students, Wenstone argues that the students' union is central to this and the vehicle through which dialogue can be conducted: 'In the student movement we value collectivism and democratic representation, but we need to ensure that the concept of the collective also serves the goal on individual student empowerment' (ibid.: 4). These ideals create some problems in implementation, although she is absolutely right to promote a democratic approach; there is a tension between participative and representative democracy. For student engagement, we would hope that there is a strong element of participation by *all* students. The problem with representation, particularly at the level of a large institution, is the *distance* between a sabbatical officer and a constituency of many thousands of students. Having said that, this model is much more democratic and accountable compared to the managerialist hierarchies that staff are currently subservient to. How truly representative are Vice-Chancellors of staff interests?

Bovill and Bulley (2011) drew on Arnstein's (1969) 'ladder of participation', based on citizen participation, to classify the degree of student activity in participation and decision making about the curriculum. Partnership is not at the top of this ladder, because that is denoted by 'students in control'. Arnstein (ibid.) describes consultation, even when it influences decision making, as 'tokenism', which might be considered harsh in the setting of HE, but her point would be that true participation requires the ability to co-create the agenda. Another model of relevance here is the continuum of industrial democracy (Pateman, 1970). Pateman describes 'pseudo-participation', another form of tokenism, an example being 'employee involvement' initiatives, where the worker is consulted on an individual basis, but predicated on the false premise that an individual employee has an equal say to a senior manager. Such a model is relevant because it acknowledges that power inequalities between managers/owners and workers only begins to be equalized by workers collectivizing through trade unions and bargaining through such a mechanism. Wenstone's (op. cit.) proposition that the student union is the vehicle for representation of students resonates with this industrial relations model. However, there is an important difference: the interests of worker and management are opposed and adversarial, whereas the interests of staff and students are not. If this is true, and there may be work to do yet in HE to align the perspectives of staff and students, then there is no reason why students' unions and universities could not work together in the spirit of *mitbestimmung*, co-determination, the German system of industrial democracy over the last 40 years.

The problem with such models is that they are one-dimensional, and, like student engagement itself, partnership is multi-dimensional. In the industrial model, the cooperative is ascribed as the most equal. However, the cooperative is different in several dimensions to other forms, because it is truly co-owned by all members as well as democratically governed and operated. The cooperative is a concept which shares a lot of features with a learning community; it has a similar ethos and principles of cooperation and mutuality.

It would appear that partnership and all that it entails offers the most fruitful way forward for student engagement as so many of the good practices for engaging students presented in this volume resonate with the principles and practices of partnership. The evidence about students engaging, built on a balance of autonomy, ownership, belonging, affiliation and community, also chimes with a partnership model and integrates the collective with the individual. This appears most practical at a local level, at module or degree or possibly school, although the latter may be too large a unit. At this level, partnership can be collective and individual, because the distance between all parties, particularly representatives and constituents, is small, and participation by all individual students and staff is possible.

There are many challenges and problems to practising partnership. There are ethical dilemmas and a myriad of issues to resolve and reach a consensus on such issues as:

- being inclusive and ensuring opportunities for all students to participate;
- the extent that participation/partnership becomes obligatory (which would remove choice and spoil the point);
- the tendency to favour (by both parties) those who are most willing, or deemed most 'capable';
- the issue of incentivization and reward;
- the relationship between the curricular and extra-curricular;
- whither the staff role; letting go;
- the point that this creates an inherently unpredictable path and unknowable future. We are co-creating in a 'disruptive' way so do not know the outcomes.

These issues are challenging, but there are many examples in this volume where a working accommodation has been reached, enabling progress to be made towards partnership. A wide range of approaches, sensitive to the context in which they occur, seems sensible. Applying *phronesis* can address any ethical issues too. The transitional nature of being a student presents a challenge of continuity, but also gives a regular injection of fresh ideas and a continuous and necessary sense of radicalism.

What started for me as an approach to enhance student engagement and build community in my day job has evolved naturally into partnership, working in a large and complex degree in a very traditional, risk averse university. That journey has been emancipatory for both myself and the students involved, but also immensely rewarding. That, and the way that so many other 'engagement projects' have evolved in a similar fashion, makes a compelling case that the future of student engagement lies in partnership and that all barriers can be overcome.

Bibliography

Allen, H. and Herron, C. (2003) 'A mixed-methodology investigation of the linguistic and affective outcomes of summer study abroad', *Foreign Language Annals* 36, 3: 370–385.

Anderson, L. (2006) 'Analytic autoethnography', *Journal of Contemporary Ethnography* 35, 4: 373–395.

Andrew, A., McGuiness, C., Reid, G. and Corcoran, T. (2008) 'Greater than the sum of its parts; transition into the first year of undergraduate nursing', *Nurse Education in Practice* 91: 13–21.

Arambewela, R. and Hall, J. (2009) 'An empirical model of international student satisfaction', *Asia Pacific Journal of Marketing and Logistics* 21, 4: 555–569.

Aristotle (1953) *The Nichomachean Ethics*, trans. J.A.K. Thomson, London: Penguin.

Arnstein, S. (1969) 'A ladder of citizen participation,' *Journal of the American Institute of Planners* 35, 4: 216–224.

Askham, P. (2008) 'Context and identity: exploring adult learners' experiences of higher education', *Journal of Further and Higher Education* 32, 1: 85–97.

Astin, A. (1977) *Four Critical Years: Effects of College on Beliefs, Attitudes and Knowledge*, San Francisco: Jossey-Bass.

Astin, A. (1984) 'Student involvement: a developmental theory for Higher Education', *Journal of College Student Development* 40, 5: 518–529.

Astin, A. (1985) *Achieving Educational Excellence*, San Francisco: Jossey-Bass.

Astin, A. (1991) *Assessment for Excellence: The Philosophy and Practice of Assessment and Evaluation in Higher Education*, New York: McMillan.

Astin, A. (1993) *What Matters in College? Four Critical Years Revisited*, San Francisco: Jossey-Bass.

Astin, A. (1999) 'Involvement in learning revisited: lessons we have learned', *Journal of College Student Development* 40, 5: 587–598.

Banning, J. (1989) 'Impact of college environment on freshman students'. In Upcraft, L., Gardner, J. and Associates (eds) *The Freshman Year Experience*, San Francisco: Jossey-Bass.

Barnett, R. (2007) *A Will to Learn: Being a Student in an Age of Uncertainty*, Maidenhead: Open University Press and Society for Research in Higher Education.

Baxter Magolda, M. (1992) *Knowing and Reasoning in College: Gender-Related Patterns in Students' Intellectual Development*, San Francisco: Jossey-Bass.

Becker, H., Geer, B., Hughes, E. and Strauss, A. (1961) *Boys in White: Student Culture in Medical School*, Chicago: University of Chicago Press.

Bentham, J. (2005) *An Introduction to the Principles of Morals and Legislation*, London: Adamant Media Corporation.

Bernstein, J. (2006) 'Suffering injustice: misrecognition as moral injury in critical theory', *International Journal of Philosophical Studies* 13, 3: 303–324.

Bhattacharyya, G., Ison, L. and Blair, M. (2003) *Minority Ethnic Attainment and Participation in Education and Training: The Evidence*, London: DfES.

BIS (2010) *Full Time Young Participation By Socio-Economic Class*. Online. Available HTTP: <http://webarchive.nationalarchives.gov.uk/+/http://stats.bis.gov.uk/he/FYPSEC_2010_final.pdf> (accessed 14 February 2012).

BIS (2011) *Students at the Heart of the System*. Online. Available HTTP: <http://www.parliament.uk/business/committees/committees-a-z/commons-select/business-innovation-and-skills/inquiries/the-future-of-higher-education//> (accessed 21 January 2013).

Bland, D. (2006) 'Researching educational disadvantage: using participatory research methods to engage marginalised students with education', unpublished PhD Thesis, Queensland University of Technology.

Bloxham, S. and West, A. (2007) 'Learning to write in Higher Education: students' perceptions of an intervention in developing understanding of assessment criteria', *Teaching in Higher Education* 12, 1: 77–89.

Boud, D. and Associates (2010) *Assessment 2020: Seven Propositions for Assessment Reform in Higher Education*, Sydney: Australian Learning and Teaching.

Boud, D. and Molloy, E. (2013) 'Rethinking models of feedback for learning: the challenge of design', *Assessment and Evaluation in Higher Education* 38, 6: 698–712.

Bovill, C. (2013a) 'Students and staff co-creating curricula: a new trend or an old idea we never got around to implementing?' In Rust, C. (ed.) *Improving Student Learning Through Research and Scholarship: 20 Years of ISL*. Oxford: Oxford Centre for Staff and Learning Development.

Bovill, C. (2013b) 'An investigation of co-created curricula within higher education in the UK, Ireland and the USA', *Innovations in Education and Teaching International* (in press).

Bovill, C. and Bulley, C. (2011) 'A model of active student participation in curriculum design: exploring desirability and possibility'. In Rust, C. (ed.) *Improving Student Learning, Proceedings of the ISSOTL/ISL Conference, October 2010*, Oxford: Oxford Centre for Staff and Learning Development.

Bovill, C., Cook-Sather, A. and Felten, P. (2011) 'Students as co-creators of teaching approaches, course design, and curricula: implications for academic developers', *International Journal for Academic Development* 16, 2: 133–145.

Bowl, M. (2001) 'Experiencing the barriers: non-traditional students entering Higher Education', *Research Papers in Education* 16, 2: 141–160.

Bowman, N. (2010) 'Can 1st-year college students accurately report their learning and development?', *American Educational Research Journal* 47: 466–496.

Brain, K., Layer, G. and Reid, I. (2004) 'Solid bedrock or shifting sands? The risky business of laying foundations', *Journal of Policy and Practice* 1, 2: 134–150.

Bransford, J.D., Brown, A. L. and Cocking, R. R. (eds) (1999) *How People Learn: Brain, Mind, Experience, and School*, Washington, DC: National Academy Press.

Brennan, J., Edmunds, R., Houston, M., Jary, D., Lebeau, J., Osborne, M. and Richardson, J. (2010) *Improving What is Learned at University*, London: Routledge.

British Educational Research Association (2011) *Ethical Guidelines for Educational Research*, London: BERA.

Broughan, C. and Grantham, D. (2012) 'Helping them succeed: the staff-student relationship'. In Clouder, L., Broughan, C., Jewell, S. and Stevenson, G. (eds) *Improving Student Engagement and Development Through Assessment*, London: Routledge.

Brown, H. and Edelmann, R. (2000) 'Project 2000: a study of expected and experienced stressors and support reported by students and qualified nurses', *Journal of Advanced Nursing* 31, 4: 857–864.

Bryson, C. (2004) 'What about the workers? The expansion of higher education and the transformation of academic work', *Industrial Relations Journal* 35, 1: 38–57.

Bryson, C. (2010) 'Enhancing student integration and success through a holistic engagement approach', Retention Convention: What Works? Student Retention and Success Conference, Leeds, 3–4 March.

Bryson, C. (2012) 'A holistic student engagement approach via partnership and peer mentoring in a research intensive university'. In Thomas, L. (ed.) *Compendium of Effective Practice: Proven ways to improve student retention and success*, York: HEA.

Bryson, C. (2013) 'Creating space for student autonomy and engagement through partnership and letting go'. In Bilham, T. (ed.) *For the Love of Learning: Innovations From Outstanding University Teachers*, Basingstoke: Palgrave Macmillan.

Bryson, C. and Hand, L. (2007) 'The role of engagement in inspiring teaching and learning', *Innovations in Teaching and Education International* 44, 4: 349–362.

Bryson, C. and Hand, L. (2008) 'An introduction to student engagement'. In Hand, L. and Bryson, C. (eds) *SEDA Special 22: Aspects Of Student Engagement*, London: Staff and Educational Development Association.

Bryson C. and Hardy, C. (2010) 'What students tell us about what influences their engagement with communities within HE', SEDA Conference, Leeds, 6–7 May.

Bryson C. and Hardy, C. (2012) 'The nature of academic engagement: what the students tell us'. In Solomonides, I., Reid, A. and Petocz, P. (eds) *Engaging with Learning in Higher Education*, Faringdon: Libri.

Buber, M. (2004) *I and Thou*, London: Continuum.

Burke, P.J. and Stets, J.E. (2009) *Identity Theory*, New York: Oxford University Press.

Butler, J. (1997) *Excitable Speech: A Politics of the Performative*, London: Routledge.

Byram, M. and Feng, A. (2006) 'Introduction'. In Byram, M. and Feng, A. (eds) *Living and Studying Abroad: Research and Practice*, Clevedon: Multilingual Matters.

Carini, R., Kuh, G. and Klein, S. (2006) 'Student engagement and student learning: testing the linkages', *Research in Higher Education* 47: 1–32.

Case, J. (2007) 'Alienation and engagement', *Teaching in Higher Education* 12, 1: 119–133.

Chandler, D. (2007) *Semiotics: The Basics*, 2nd edition, London: Routledge.

Chickering, A. and Gamson, Z. (1987) 'Seven principles for good practice'. In Chickering, A. and Gamson, Z. (1991) *New Directions for Teaching and Learning: Vol. 47. Applying the Seven Principles for Good Practice in Undergraduate Education*, San Francisco: Jossey-Bass.

Christie H., Tett, L., Cree, V., Hounsell, J. and McCure, V. (2007) 'A real rollercoaster of confidence and emotions: learning to be a university student', *Studies in HE* 33, 5: 567–581.

Claxton, G. (2011) 'Higher Education as epistemic apprenticeship', keynote speech to the NAIRTL/CELT annual conference, Galway, June, 2011.

Coakley, A. (1997) 'Nurse education: attrition rates in the UK', *Nursing Standard* 11, 48: 45–47.

Coates, H. (2006) *Student Engagement in Campus Based and On-Line Education. University Connections*, London: Routledge.

Coffey, A. (1999) *The Ethnographic Self: Fieldwork and the Representation of Identity.* London: Sage Publications.

Cohen, A.D., Paige, R.M., Shively, R.L., Emert, H.A. and Hoff, J.G. (2005) *Maximizing Study Abroad Through Language and Culture Strategies: Research on Students, Study Abroad Program Professionals, and Language Instructors*, University of Minnesota: Centre for Advanced Research on Language Acquisition.

Colley, H. (2006) 'Learning to labour with feeling: class, gender and emotion in childcare education', *Contemporary Issues in Early Childhood* 7, 1: 15–29.

Colvin, J. and Ashman, A. (2010) 'Roles, risks and benefits of peer mentoring relationships in Higher Education', *Mentoring and Tutoring: Partnership in Learning* 18, 2: 121–134.

Cook, A. and Rushton, B. (2008) *Student Transition: Practices and Policies to Promote Retention*, London: Staff and Educational Development Association.

Cornwall, A. and Jewkes, R. (1995) 'What is participatory research?', *Social Science and Medicine* 41, 12: 1667–1676.

Crawford, K. (2012) 'Rethinking the student/teacher nexus: students as consultants on teaching in higher education'. In Neary, M., Stevenson, H. and Bell, L. (eds) *Towards Teaching in Public: Reshaping the Modern University*, London: Continuum.

Davies, C. (1999) *Reflexive Ethnography: A Guide to Researching Self and Others*, London: Routledge.

Davies, R., Hope, M. and Robertson, A. (2010) *Student-Led Teaching Awards: Lessons From a Leading Higher Education Initiative in Scotland*, Edinburgh: Higher Education Academy Scotland.

Denzin, N. and Lincoln, Y. (1994) 'Introduction'. In Denzin, N. and Lincoln, Y. (eds) *Handbook of Qualitative Research*, Thousand Oaks, CA: Sage Publications, 1–17.

Denzin, N. and Lincoln, Y. (2005) 'Introduction'. In Denzin, N. and Lincoln, Y. (eds) *Handbook of Qualitative Research*, 3rd edition, Thousand Oaks, CA: Sage Publications: 1–32.

Dewey, J. (1916) *Democracy and Education: An Introduction to the Philosophy of Education*, New York: Macmillan.

DfEE (1998) *The Learning Age: A Renaissance for a New Britain.* Online. Available HTTP: <http://www.lifelonglearning.co.uk/greenpaper/> (accessed 14 February 2012).

DfEE (2000) *David Blunkett's Speech on Higher Education.* Online. Available HTTP: <http://cms1.gre.ac.uk/dfee/#speech> (accessed 14 February 2012).

Di Pietro, G. and Page, L. (2008) 'Who studies abroad?: evidence from France and Italy', *European Journal of Education* 43, 3: 389–398.

Docherty, D. (2011) *Universities Need to Work Harder to Turn UK Students Into Global Graduates*, The Guardian Higher Education Network. Online. Available HTTP: <http://www.guardian.co.uk/higher-education-network/blog/2011/nov/29/universities-uk-students-global-graduates> (accessed 20 December 2011).

Dubet, F. (1994) 'Dimensions et figures de l'expérience étudiante dans l'université en masse', *Revue Française de Sociologie* 35, 4: 511–532.

Eagleton, T. (2008) *Trouble with Strangers: A Study of Ethics*, Chichester: Wiley-Blackwell.

Ecclestone, K., Biesta, G. and Hughes, M. (2010) 'The role of identity, agency and structure'. In Ecclestone, K., Biesta, G. and Hughes, M. (eds) *Transitions and Learning Through the Lifecourse*, London: Routledge.

Edvardsson, D., Rasmussen, B.H. and Riessman, C.K. (2003) 'Ward atmospheres of horror and healing: a comparative analysis of narrative', *Health* 7, 4: 377–396.

Edward, N.S. (2003) 'First impressions last: an innovative approach to induction', *Active Learning in Higher Education* 4: 226.

Ellis, C. (2004) *The Ethnographic I: A Methodological Novel About Autoethnography*, Oxford: AltaMira Press.

Ellis, C. and Bochner, A. (2000) *Ethnographically Speaking: Autoethnography, Literature and Aesthetics*, Oxford: AltaMira Press.

Ellsworth, E. (1992) 'Why doesn't this feel empowering: working through the repressive myths of critical pedagogy'. In Luke, C. and Gore, J. (eds) *Feminism and Critical Pedagogy*, London: Routledge, 90–119.

Engle, L. and Engle, J. (2003) 'Study abroad levels: towards a classification of program types', *Frontiers: The Interdisciplinary Journal of Study Abroad* 9: 1–20.

Engle, L., and Engle, J. (2004) 'Assessing language acquisition and intercultural sensitivity development in relation to study abroad program design', *Frontiers: The Interdisciplinary Journal of Study Abroad* 10: 219–236.

Feldman, K. and Newcomb, T. (1969) *The Impact of College on Students*, San Francisco: Jossey-Bass.

Fergy, S., Heatley, S., Morgan, G. and Hodgson, D. (2008) 'The impact of pre-entry study skills training programmes on students' first year experience in health and social care programmes', *Nurse Education in Practice* 8, 1: 20–30.

Fielding, M. (2001) 'Students as radical agents of change', *Journal of Educational Change* 2: 123–141.

Fleming, H. (2009) 'Peer assisted learning in Bournemouth: an established and integral component of university student support'. In Potter, J. and Hampton D. (eds) *Students Supporting Students*, SEDA Special 26, London: SEDA, 9–14.

Foster, E., Lawther, S. and McNeil, J. (2011a) 'Learning developers supporting early student transition'. In Hartley, P., Hildson, J., Keenan, C., Sinfield, S. and Verity, M. (eds) *Learning Development in Higher Education*, Basingstoke: Palgrave Macmillan.

Foster, E., Lawther, S., Keenan, C., Bates, N., Colley, B. and Lefever, R. (2011b) *The HERE Project Final Report*. Online. Available HTTP: <http://www.heacademy. ac.uk/resources/detail/what-works-student-retention/HERE_Project_What_ Works_Final_Report> (accessed 15 January 2013).

Foster, E., Lawther, S., Lefever, R., Bates, N., Keenan, C. and Colley, B. (2012c) 'HERE to stay? An exploration of student doubting, engagement and retention in three UK universities'. In Solomonides, I., Reid, A. and Petocz, P. (eds) *Engaging with Learning in Higher Education*, Faringdon: Libri Publishing.

Foster, E., Lawther, S., Lefever, R., Bates, N., Keenan, C. and Colley, B. (2012d) *The HERE Project Toolkit: A Resource For Programme Teams Interested in Improving Student Engagement and Retention*, London: Paul Hamlyn Foundation. Online. Available HTTP: <http://www.improvingthestudentexperience.com/library/UG_ documents/Toolkit_-_HERE_Project.pdf> (accessed 9 July 2013).

Frawley, W. (2003) *International Encyclopaedia of Linguistics*, 2nd edition, New York: Oxford University Press.

Fredricks, J., Blumenfeld, P. and Paris, A. (2004) 'School engagement: potential of the concept, state of the evidence', *Review of Educational research* 74, 1: 59–109.

Freestone, P. and Geldens, P. (2008) '"For more than just the postcard": student exchange as a tourist experience', *Annals of Leisure Research* 11, 1/2: 41–56.

Freire, P. (1972) *Pedagogy of the Oppressed*, Harmondsworth: Penguin.

Fromm, E. (1978). *To Have or To Be?* London: Jonathan Cape.

Fuller, A. (2001) 'Credentialism, adults and part-time higher education in the United Kingdom: an account of rising take up and some implications for policy', *Journal of Education Policy* 16, 3: 233–248.

Giroux, H. (1983) *Theory and Resistance in Education. A Pedagogy for the Opposition*, London: Heinemann.

Godwin, L. and Neville, M. (2008) 'Learning from a whole-system, strength-based approach: a case of collaborative curriculum development', *The Journal for Quality and Participation* Spring: 11–14.

Goffman, E. (1959) *The Presentation of Self in Everyday Life*, New York: Doubleday Anchor Books.

Goodall, Jr. H. (2000) *Writing the New Ethnography*. Lanham, MD: Rowman & Littlefield Publishers.

Gordon, J., Ludlum, J. and Hoey, J. (2008) 'Validating NSSE against student outcomes: are they related?' *Research in Higher Education* 49: 19–39.

Greenbank, P. (2007) 'From Foundation to Honours degree: the student experience', *Education and Training* 49, 2: 91–102.

Griffin, P., Coates, H., Mcinnis, C. and James, R. (2003) 'The development of an extended Course Experience Questionnaire', *Quality in Higher Education* 9, 3: 259–266.

Grosset, J. (1991) 'Patterns of integration, commitment, and student characteristics and retention among younger and older students', *Research in Higher Education*. 32, 2: 159–178.

Gubrium, J. (1993) *Speaking of Life: Horizons of Meaning for Nursing Home Residents*, New York: Aldine de Gruyter.

Gump, S.E. (2007) 'Classroom research in a general education course: exploring implications through an investigation of the sophomore slump', *The Journal of General Education* 56: 105–125.

Hagel, P., Can, R. and Devlin, M. (2012) 'Conceptualising and measuring student engagement through the Australasian Survey of Student Engagement (AUSSE): a critique', *Assessment and Evaluation in Higher Education* 37, 4: 475–486.

Haggis, T. (2004) 'Meaning, identity and "motivation": expanding what matters in understanding learning in Higher Education?' *Studies in Higher Education* 29, 3: 335–352.

Hamshire, C., Cullen, W.R. and Wibberley, C. (2009) 'Autonomy, motivation and IT skills: impacts on student engagement with eLearning in level 4 Physiotherapy students', *PRIME: Proceedings of the PRHE Conference* 3, 2: 37–48.

Hamshire, C., Willgoss, T. and Wibberley, C. (2011) '"The placement was probably the tipping point:" the narratives of recently discontinued students', *Nurse Education in Practice* 12, 4: 182–186.

Hamshire, C., Willgoss, T. and Wibberley, C. (2013a) 'What are reasonable expectations? Healthcare student perceptions of their programmes in the North West of England', *Nurse Education Today* 33, 2: 173–179.

Hamshire, C., Willgoss, T. and Wibberley, C. (2013b) 'Should I stay or should I go? A study exploring why healthcare students consider leaving their programme', *Nurse Education Today* 33, 8: 889–895.

Hamza, A. (2010) 'International experience: an opportunity for professional development in higher education', *Journal of Studies in International Education* 14, 1: 50–69.

Hand, L. and Bryson, C. (2008) *Student Engagement*, London: Staff and Educational Development Association.

Hardy, C. and Bryson C. (2009) *Student Engagement: Paradigm Change or Political Expediency?*, ADM-HEA. Online. Available HTTP: <http://www.adm.heacademy. ac.uk/resources/features/student-engagement-paradigm-change-or-political-expe diency/> (accessed 10 May 2013).

Harrington, K. and O'Neill, P. (2010) 'Using student writing mentors to help first years adapt to university writing,' keynote speech at the Student Writing in Transition Synposium, Nottingham Trent University, 14 September 2010. Online. Available HTTP: <http://www.writenow.ac.uk/wp-content/uploads/2010/11/ntu-writing-in-transition-keynote-2010-final.pptx> (accessed 3 July 2013).

Harvey, L. (2009) *Review of Research Literature Focussed on Foundation Degrees*, Foundation Degree Forward. Online. Available HTTP: <http://www.heacademy.ac.uk/ assets/documents/fdf/Review-of-research-literature-focussed-on-foundation-degrees.pdf> (accessed 14 February 2012).

Hatch, J. and Wisniewski, R. (1995) 'Life history and narrative: questions, issues, and exemplary works'. In Hatch, J. and Wisniewski, R. (eds) *Life History and Narrative*, London: The Falmer Press, 113–135.

Hays, D.G. and Singh, A. (2012) *Qualitative Enquiry in Clinical and Education Settings*, New York: The Guilford Press.

HEA (2010) *Research and Evidence Base for Student Engagement*. Online. Available HTTP: <http://www.heacademy.ac.uk/ourwork/universitiesandcolleges/alldisplay?type= resourcesandnewid=ourwork/studentengagement/Research_and_evidence_base_ for_student_engagementandsite=york> (accessed 9 December 2010).

HEA (2012) *Life Outside the Classroom*. Online. Available HTTP: <http://www.hea cademy.ac.uk/resources/detail/internationalisation/ISL_Life_outside_classroom> (accessed 1 October 2012).

HEA (2013) *Dimensions of Student Engagement*. Online. Available HTTP: <http:// www.heacademy.ac.uk/resources/detail/studentengagement/Dimensions_ student_engagement> (accessed 4 April 2013).

Healey, M. and Jenkins, A. (2009) *Developing Undergraduate Research and Inquiry*. York: HE Academy. Online. Available HTTP: <www.heacademy.ac.uk/assets/York/ documents/resources/publications/DevelopingUndergraduate_Final.pdf> (accessed 20 July 2013).

Healey, M., Mason O'Conner, K. and Broadfoot, P. (2010) 'Reflections on engaging students in the process and product of strategy development for learning, teaching and assessment: an institutional case study', *International Journal of Academic Development* 15, 1: 19–32.

HEFCE (2000) *Foundation Degree Prospectus*. Online. Available HTTP: <http:// www.hefce.ac.uk/pubs/hefce/2000/00_27.htm> (accessed 14 February 2012).

HEFCE (2010a) *Foundation Degrees: Key Statistics 2001/2–2009/10*. Online. Available HTTP: <https://www.hefce.ac.uk/media/hefce/content/pubs/2010/201012/ 10_12.pdf> (accessed 2 July 2012).

HEFCE (2010b) *Summative Evaluation of the Lifelong Learning Network Programme*. Online. Available HTTP: <http://www.hefce.ac.uk/pubs/rereports/year/2010/summativeevaluationofthelifelonglearningnetworkprogramme/#d.en.64131> (accessed 14 February 2012).

HEFCE (2013) *Higher Education in England: Impact of the 2012 Reforms*. Online. Available HTTP: <http://www.hefce.ac.uk/media/hefce/content/about/introduction/aboutheinengland/impactreport/Impact-report.pdf> (accessed 1 May 2013).

HEPI (2009) *Male and Female Participation and Progression in Higher Education*. Online. Available HTTP: <http://www.hepi.ac.uk/files/41Maleandfemaleparticipation.pdf> (accessed 2 July 2012).

Hesse-Biber, S.N. and Leavy, P. (2011) *The Practice of Qualitative Research*, London: Sage.

Hockings, C. (2010) 'Reaching the students that student-centred learning cannot reach', *British Educational Research Journal* 35, 1: 83–98.

Hockings, C. (2011) 'Hearing voices, creating spaces: the craft of artisan teaching in a mass Higher Education system', *Critical Studies in Education* 52, 2: 1–15.

Hockings, C., Cooke, S. and Bowl, M. (2007) '"Academic engagement" within a widening participation context: a 3D analysis', *Teaching in Higher Education* 12, 5–6: 721–733.

Holdsworth, C. and Morgan, D. (2005) *Transitions in Context Leaving Home, Independence and Adulthood*, Maidenhead: Open University Press.

Holmes, L. (1995) 'Competence and capability: from confidence trick to the construction of the graduate identity', paper presented at the Higher Education for Capability Conference, UMIST, November.

Holstein, J.A. and Gubrium, J.F. (2000) *The Self We Live By: Narrative Identity in a Postmodern World*, New York: Oxford University Press.

Honkimaki, S., Tynjala, P. and Valkonen, S. (2004) 'University students' study orientations, learning experiences and study success in innovative courses', *Studies in Higher Education* 29, 4: 431–449.

Horstmanshof, L. and Zimitat C. (2003) 'Do extracurricular roles impact on retention? A social exchange theory perspective', paper presented at 7th Pacific Rim First Year in Higher Education Conference, Queensland University of Technology, July.

Hutchings, P. (2005) *Building Pedagogical Intelligence*, Carnegie Perspectives: a different way to think about teaching and learning, Stanford: Carnegie Foundation for the Advancement of Teaching. Online. Available HTTP: <http://www.carnegiefoundation.org/perspectives/building-pedagogical-intelligence> (accessed 9 July 2013).

Institute of International Education (2012) *Project Atlas: Atlas of Student Mobility: United Kingdom*. Online. Available HTTP: <http://www.iie.org/Services/Project-Atlas/United-Kingdom> (accessed 1 September 2012).

Israel, M. and Hay, I. (2006) *Research Ethics for Social Scientists*, London: Sage.

Jary, D. and Lebeau, Y. (2009) 'The student experience and subject engagement in UK sociology: a proposed typology', *British Journal of the Sociology of Education* 30: 697–712.

Johnes, G. and McNabb, R. (2004) 'Never give up on the good times: student attrition in the UK', *Oxford Bulletin of Economics and Statistics* 66: 23–47.

Johnston, B. (2010) *The First Year at University: Teaching Students in Transition*, Glasgow: McGraw-Hill.

Kahu, E. (2013) 'Framing student engagement in Higher Education', *Studies in Higher Education* 38, 5: 758–773.

Kangas, I. (2001) 'Making sense of depression: perceptions of melancholia in lay narratives', *Health* 5, 1: 76–92.

Kant, I. (1997) *Critique of Practical Reason*, Cambridge: Cambridge University Press.

Kant, I. (1998) *Groundwork of the Metaphysics of Morals*, Cambridge: Cambridge University Press.

Kantanis, T. (2000) 'The role of social transition in students' adjustment to the first-year of university', *Journal of Institutional Research* 9, 1. Online. Available HTTP: <http://www.aair.org.au/jir/May00/Kantanis.pdf> (accessed 1 April 2009).

Kay, J., Owen, D. and Dunne, E. (2012) 'Students as change agents: student engagement with quality enhancement of learning and teaching'. In Somolonides, I., Reid, A. and Petocz, P. (eds) *Engaging with Learning in Higher Education*, Faringdon: Libri, 359–380.

Kelly, G. (1991) *The Psychology of Personal Constructs: Vol I A Theory of Personality*, London: Routledge.

Kember, D. (2001) 'Beliefs about knowledge and the process of teaching and learning as a factor in adjusting to study in higher education', *Studies in Higher Education* 26, 2: 205–221.

Kember, D., Lee, K. and Li, N. (2001) 'Cultivating a sense of belonging in part-time students', *International Journal of Lifelong Education* 20, 4: 326–341.

Kember, D., Hong, C. and Ho, A. (2013) 'From model answers to multiple perspectives: adapting study approaches to suit university study,' *Active Learning in Higher Education* 14, 1: 23–35.

Kemmis, S. (2012) '*Phronesis*, experience and the primacy of praxis'. In Kinsella, E.A. and Pitman, A. (eds) *Phronesis as Professional Knowledge: Practical Wisdom in the Professions*, Rotterdam: Sense Publishers.

Kift, S. (2009) *Final Report for ALTC Senior Fellowship Programme*, Sydney: Australian Learning and Teaching Council. Online. Available HTTP: <http://www.altc.eud.au/resource-first-year-learning-experience-kift-2009> (accessed 14 September 2012).

Kift, S., Nelson, K. and Clark, J. (2010) 'Transition pedagogy: a third generation approach to FYE – a case study of policy and practice for the Higher Education sector', *The International Journal of the First Year in Higher Education* 1, 1: 1–20.

Knight, T., Tennant, R., Dillon, L. and Weddell, E. (2006) *Evaluating the Early Years Sector Endorsed Foundation Degree: A Qualitative Study of Students' Views and Experiences*. Online. Available HTTP: <http://www.education.gov.uk/publications/standard/publicationDetail/Page1/RR751> (accessed 14 February 2012).

Krause, K. (2005) 'Understanding and promoting student engagement in university learning communities', keynote paper presented at the James Cook University Symposium, James Cook University, September.

Krause, K. and Coates, H. (2008) 'Students' engagement in first-year university', *Assessment and Evaluation in Higher Education* 33, 5: 493–505.

Krause, K., Hartley, R., James, R. and McInnis, C. (2005) *The First Year Experience in Australian Universities: Findings From a Decade of National Studies*. Online. Available HTTP: <http://www.griffith.edu.au/__data/assets/pdf_file/0006/37491/FYEReport05.pdf> (accessed 14 February 2012).

Kreisberg, S. (1992) *Transforming Power: Domination, Empowerment and Education*, Albany, NY: SUNY Press.

Kress, G. (2003) *Literacy in the New Media Age*, London: Routledge.

Kuh, G. (2001) 'Assessing what really matters to student learning: inside the National Survey of Student Engagement', *Change* 33, 3: 10–17.

Kuh, G. (2008) *High Impact Practices: What They Are, Who Has Access to Them and Why They Matter*. Online. Available HTTP: <http://www.neasc.org/downloads/aacu_high_impact_2008_final.pdf> (accessed 12 February 2012).

Kuh, G. and Hu, S. (2001) 'The effects of student faculty interaction in the 1990s', *Review of Higher Education* 24, 3: 309–332.

Kuh, G., Cruce, T., Shoup, R., Kinzie, G. and Gonyea, R. (2008a) 'Unmasking the effects of student engagement on first-year college grades and persistence', *The Journal of Higher Education* 79, 5: 540–563.

Kuh, G., Kinzie, J., Buckley, J., Bridges, B. and Hayek, J.C. (2008b) *What Matters to Student Success: A Review of the Literature (ASHE Higher Education Report)*, San Francisco: Jossey-Bass.

Kuh, G., Kinzie, J., Schuh, J. and Whitt, E. (2010) *Student Success in College: Creating Conditions That Matter*, San Francisco: Jossey-Bass.

LaNasa, S., Cabrera, C. and Trangsrud, H. (2009) 'The construct validity of student engagement: a confirmatory factor analysis approach', *Research in Higher Education* 50, 315–332.

Lave, J. and Wenger, E. (1991) *Situated Learning: Legitimate Peripheral Participation*, Cambridge: Cambridge University Press.

Lave, J. and Wenger, E. (1998) *Communities of Practice: Learning, Meaning, and Identity*, Cambridge: Cambridge University Press.

Leach, L. and Zepke, N. (2012) 'Student engagement in learning; facets of a complex interaction'. In Solomonides, I., Reid, A. and Petocz, P. (eds) *Engaging with Learning in Higher Education*, London: Libri.

Lechte, J. (2008) *50 Key Contemporary Thinkers: From Structuralism to Post-Humanism*, 2nd edition, London: Routledge.

Lefever, R. (2012) 'Student understandings of belonging', *Journal of Applied Research in Higher Education* 4, 2: 126–141.

Lemert, C. and Branaman, A. (eds) (1997) *The Goffman Reader*, Oxford: Blackwell Publishing Ltd.

Levett-Jones, T.L., Lathlean J., Maquire J. and McMillan, M. (2007) 'Belongingness: a critique of the concept and implications for nursing education', *Nurse Education Today* 27: 210–218.

Lewin, R. (ed.) (2009) *The Handbook of Practice and Research in Study Abroad: Higher Education and the Quest for Global Citizenship*, New York: Routledge.

Little, B. (2005) 'Policies towards work-focused Higher Education: are they meeting employer's needs?', *Tertiary Education and Management* 11, 2: 131–146.

Little, B., Locke, W., Scesa, A. and Williams, R. (2009) *Report to HEFCE on Student Engagement*, London: CHERI.

Little, S. (ed) (2011) *Staff-Student Partnerships in Higher Education*, London: Continuum.

Lizzio, A. and Wilson, K. (2009) 'Student participation in university governance: the role conceptions and sense of efficacy of student representatives on departmental committees,' *Studies in Higher Education* 10, 3: 69–84.

Lowe, H. and Cook, A. (2003) 'Mind the gap: are students prepared for Higher Education', *Journal of Further and Higher Education* 27, 1: 53–76.

Macfarlane, B. (2012) 'Ambition, boredom, friendship and love: what they tell us about research ethics', *Research Intelligence*, London: BERA.

Mackie, S. (2001) 'Jumping the hurdles: undergraduate student withdrawal behaviour', *Innovation in Education and Teaching International* 38, 3: 265–276.

Mann, S. (2001) 'Alternative perspectives on the student experience: alienation and engagement', *Studies in Higher Education* 26, 1: 7–19.

Mann, S. (2005) 'Alienation in the learning environment: a failure of community?', *Studies in Higher Education* 30, 1: 43–55.

Marsh, H. (1987) 'Students' evaluations of university teaching: research findings, methodological issues, and directions for future research,' *International Journal of Educational Research* 11, 3: 253–388.

Marton, F. and Saljo, R. (1976) 'On qualitative differences in learning: outcome and process', *British Journal of Educational Research* 46: 4–11.

Mascia-Lees, F.E. (2011) *A Companion to the Anthropology of the Body and Embodiment*, Chichester: John Wiley and Sons.

Mautner, T. (2000) *Dictionary of Philosophy*, London: Penguin.

McCormick, A., Gonyea, R. and Kinzie, J. (2013) *Refreshing Engagement: NESSE at 13, Change*, May/June 2013. Online. Available HTTP: <http://www.changemag.org/index.html> (accessed 5 July 2013).

McCracken. G. (1988) *The Long Interview: Qualitative Research Methods Series 13*, Newbury Park, CA: SAGE Publications.

McCulloch, A (2009) 'The student as co-producer: learning from public administration about the student-university relationship', *Studies in Higher Education* 34, 2; 171–183.

McCune, V. (2009) 'Final year Biosciences students' willingness to engage: teaching, learning environments, authentic learning experiences and identities', *Studies in Higher Education* 34, 3: 347–361.

McGivney, V. (2003) *Staying or Leaving the Course*, 2nd edition, Leicester: National Institute of Adult Continuing Education.

McInnis, C. (2001) *Signs of Disengagement? The Changing Undergraduate Experience in Australian Universities*, Melbourne: CSHE. Online. Available HTTP: <http://eprints.unimelb.edu.au/archive/00000094/01/InaugLec23%5F8%5F01.pdf> (accessed 6 May 2006).

McInnis, C. (2005) 'Reinventing student engagement and the learning community: strategic directions for policy, research and practice', keynote presented at the HEA Conference, Edinburgh.

McInnis, C. and James, R. (1995) *First Year on Campus: Diversity in the Initial Experiences of Australian Undergraduates*, Melbourne: Melbourne University Press.

McLeod, M. and Wainwright, P. (2009) 'Researching the study abroad experience', *Journal of Studies in International Education* 13, 1: 66–71.

Metcalfe, D., Gibson, C. and Lambert, C. (2011) 'A collaborative foray into undergraduate publishing'. In Little, S. (ed) (2011) *Staff-Student Partnerships in Higher Education*, London: Continuum.

Meyer, J. and Land, R. (2003) 'Threshold concepts and troublesome knowledge: linkages to ways of thinking and practising'. In Rust, C. (ed.) *Improving Student Learning: Theory and Practice Ten Years On*, Oxford: Oxford Centre for Staff and Learning Development (OCSLD).

Meyer, J. and Land, R. (2005) 'Threshold concepts and troublesome knowledge: epistemological considerations and a conceptual framework for teaching and learning', *Higher Education* 49, 3: 373–388.

Million+, NUS (2012) *Never Too Late to Learn*. Online. Available HTTP: <http://www.millionplus.ac.uk/research/never-too-late-to-learn> (accessed 2 July, 2012).

Morosanu, L., Handley, K. and O'Donovan, B. (2010) 'Seeking support: researching first-year students' experiences of coping with academic life', *Higher Education Research and Development* 29, 6: 665–678.

Mulholland, J., Anionwu, E.N., Atkins, R., Tappern, M. and Franks, P.J. (2008) 'Diversity, attrition and transition into nursing', *Journal of Advanced Nursing* 64, 1: 49–59.

Murphy, L., Mufti, E. and Kassem, D. (2009) 'How people learn'. In Murphy, L., Mufti, E. and Kassem, D. (eds) *Education Studies: An Introduction*, Milton Keynes: Open University Press.

Naidoo, R. and Jamieson, I. (2005) 'Empowering participants or corroding learning? Towards a research agenda on the impact of student consumerism in Higher Education', *Journal of Education Policy* 20, 3: 276–281.

National Audit Office (2007) *Staying the Course: The Retention of Students in Higher Education*. Online. Available HTTP: <http://image.guardian.co.uk/sys-files/Education/documents/2007/07/25/Retention_26.07.2007.pdf > (accessed 14 February 2012).

Neary, M. (2010) *Student as Producer: Research Engaged Teaching and Learning at the University of Lincoln User's Guide 2010-11*, Lincoln: University of Lincoln. Online. Available HTTP: <http://studentasproducer.lincoln.ac.uk/files/2010/11/user-guide.pdf> (accessed 2 May 2012).

Neary, M. with Winn, J. (2009) 'Student as producer: reinventing the undergraduate curriculum'. In Neary, M., Stevenson, H. and Bell, L. (eds) (2009) *The Future of Higher Education: Policy, Pedagogy and the Student Experience*, London: Continuum, 192–210.

Nelson, K., Kift, S. and Clarke, J. (2012) 'A transition pedagogy for student engagement and first-year learning, success and retention'. In Solomonides, I., Reid, A. and Petocz, P. (eds) *Engaging with Learning in Higher Education*, Faringdon: Libri.

Nettleton, S., Watt, I., O'Malley, L. and Duffey, P. (2005) 'Understanding the narratives of people who live with medically unexplained illness', *Patient Education and Counseling* 56, 2: 205–210.

Nicol, D. (2009). *Transforming Assessment and Feedback: Enhancing Integration and Empowerment in the First Year*, Mansfield: The Quality Assurance Agency for Higher Education.

Nicol, D. (2010) *The Foundation for Graduate Attributes: Developing Self-Regulation Through Self and Peer Assessment*, London: The Quality Assurance Agency for Higher Education.

Nixon, J. (2012) *Interpretive Pedagogies for Higher Education: Arendt, Berger, Said, Nussbaum and their Legacies*, London: Continuum/Bloomsbury.

Noel, J. (1999) 'On the varieties of *phronesis*', *Educational Philosophy and Theory* 31, 3: 273–289.

North, W. (1995) *Handbook of Semiotics*, Bloomington: Indiana University Press.

National Survey of Student Engagement (NSSE) (no date) *North American Survey of Student Engagement* Online. Available HTTP: <http://nsse.iub.edu/> (accessed 4 April 2013).

Northedge, A. (2003) 'Enabling participation in academic discourse', *Teaching in Higher Education* 8, 2: 169–180.

Nottingham Trent Students' Union (2012) *Nominate Your Outstanding Teacher or Support Team*, Nottingham. Online. Available HTTP: <http://www.trentstudents. org/general/news/index.php?page=articleandnews_id=326783> (accessed 28 April 2013).

NUS (2010) *Student Engagement Hub*. Online. Available HTTP: <http://www. nusconnect.org.uk/campaigns/highereducation/student-engagement-hub/> (accessed 9 December 2010).

Nygaard, C., Brand, S., Bartholomew, P. and Millard, L. (2013) *Student Engagement – Identity, Motivation and Community*, Faringdon: Libri.

Ozga, J. and Sukhnandan, L. (1998) 'Undergraduate non-completion: developing an explanatory model', *Higher Education Quarterly* 52: 316–333.

Pace, R. (1982) *Achievement and the Quality of Student Effort*, Report to the Department of Education, Washington, DC.

Pascarella, E. and Terenzini, P. (1991). *How College Affects Students: Findings and Insights From Twenty-Years of Research* (1st ed.), San Francisco: Jossey-Bass.

Pascarella, E. and Terenzini, P. (2005) *How College Affects Students Volume 2: A Third Decade of Research*, San Francisco: Jossey-Bass.

Pateman, C. (1970) *Participation and Democratic Theory*, Cambridge: Cambridge University Press.

Perry, R. (1991) 'Perceived control in college students: implications for instruction in Higher Education', *Higher Education: Handbook of Theory and Research* 7: 1–56.

Perry, W. (1999) *Forms of Intellectual and Ethical Development in the College Years: A Scheme*, New York: Harcourt Brace.

Polkinghorne, D. (1995) 'Narrative configuration in qualitative analysis', *International Journal of Qualitative Studies in Education* 8: 8–25.

Porter, S. (2009) *Do College Student Surveys Have Any Validity?*, Annual meeting of the Association for the Study of Higher Education, Vancouver, British Columbia, Canada, November.

Prentice, D. (1999) *Cultural Divides: Understanding and Overcoming Group Conflicts*, New York: Russell Sage Foundation.

Price, M., Rust, C., O'Donovan, B. and Handley, K. (2012) *Assessment Literacy: The Foundation for Improving Student Learning*, Oxford: OCSLD.

Purnell, S. and Foster, E. (2008) 'Transition and engagement'. In Hand, L. and Bryson, C. (eds) *Student Engagement: SEDA Special 22*, London: Staff and Educational Development Association.

Quality Assurance Agency (2012) *UK Quality Code for Higher Education: Part B: Assuring and Enhancing Academic Quality: Chapter B5: Student Engagement*, Gloucester: The Quality Assurance Agency for Higher Education.

Ramsden, P. (1992) *Learning to Teach in Higher Education*, London: Routledge.

Reay, D., David, M. and Ball, S. (2005) *Degrees of Choice, Social Class, Gender and Race in Higher Education*, Stoke-on-Trent: Trentham Books.

Reid, A. and Solomonides, I. (2012) 'Student engagement with capability development'. In Solomonides, I., Reid, A. and Petocz, P. (eds) *Engaging with Learning in Higher Education*, London: Libri.

Reid, A., Abrandt Dahlgren, M., Petocz, P. and Dahlren, L. (2011) *From Expert Student to Novice Professional*, Dordrecht: Springer.

Reisinger, Y. and Turner, L.W. (2003) *Cross-Cultural Behaviour in Tourism: Concepts and Analysis*, Oxford: Butterworth-Heinemann.

Rich, A. (1986) *Blood, Bread and Poetry: Selected Prose 1979–1986*, New York: Norton.

Roberts, C., Watkin, M., Oakey, D. and Fox, R. (2003) 'Supporting student "success": what can we learn from the persisters', paper presented at the Education in a Changing Environment Conference, University of Salford, September.

Rogers, C. and Freiberg, H. (1969) *Freedom to learn*, 3rd edition, New York: Macmillan.

Rust, C., O'Donovan, B. and Price, M. (2005) 'A social constructivist assessment process model: How the research literature shows us this could be best practice', *Assessment & Evaluation in Higher Education* 30, 3: 231–240.

Sadler, R. (2013) 'Opening up feedback: teaching learners to see'. In Merry, S. et al. (eds), *Reconceptualising Feedback in Higher Education: Developing Dialogue With Students*, London: Routledge.

Sambell, K. (2010) 'Enquiry-Based Learning and formative assessment environments: student perspectives', *Practitioner Research in Higher Education* 4, 1: 52–61.

Sambell, K. and Graham, L. (2013) 'Developing assessment literacy: students' experiences of working with exemplars to improve their approaches to assignment writing,' 4th Assessment in Higher Education conference, Birmingham, July.

Sambell, K., McDowell, L. and Montgomery, C. (2012). *Assessment for Learning in Higher Education*, London, Routledge.

Sambell, K., McDowell, L. and Montgomery, C. (2013) *Assessment for Learning in Higher Education*, London: Routledge

Sanders, C. (2004) *The Cambridge Companion to Saussure*, Cambridge: Cambridge University Press.

Schon, D. (1983) *The Reflective Practitioner: How Professionals Think in Action*, London: Temple Smith.

Schwandt, T. (1994) 'Constructivist, interpretivist approaches to human inquiry'. In Denzin, N. and Lincoln, Y. (eds). *Handbook of Qualitative Research*, Thousand Oaks, CA: Sage Publications, 118–137.

Sen, A. (2001) *Development as Freedom*, Oxford: Oxford Paperbacks.

Sikes, P. (2010) 'The ethics of writing life history a narrative in educational research'. In Bathmaker, A.-M. and Harnett, P. (eds) *Exploring Learning, Identity and Power through Life History and Narrative Research*, London: Routledge.

Silver, J. (2006) *Teachers 'Bullied By Online Grading'*, Homepage of BBC. Online. Available HTTP: <http://news.bbc.co.uk/1/hi/uk/6139626.stm> (accessed 23 April 2013).

Sissel, P.A., Hansman, C.A. and Kasworm, C.E. (2001) 'The politics of neglect: adult learners in Higher Education', *New Directions for Adult and Continuing Education* 91: 17–27.

Solomonides, I. and P. Martin (2008) 'All this talk of engagement is making me itch: an investigation into the conceptions of "engagement" held by students and tutors'. In Hand, L. and Bryson, C. (eds) *SEDA Special 22: Aspects of Student Engagement*, London: Staff and Educational Development Association.

Solomonides, I., Reid, A. and Petocz, P. (2012a) *Engaging with Learning in Higher Education*, Faringdon: Libri.

Solomonides, I., Reid, A. and Petocz, P. (2012b) 'A relational model of student engagement'. In Solomonides, I., Reid, A. and Petocz, P. (eds) *Engaging with Learning in Higher Education*. Faringdon: Libri, 11–24.

Stake, R.E. (1995) *The Art of Case Study Research*, London: Sage.

Stamm, T., Lovelock, L., Stew, G. et al. (2008) 'I have mastered the challenge of living with a chronic disease: life stories of people with rheumatoid arthritis', *Qualitative Health Research* 18, 5: 658–669.

Steele, R., Lauder, W., Caperchione, C. and Anastasi, J. (2005) 'An exploratory study of the concerns of mature access to nursing students and the coping strategies used to manage these adverse experiences', *Nurse Education Today* 25, 7: 573–581.

Stott, A. (2006) 'Exploring factors affecting attrition of male students from an undergraduate nursing course: a qualitative study', *Nurse Education Today* 27: 325–332.

Strauss, A and Corbin, J. (1990) *Basics of Qualitative Research: Grounded Theory Procedures and Techniques*, Newbury Park, CA: SAGE Publications.

Stryker, S. and Burke, P.J. (2000) 'The past, present and future of an identity theory', *Social Psychology Quarterly* 63, 4: 284–297.

Taylor, C. (2012) 'Student engagement, practice architectures and *phronesis* in the student transitions and experiences project', *Journal of Applied Research in Higher Education* 4, 2: 109–125.

Taylor, C. and Robinson, C. (2009) 'Student voice: theorising power and participation', *Pedagogy, Culture and Society* 17, 2: 161–175.

Taylor, P., Wilding, D., Mockridge, A. and Lambert, C. (2012) 'Reinventing engagement'. In Somolonides, I., Reid, A. and Petocz, P. (eds) *Engaging with Learning in Higher Education*, Faringdon: Libri, 259–278.

Teichler, U. (1998) 'Massification: a challenge for institutions of Higher Education', *Tertiary Education and Management* 4, 1: 17–27.

Thomas, L. (2002) 'Student retention in Higher Education: the role of institutional habitus', *Journal of Education Policy* 17, 4: 423–442.

Thomas, L. (2012a) 'Building student engagement and belonging in Higher Education at a time of change: final report from the "What Works? Student Retention and Success programme"', a report for the Higher Education Academy. York: Higher Education Academy.

Thomas, L. (2012b) 'What works? Facilitating an effective transition into Higher Education', *Widening Participation and Lifelong Learning* 14. Online. Available HTTP: <http://wpll-journal.metapress.com/content/3628kq59204r7107/fulltext.pdf> (accessed 6 July 2013).

Thomas, L. (2012c) *Building Student Engagement and Belonging in Higher Education at a Time of Change: A Summary of Findings and Recommendations from the What Works? Student Retention and Success Programme*, York: Paul Hamlyn Foundation, HEFCE, HEA and Action on Access.

Thoreau, H.D. (1857) *Journal, 2 July 1857* Online. Available HTTP: <http://www.walden.org/Library/Quotations/Observation> (accessed 11 November 2013).

Tinto, V. (1975) 'Dropout from Higher Education: a theoretical synthesis of recent research', *Review of Educational Research* 45, 1: 89–125.

Tinto, V. (1987) *Leaving College: Rethinking the Causes and Cures of Student Attrition*, Chicago and London: University of Chicago Press.

Tinto, V. (1998) 'Colleges as communities: taking research on student persistence seriously', *Review of Higher Education* 21, 2: 167–177.

Tinto, V. (2006) 'Research and practice of student retention: what next?', *College Student Retention* 8, 1: 1–19.

Trowler, V. (2010) *Student Engagement Literature Review*. Online. Available HTTP: <http://www.heacademy.ac.uk/assets/York/documents/ourwork/studentengagement/StudentEngagementLiteratureReview.pdf> (accessed 9 December 2010).

Trowler, V. and Trowler, P. (2010) *Student Engagement Evidence Summary*, York: Higher Education Academy.

Tynjala, P. (1997) 'Developing education students' conceptions of the learning process in different learning environments', *Learning and Instruction* 7: 277–292.

UK Council for International Student Affairs (2012) *The Prime Minister's Initiative for International Education – PMI Student Experience Strand*. Online. Available HTTP: <http://www.ukcisa.org.uk/pmi/index.php> (accessed 25 June 2012).

UKCOSA (2004) *Broadening Our Horizons: International Students in UK Universities and Colleges – Report of the UKCOSA Survey*, London: UKCOSA: The Council for International Education. Online. Available HTTP: <http://www.ukcisa.org.uk/files/pdf/about/reports/BOHreport.pdf> (accessed 1 September 2012).

Unistats (2012) The Official Website for Comparing UK Higher Education Course Data. Online. Available HTTP: <http://unistats.direct.gov.uk/> (accessed 19 March 2013).

Upcraft, M. and Gardner, J. (1989) *The Freshman Year Experience: Helping Students Survive and Succeed in College*, San Francisco: Jossey-Bass.

Upcraft, L., Gardner, J. and Barefoot, B. (2005) 'The first year of college revisited'. In Upcraft, L., Gardner, J. and Barefoot, B. (eds) *Challenging and Supporting the First-Year Student: A Handbook for Improving the First Year of College*, 1st edition, San Francisco: Jossey-Bass.

UUK (2011) *Patterns and Trends in UK Higher Education*. Online. Available HTTP: <http://www.universitiesuk.ac.uk/Publications/Documents/Patterns AndTrendsinUKHigherEducation.pdf> (accessed 14 February 2012).

UUK (2012) *A Picture of Health and Education*. Online. Available HTTP: <http://www.universitiesuk.ac.uk/Publications/Pages/Apictureofhealthandeducation.aspx> (accessed 10 July 2012).

Van der Velden, G. (2012). 'Institutional level student engagement and organisational cultures', *Higher Education Quarterly* 66, 3: 227–247.

Van Gennep, A. (2004) *Rites of Passage*, London: Routledge.

Van Hoof, H. (2005) 'Wine is for drinking, water is for washing: student opinions about international exchange programs', *Journal of Studies in International Education* 9, 1: 42–61.

Vygotsky, L. (1978) *Mind and Society: The Development of Higher Psychological Processes*, Cambridge, MA: Harvard University Press.

Webster, L. and Mertova, P. (2007) *Using Narrative Inquiry as a Research Method: An Introduction to Using Critical Event Narrative Analysis in Research on Learning and Teaching*, London: Routledge.

Wenger, E. (1999) *Communities of Practice: Learning, Meaning, and Identity*, Cambridge: Cambridge, University Press.

Wenstone, R. (2012) *Manifesto for Partnership*, London, NUS. Online. Available HTTP: <http://www.nusconnect.org.uk/news/article/highereducation/Rachel-Wenstone-launches-a-Manifesto-for-Partnership/> (accessed 2 February 2013).

Werder, C. and Otis, M. (eds) (2010) *Engaging Student Voices in the Study of Teaching And Learning*, Sterling, VA: Stylus.

Whitaker, R. (2008) *Quality Enhancement Themes: The First Year Experience: Transition to and During the First Year*, Mansfield. Online. Available HTTP: <http://www.enhancementthemes.ac.uk/docs/publications/transition-to-and-during-the-first-year.pdf> (accessed 9 July 2013).

Wiles, R. (2012) *What Are Qualitative Research Ethics?*, London: Bloomsbury Press.

Williams, C. (1982) *The Early Experiences of Students on Australian University Campuses*, Sydney: University of Sydney.

Williams, C. and Johnson, L. (2011) 'Why can't we be friends?: Multicultural attitudes and friendships with international students', *International Journal of Intercultural Relations* 35, 1: 41–48.

Willis, D. (1993) 'Academic involvement at university', *Higher Education* 25, 2: 133–150.

Wintrup, J., James, E., Humphris, D. and Bryson, C. (2012) 'Emotional work: students realising, negotiating and overcoming barriers', *Journal of Applied Research in Higher Education* 4, 2: 170–185.

Wintrup, J., James, E. and Humphris, D. (2013) 'Beyond inequality? A case study of progression, achievements and experiences of health and care workers in Higher Education, 2005-2011', *Widening Participation and Lifelong Learning* 14, 3: 172–189.

Wittgenstein, L. (2007) *Tractatus Logico-Philosophicus*. Translated from the German by C.K. Ogden. New York: Cosimo Classics.

Woodward, K. (2004) *Questioning Identity: Gender, Class, Ethnicity*, 2nd edition, London: The Open University.

Yang, R.P.-J., Noels, K.A. and Saumure, K.D. (2006) 'Multiple routes to cross-cultural adaptation for international students: mapping the paths between self-construals, English language confidence, and adjustment', *International Journal of Intercultural Relations* 30, 4: 487–506.

Ylijoki, O.-H. (2000) 'Disciplinary cultures and the moral order of studying: a case of four Finnish university departments', *Higher Education* 39, 3: 339–362.

Yorke, M. (1999) *Leaving Early: Undergraduate Non-completion in Higher Education*, London: Falmer Press.

Yorke, M. (2000) 'Smoothing the transition into Higher Education: what can be learned from student non-completion', *Journal of Institutional Research* 9, 1. Online. Available HTTP: <http://www.aair.org.au/articles/volume-9-no-1/9-1-smoothing-the-transition-into-higher-education-what-can-be-learned-from-student-non-completion> (accessed 17 November 2012).

Yorke, M. and Longden, B. (2008) 'The first-year experience in Higher Education in the UK', final report for the Higher Education Academy, York: Higher Education Academy.

Yow, V. (1994) *Recording Oral History: A Practical Guide for Social Scientists*, Thousand Oaks, CA: SAGE Publications.

Zepke, N. (2011) 'Understanding teaching, motivation and external influences in student engagement: how can complexity theory help?', *Research in Post-Compulsory Education* 16, 1–13.

Zepke, N. and Leach, L. (2005) 'Integration and adaption: approaches to the student retention and achievement puzzle', *Active Learning in Higher Education* 6, 1: 46–59.

Zepke, N. and Leach, L. (2010) 'Improving student engagement: ten proposals for action', *Active Learning in Higher Education* 11, 3: 167–177.

Zyngier, D. (2008) '(Re)conceptualising student engagement: doing education not time', *Teaching and Teacher Education* 24: 1765–1776.

Index